C.W. (Robert) Willies

26 January, 2011

Barnsley Libraries — PENISTONE

P.S.2027

1/11   **Return Date**

SIGNED + DONATED BY THE AUTHOR
LOCAL HISTORY.

2 8 MAR 2011

- 6 AUG 2011
- 2 JUL 2012

JUL 18

04. JUN
24.

3805900465131 3

NO ESCAPING OUR ROOTS

A Family History, which is largely biographical, is certain to have overlooked some key events and achievements of family members. Hopefully present and future generations will be inspired to restore the balance.

Here are two quotations, from the work of Thomas Carlyle (1795-1881), which are pertinent; both are from *Critical and Miscellaneous History Essays*.

"History is the essence of innumerable biographies."

"A well written life is almost as rare as a well spent one."

Robert Willis
December 2009

NO ESCAPING OUR ROOTS

300 years of Family History

by
G R T (Robert) Willis MBE DFC

To
Catherine, Ian, Andrew and Howard.

'Though leaves are many, the root is one'
W B Yeats (1865-1939) 'The coming of Wisdom with Time'

Copyright © by GRT Willis.
First published in Great Britain 2009 by GRT (Robert) Willis,
19 Rectory Lane, Emley, Huddersfield.

Typesetting and Reprographics by
Paulette Huntington,
4 Summer Lane, Emley, Huddersfield.

All rights reserved.

ISBN 978 0 9564080 0 6

By the same author 'No Hero, Just A Survivor'.

CONTENTS

Foreword
Introduction
Acknowledgements

1: Laying the Foundation
2: Preserving the memory of a Derbyshire tragedy
3: George Hamlet Willis: A Pivotal Ancestor
4: New Horizons – The Impact of the Martins
5: Robert Thomas Willis 1920-1955: Overcoming a generation split
6: Florence Elsie Willis
7: The Nowell and Palframan family history
8: The Robert Willis Story (GRTW) 1921-1946
9: Post war reconciliation and healing
10: The Willis family business 1946-1955
11: Reflections on a changing social scene and family life
12: Enterprise, growth and ambition 1955-1981
13: Success, then facing disaster with a rewarding conclusion
14: Not quite retirement
15: The Willis family 1701-2008
16: The Nowell and Palframan families 1750-2008
17: Today's Players
Epilogue

Appendix: The Willis, Martin, Hyland, Lowe, Hind, Nowell and Palframan Family Trees

FOREWORD

One of the most profound changes in the nation's daily life over the past three hundred years has been engineered by the food industry. The changes have brought immeasurable benefits to populations in many regions around the world, particularly in health and individual quality of life. The impact on public institutions and businesses of all sizes, whether in the service or manufacturing sector, has been profound. Many enterprises fall away, new arrivals come in, governments regulate, economies expand and populations acquire new powers to choose. We are called consumers. This book is a microcosm of how this revolution and social change impacted upon my family who, on the one hand, moved from farm work in North Derbyshire to factory work in Eyam and then sought new opportunities in the expanding coal fields and manufacturing towns of Yorkshire, in the late 19th century. On the other hand, the Nowell and Palframan families moved from humble beginnings in Leeds, to seek new opportunities in the rag (shoddy) trade of Dewsbury and the building trade in the expanding resorts of East Yorkshire.

The story is one of success and disappointment, of family tensions and disputes, of the impact of two world wars and of tragedy, but above all of deep family bonds and the determination to adapt to change and give future generations a more secure future for their chosen way of life. Writing in 'The Times' in December 2002, Dame Stella Rimington, the former head of MI5, emphasised that "archives have long remained one of our few untapped treasures. These archives provide the bedrock for our understanding of the past. They show us and future generations, how we came to be what we are as a nation, a community or as an individual". Source material for this book comes from the Willis family business records, letters and documents related to business and family activities, together with personal memories from today's family members, supplemented by research at the National Archives, Kew. To collate and assist in the interpretation and typing of all the materials, we owe a special word of thanks to my part time secretary, Paulette Huntington, working at Greenways from 1996 to the present day.

From a market stall in Leeds to a 'house shop' grocery store, of the late 19th century, based in Barnsley, South Yorkshire, there evolved in the late 20th century, a retail chain of over thirty stores and four cash and carry warehouses, with a central distribution depot and head office. There are many lessons in this history which, hopefully, will show future generations where they came from and perhaps encourage them to tread a path which fosters a sense of personal satisfaction, besides bringing benefit to the community in which they work and reside. From the Nowell/Palframan family came the great Yorkshire traits of steadfastness, character and Christian spirit to temper the restless Willis character. Both the Nowell and Palframan families seized opportunities in the expanding industrialisation of Yorkshire through their own textile and building enterprises.

Nothing is possible in business without the support and dedication of the team leaders who collectively make it all happen. To all the past directors, of the several enterprises

I created on the back of the inherited Willis business, I extend my warmest thanks for their confidence and support. However, there were several key individuals, who should be named. Most important of all was my wife Joan, whose patience and commitment in her personal support was unsurpassed. To my three successive personal secretaries of over thirty five years, Dorothy Hill, Dorothy Dyson and Joan Crofts I owe a debt which can never be repaid, as they kept open all the lines of communication. No less important were Janet Hardwick, who worked for the company, in charge of accounts, all her working life, and Anne Strutt who made sure that the central administration never failed. Over these thirty five years there were five main board directors who, each in their own way, filled a key role namely, my brother Derek, two sons Ian and Andrew, Ivor Winetroube and that very special person, Stanley Corbishley. Stanley, with his great sense of humour, was always on hand to smooth the way and reduce the tensions. To all of them, my sincere thanks for their loyalty and support, given through all the changes and challenges we faced in the latter half of the 20th century.

Family history research is a long and arduous task. All I can hope to do is to give a starting line for future generations to explore before 1700. However, there are many family activities over the past 300 years which require further research and perhaps a different interpretation to some of my conclusions. One has to draw the line somewhere. All I can do, in 2009, is to publish what I know and to extend sincere apologies for all errors, false conclusions or omissions.

INTRODUCTION

Before reading this book it is as well to remember that 'The House Shop' played a major role in the Willis family story from the late 19th century and the early 20th century. Home shops or corner shops were very much a product of the Industrial Revolution. Before this time the grocery trade was largely conducted with the middle class and the higher income groups of society through agents allied to the sugar plantations of America and the West Indies or to such companies as the East India Company. The stock in trade of these establishments was centred around luxuries consisting almost entirely of imported foodstuffs and products which could not be made in the kitchens of the wealthy. As trade across the world expanded, particularly to new territories in the east, companies, such as the East India Company, brought in new and exotic foodstuffs, such as a variety of teas, sugars, coffee, dried fruits and spices. At the same time the general population largely depended upon the cottage home to provide their own baked bread with flour from the local mill together with potatoes and vegetables from their gardens or a small allotment, or in lieu of wages from the farmer or landlord. This basic diet could be supplemented with fowl, game and some meat, again if allowed by the employer or landlord. The changes brought about by the textile mill, the weaving shed, the iron foundry and the coal industry brought increasing migration to towns and cities to create an urban way of life not experienced before. Wages, although pitifully small, were to provide the only means to sustain life, through the availability of the basic necessities from small grocers and drapers now being established as 'house shops' or travelling shops in the mean urban streets of town and city. Town and city centres, previously dominated by markets, soon experienced a rapid growth in department stores, high class grocers and specialist shops, all to cater for the increasingly mobile, wealthy and expanding merchant class and middle class.

Much more research is required on the Nowell/Palframan family story. Where did they really come from prior to moving into Leeds? With limited research, I have tried to give a few answers as they progressed from humble urban surroundings to a better lifestyle in the 20th century.

The Martin family, as written here, only goes back to the mid 19th century. Here too, much research will have to be undertaken starting at the marriage of William Albert Martin and Elizabeth Lightfoot in 1872 and going back further in time. The parish registers in Coventry could be a starting point, together with early census records from 1841 and genealogical records from the internet.

The Willis family story is very much one of commercial enterprise, sparked off by the Industrial Revolution. In many ways it does reflect the pressures and demands made upon families as they came to terms with world wars, technological advances and the ever changing social environment. At least it must be important for all generations to know where they came from and then, hopefully, they can build a better future for themselves and future generations.

CHAPTER 1

LAYING THE FOUNDATION

Much has been written and researched about the changing social scene in Victorian England as the country expanded its manufacturing capacity and extended its trading activities to all corners of the world. From the time of the Great Exhibition in 1851 the country witnessed a dramatic expansion of its towns and cities where the manufacturing processes were centred. Opportunities beckoned, particularly if you were prepared to face the crowded, squalid, unsanitary conditions of urban housing. Barnsley was an old market town in South Yorkshire positioned in the centre of a reasonably prosperous rural community. Since the time of James I the town had been engaged in wire manufacturing, followed by linen and glass manufacturing, expanded and developed from the beginning of the 19th century.

It was all to change, as the demand for coal, and its conversion to coke expanded to feed the steel mills of Rotherham and Sheffield. Deep shafts were sunk in the Dearne Valley where particularly rich and broad seams of coal were readily available. A vast network of railway lines, connecting all the mines was rapidly built from 1860 to 1880. Employment opportunities attracted families from Scotland and the North East. To work in the 'Pits', as these mines were called, demanded a very strong physique accompanied by an ever frequent risk of injury. But perhaps as life could still be better than that of a 'tied' rural labourer, young families flocked to the towns where the pit or the mill offered work and very modest money wages.

In the reign of Henry II (1154-1189), the lands on which Barnsley stood were wholly taken into the possession of the monks of St John of Pontefract. During the reign of Henry III (1216-1272) a market and fair charter was granted by the king in 1249, with Wednesday of each week designated Market Day. By the beginning of the 20th century Barnsley was a typical industrial town of the north with a population of around 70,000 souls. The main industry was coal, followed by glass making and linen manufacturing. The last linen mill closed down for good shortly after WWII. Coal disappeared in the latter part of the 20th century. Glass manufacturing still survives in 2008. Today it is a prosperous town, covering a wide area with a population of over 200,000 supporting dozens of small, medium and some large sized enterprises engaged in the service sector, manufacturing and public administration.

In the comparatively small and rather remote town of Eyam in Derbyshire John Willis (1840-1898) was employed as a shoe maker in one of several shoe factories or workshops based in the town. In 1870, at the age of 30 John, with his wife Emma, already had a small family of two sons, George Hamlet born in 1867 and Henry born in 1870. As testified by the tombstone in Eyam churchyard, the Willis family had lived and worked in Eyam for at least the past one hundred years. John was ambitious, he knew that the growing industrial towns of the north, with their expanding population of working class families, would require shoes – at least for the adults. Why not do as so many others had done, migrate to a growing urban population and establish himself as an independent shoe maker? The decision was made, the money was saved, with John arriving in Barnsley in early 1871 with his wife Emma and two sons. They probably travelled to Barnsley with their luggage by a horse drawn wagon taking shoes to Barnsley market and other markets in South Yorkshire. No doubt John had explored the prospects in Barnsley before he moved from Eyam. They took up residence at 2 Court, 5 Buckley Street, a tenement in the centre of Barnsley, off New Street. New Street had just been newly paved and was surrounded by a mass of small streets and courts. As they settled in the oldest son, George Hamlet, was three with the baby Henry, always called Harry, just over one year old. Edith was born in 1873 and died in infancy. Success was not to be found in Barnsley, with the family soon moving to Leeds in either 1872 or 1873, taking up residence at 19 Ashfield Place, east Leeds. Three more children were born in Leeds, Bernard in 1874, John in 1875 and then Walter, who died in infancy. One can only assume that John senior pursued his trade as a shoe maker with reasonable success. Both John and his wife Emma died in Pontypool, ten miles north of Newport, South Wales in 1898 at the age of fifty eight. By this time George Hamlet had already established his grocery shop at 163 Sheffield Road, Barnsley in 1891. With George Hamlet established in Barnsley, and the other three sons striking out on their own, John and Emma moved to Pontypool, presumably into a modest retirement. Child bearing and the strain of a working class life in the Victorian era took its toll as they both passed into history.

Moving back in time, George Hamlet left school at thirteen and was apprenticed to a grocer in the centre of Leeds, who quite possibly had a stall in the open market. We pick up his story as a stall holder for his employer and later on his own account in Leeds open and covered markets from 1886 to 1891. A market stall in the open market would be just a trestle table about four feet by six feet, on which would be displayed the merchandise for sale. Around 1888 he moved as an independent stall holder into the covered market which would provide more space for the Irish produce which was George Hamlet's stock in trade. What is not in doubt is that the young and very intelligent George Hamlet acquired an intimate knowledge of the grocery business and its range of produce, affordable to working class families. By the time he opened his grocery store at 163 Sheffield Road, Barnsley in 1891 he had certainly equipped himself with a wide understanding of how to care for customer needs and obtain a wide range of food products from many and varied suppliers. Market days in Leeds were Tuesday and Saturday. George Hamlet's original employer would additionally have a grocery store in the city. The wage of an apprentice, if he lived over the shop, would be very modest indeed, measured in shillings at the most. However, enough money was saved by George Hamlet by the age of 21 to be able to rent a stall in Leeds covered market, then a shop in Barnsley followed three years later in 1891. Amidst all this activity came marriage, at the age of twenty three, to Mary Louisa Hyland from Corrawallen, County Leitrim in Northern Ireland. George Hamlet was not the only young man in Leeds market at this time striving for success. He must have rubbed shoulders with Michael Marks who founded his Penny Bazaar in 1884, just three years before George Hamlet founded the Willis enterprise. By 1890 Michael Marks had established five Penny Bazaars in northern towns.

One could say that the Willis grocery business was founded upon imported Irish farm products particularly eggs and ham. In a large market, such as Leeds, an enterprising young man would soon learn where all the products for sale came from. From the 1830s to 1860 there had been a rapid expansion of small grocery stores in the towns and cities of England. No longer were tea, sugar and spices the preserve of the 'high class' grocery store. A new type of store for the growing working class population of the cities rapidly developed, continuing into the 20th century. These family stores, created in their thousands were either house shops in the terraces off main streets or corner house shops similarly located. Essentially, they were 'one stop' shops stocking a wide range of imported and home produced provisions plus small sundries. It could be tea from India, sardines from Morocco, butter from Denmark, bacon and eggs from Ireland, currants from Greece and much more. Basic household necessities were soon added to the inventory, from candles to washing and cleaning aids.

George Hamlet, in the late 1880s was soon on his way to Ireland to purchase and bring back to Leeds, Irish farm products. By the time he was twenty one in 1888 he was doing this journey on his own account for his stall in Leeds covered market. The journey started by taking a train from Leeds to Liverpool, steamship to Belfast and then to the village of Corrawallen in County Leitrim. He became a vital link between this small Irish farming community and the outside world.

Corrawallen was, and still remains today, a small Protestant village with the fine, beautifully kept Parish Church of St Columbia. Contacts in Leeds must have introduced George Hamlet to this very remote corner of Ireland.

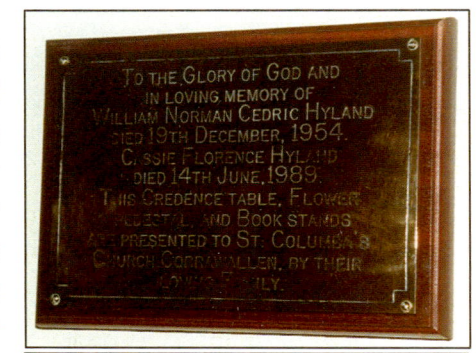

The Hyland Dynasty, memorial at St Cuthbert's, Corrawallen.

Corrawallen, situated amongst the lakes east of Loch Allen, with the nearest coast at Sligo Bay in north western Ireland, was the centre of a small farming community guided by the Hyland family, owners of the Post Office. From the Parish Register of 1857 we learn that Thomas Hyland, the father of Mary Louisa had a lease on a house, office and land, with a rateable value of £13/10/-. This was the largest holding in the village, leased from the landlord, one John Godley. The Hyland family house, next to the Post Office, is quite an imposing Victorian two storey mansion, probably built in the late 19th century and which inevitably attracted the attention of George Hamlet. He was soon to pay court to and ultimately marry in 1890 Mary Louisa Hyland born on 22 April 1858, the only daughter of Thomas Hyland.

Thus were the foundations laid for the Willis Grocery enterprises.

CHAPTER 2

PRESERVING THE MEMORY OF A DERBYSHIRE TRAGEDY
A Snapshot from the Willis Family History

In April 1758 a young couple, known as Alan and Clara called at the Royal Oak Inn, Stoney Middleton, Derbyshire to have their horses rested and fed. The couple were identified, by the landlord, as a lady and gentleman due to their dress and the quality of their horses and baggage. It was also noted that the lady's horse with its fine red morocco saddle must have belonged to a member of the gentry. Alan's horse also carried two large saddle bags, which were quite full, and were carried by Alan into the inn. They were offered a night's lodging but declined as they wanted to push on with their journey over Winnats Pass in good daylight.

It was 'bargain' night at the Royal Oak, with several miners from the local lead mines over indulging. They were curious to see this couple and quickly guessed that they were eloping and on their way to the Peak Forest Chapel to be married. This Chapel was visited for hasty marriages from all districts of Derbyshire, where the minister granted marriage certificates and provided wills. The Chapel did not fall under any parochial or Episcopal jurisdiction. The register just contained the names of the parties without any other details being recorded.

Five drunken miners left the Royal Oak and after another meeting in a local mine known as the Odin mine, determined to waylay the couple at Winnats Pass to rob them of all their possessions. Later that day the couple were duly waylaid, dragged into a nearby barn, and to avoid detection were brutally murdered. The murdered couple were buried in the nearby forest, to be discovered by lead mining operations ten years later. The murderers were never caught but apparently they all had early deaths, including one suicide. The last miner of the five to die gave a written, signed account of the terrible tragedy on his death bed.

When the tragedy happened our direct descendant William Willis, was a groomsman at the Duke of Devonshire's establishment at Chatsworth, later a tenant farmer on the Chatsworth Estate. The abandoned horse, ridden by Clara, still carrying the red morocco saddle and bridle had been found wandering in the forest and brought to Chatsworth. At that time the Duke of Devonshire was a tenant to the Duchy of Lancaster which involved the manorial right of Castleton and the area of Winnats Pass. William Willis ultimately acquired Clara's saddle and bridle, handing it on to his wife Abigail on his death. After Abigail's death the saddle was handed down in the family and exhibited in various local museums in the Castleton area. It is currently in the care of and an exhibit in the city museum at Derby.

After working at Chatsworth, William married Abigail Hadfield at Tideswell in 1749, later leaving Chatsworth to take up a tenancy at Barn Top Farm, Grindleford Bridge. The family continued to farm at Grindleford Bridge, but

George Willis, grandson of William, who married Elizabeth Hind in 1836, moved to Eyam and was employed in one of the shoe making establishments in this small town. Over the centuries the direct line to GRT Willis, in the 20th century, was firstly farming, then shoe making, followed by a grocery stall in Leeds market, and culminating in a major wholesale and retail food distribution business based in Barnsley.

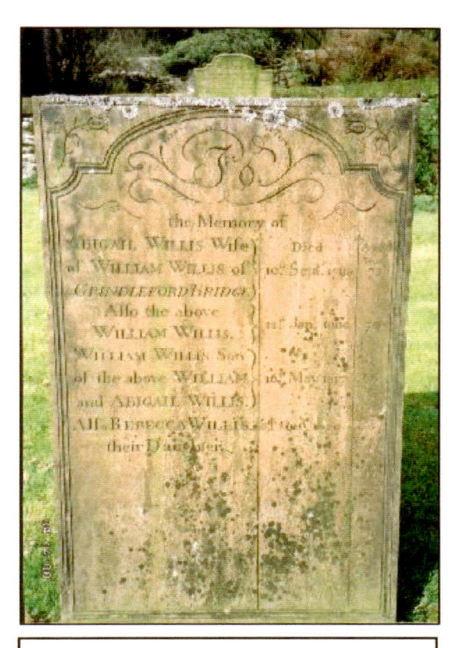

Gravestone of Abigail and William Willis, of Grindleford Bridge, in the graveyard at Eyam.

CHAPTER 3

GEORGE HAMLET WILLIS:
A PIVOTAL ANCESTOR
The story of his family, business and achievements

By any measure George Hamlet, born on 17 October 1876, the oldest of the six children of John and Emma Willis, was a remarkable character. It was he, with a very modest education who moved up from the artisan class and before that of the farm labourer society, to become one of the wealthiest and most respected citizens of the small industrial town of Penistone in South Yorkshire.

In November 1999, I received a letter from the Assistant Editor of the Barnsley Chronicle to let me know that a Mrs Monica Hoyland of Penistone wished to get in touch with me, as she, Monica was the daughter of my grandfather, George Hamlet. I made immediate contact as it was certainly a family tragedy that my grandfather had disinherited his only son back in 1926. Monica was inspired to make contact after reading a review of my book 'No Hero, Just A Survivor', in the Barnsley Chronicle a few days before. I was not aware that either of George Hamlet's two daughters, by his third marriage, were still alive or in what part of the country they lived. Contact by phone was quickly established with Monica inviting Joan and myself to her bungalow in Penistone for tea. We discovered a very sprightly lady of 87, living quite comfortably on her own in a pleasant bungalow with a small garden of which she was very proud. Her husband, Billy, had died a few years before in Penistone. She was under the care of her son Richard, living in Bury with a post as a lecturer at UMIST, a part of Manchester University. We visited Monica several times over the next few years but it soon became apparent that her knowledge of George Hamlet's personal history was very limited. However, she kindly lent us many photographs and put us in touch with her younger sister Joan, living with her husband Charles, in Woodbridge, Suffolk. Monica also gave us as much background, as she was able to, of the life style imposed upon her by her father.

Perhaps we should start with John Willis, born in Eyam, Derbyshire in 1840. It would appear that Daniel Willis, George Hamlet's great grandfather had not been able to take up a farm tenancy at Grindleford Bridge as he was the second son of William Willis at Grindleford Bridge. Daniel and his wife Mary had 10 children and, through his wife Mary Townsend, had connections in Sheffield where they were married in 1789. Putting the Willis family in the historical context of the time, we should note that we were in the reign of George III. Eight years before Daniel and Mary's wedding we lost the American colonies for ever with the surrender of British forces at Yorktown in 1781. One year later London suffered the most horrific riots in English history when 700 lives were lost and there was enormous damage to property. The riots were a resumption of old prejudices against Roman Catholics, exploited by criminal gangs and aggravated by the many other grievances such as the very low wages of the working class in London. After these riots Parliament brought in the Combination Acts, forbidding the assembly of two or more people to join together to press for higher wages or better working conditions. The great political fear was the impact of the French Revolution soon to be followed by war with France, declared by Pitt and his government in 1793. Lasting peace was not to come until 1815 after the battle of Waterloo. The effect of the war with France was to bring much increased manufacturing opportunities to the towns of northern England. There is no doubt that Daniel would be able to find employment for his children in Eyam and district where demand for shoes and clothing, needed by the armed forces, would be substantial.

However, George Hamlet's grandfather, George, would grow up in a quite difficult era, in the middle of the industrial revolution, when there were huge population shifts to big industrial cities, with more opportunities than existed in small towns located in unsuitable areas. In 1843 George's wife Elizabeth emigrated to America and was lost sight of. As their third child Mary was born in the year that Elizabeth went to America it is most likely that George and the three children went too. We assume that George and the children stayed in America but returned when Mary, the youngest, could be cared for without her mother.

Our interest now turns to John, the second child of George Willis, born in Eyam who probably worked in one of the many small shoe factories established in Eyam. However, we do know that John was a very enterprising person in travelling and seeking opportunities outside the confines of Eyam. He married Emma Lowe, from Newton Heath, Lancashire, in

1867 at Eccles, Lancashire, but was probably resident in Eyam at the time. Their first child was George Hamlet, born at Eyam, also in 1867. Only four years later in 1871, but perhaps sooner, we know that John was living at 2 Court, Buckley Street, Barnsley. According to his granddaughter Monica, John walked from Eyam to Barnsley to set up his shoe making business, moving with his wife Emma and two children to Barnsley when he found a suitable terrace house in Buckley Street. The whole area is now covered in high rise flats with Buckley Street Chapel the only surviving building from the 19th century.

Of the two children, we know that George Hamlet was 4 years old and Harry 1 year old. However, by 1873 John and his wife had established themselves at 19 Ashfield Place in Leeds. John and Emma had four more children born in Leeds, two died in infancy but Bernard born in 1874 and John born in 1875 grew to manhood. George Hamlet was certainly long enough in the Buckley Street area of Barnsley to realise, in later years, or perhaps hear from his father that the growing mining town of Barnsley offered opportunities. Whilst at Ashfield Place in Leeds, John would only be in his early forties, so clearly he would still be pursuing his occupation as a shoe maker. John and Emma both died in 1898 in their late fifties in Pontypool in South Wales. John must have retired there with Emma, to be near his wife's family who lived in Pontypool. George Hamlet, although born in Eyam, was living in 2 Court, Buckley Street, Barnsley by the age of four if not a little earlier. Three years later he was living with his parents John and Emma at 19 Ashfield Place, Leeds. Ashfield Place no longer exists, but Ashfield Close and Ashfield Terrace are shown on the Geographia Leeds Street Map of 1989 as being situated in the Seacroft area of Leeds adjacent to Cross Gates. In the late 19th century this would be a crowded area of terraces and courts, now all demolished and developed after World War II as a local authority housing and shopping area. In the 1970s RT Willis (Food Distributors) Ltd leased a supermarket from the local authority in the newly developed Seacroft shopping complex. After a few years the lease was terminated due to poor trading results. It is probable that John, Emma and their four surviving children lived in Ashfield Place until John and Emma retired to Pontypool, possibly around 1895 when John was 55 and possibly in poor health as he died three years later.

With John's death all direct connection with Eyam ceased, although George Hamlet, born in Eyam, directed that on his death he be buried in Eyam Parish Church precincts, alongside his ancestors commemorated by two tombstones in the churchyard. This wish was duly carried out on 29 December 1950. Eyam has a long history, with the area mined in Roman times for its lead which carried on until late in the 19th century, to be followed by the mining of gritstone and chalk. The Saxons came across the North Sea during the 5th and 6th centuries, first marauding and destroying all in their path, but later creating farming settlements across the country, of which Eyam was one. Quite appropriately Eyam has kept its Saxon name which translates as 'Settlement by the water'.

George Hamlet, along with his brothers, lived in the crowded tenements of Victorian Leeds until he broke out, at around the age of 19 in 1886, to open a provision shop at 163 Sheffield Road, Barnsley, to cater for the densely populated terraces and courts situated between Sheffield Road, Park Road and New Street, Barnsley. His father John had given George Hamlet his first opportunity to break out on his own by securing an apprenticeship for him in a Leeds grocery store. On taking up this apprenticeship George Hamlet would be no older than 13, having just left school. His education, quite possibly in a local church school, would equip him with the ability to read and write reasonable English, with a little arithmetic, but little more. However, this apprenticeship was the foundation of George Hamlet's whole career.

GH Willis, 163 Sheffield Road, Barnsley, c1888.

We do not know the name of the grocery business in Leeds which gave George Hamlet his initial training, but we do know that at the age of 16 he was put in charge of a market stall in Kirkgate, Leeds owned by the grocer who had accepted George Hamlet as an apprentice three years earlier. The year was 1884, which has some significance as in that year

Michael Marks, the founder of Marks & Spencer, set up his first stall, also in Kirkgate open market in Leeds. George Hamlet never claimed to have met Michael Marks at this time or later. Within two years George Hamlet had left his employment and set up his own market stall, this time in the covered market in and around the corn exchange, in the centre of Leeds. During his previous experience with his past employer he became fully acquainted with the supply chain to a Leeds grocery market stall selling groceries and provisions.

There is no doubt that in less than two years he created a thriving business in Leeds from this one stall, enabling him to explore and then acquire a shop at 163 Sheffield Road, Barnsley in 1886. With his savings he was able to fully stock and equip this new shop within three years of taking charge of his employers stall in Kirkgate, Leeds. He was to keep the Sheffield Road shop from 1891 to 1913, during which time he developed not only his retail business but developed a wholesale function as well. Moving to Barnsley at the age of 19 was quite an achievement, especially so when at the age of 23 he also married Mary Louise Hyland, the daughter of Thomas Hyland who was the leader of a small Church of Ireland community in the village of Corrawallen, near Caven, County Leitrim, Ireland. On my visits to Corrawallen in the early 1990s I took the opportunity to visit the local heritage centre at Ballinamore which provided much of the information on the Hyland family in this book. I also deduced that most probably the Hyland family emigrated from Yorkshire to Ireland in the early 19th century.

Above: Hyland House, Corrawallen, Co Leitrim. Home of Mary Louisa Hyland. (Taken in 1994)
Below: Corrawallen Post Office. (Taken in 1996)

From setting up his own grocery stall in Leeds covered market in 1885-86 George Hamlet sought out good, cheap wholesome food supplies for resale. This search took him to Ireland and Corrawallen where the family of Thomas Hyland ran the local post office, which also acted as the collecting point for local farm products designed for onward sale to a large city such as Belfast or to England if English food retailers came across. We know from photographs that George Hamlet was selling eggs from his Barnsley shop at a price of 16 eggs for 1/- (5p) to miners earning approximately 40/- per week. The journey from Ireland by George Hamlet would be made by train from Leeds to perhaps Stranraer, across by ferry to Larne, then a train journey across Ireland culminating in a horse drawn carriage or dray. George Hamlet would stay in Corrawallen overnight before the return journey with the eggs he had purchased. The eggs would be packed into small watertight wooden crates with the eggs covered in waterglass as a preservative. Thomas Hyland lived in the largest house in Corrawallen and had an attractive daughter Mary Louisa, age 27 in 1888. Corrawallen is a very remote village in western Ireland where any unmarried lady would find a young man from England very interesting indeed. Inevitably after several visits by George Hamlet to this corner of Ireland, he and Mary Louisa fell in love and were married in 1890, George Hamlet at the age of 23 and Mary Louise six years older at the age of 29. This newly married couple moved to 163 Sheffield Road, Barnsley in 1891 where their first and only child Robert Thomas was born above the shop on 4 January 1892. As far as we know the marriage of George Hamlet and Mary Louisa took place at Drumreilly Church, Church of Ireland, (pictured above) about four miles from the village of Corrawallen. Mary Louisa moved to Barnsley after George Hamlet had completed furnishing his new house shop in Sheffield Road.

It must have been quite a culture shock for Mary Louisa, coming from a quiet rural background where the general farming community, all tenants of a landlord, struggled to feed and clothe themselves and their families, to move to a crowded, noisy, urban environment. It transpires that Mary Louisa was not a very fit woman, suffering from emphysema. George Hamlet, possibly through his membership of his local church, thought to be the Parish Church of Wortley, near High Green, close to Sheffield, obtained the support of a retired milliner Ann Varley, who lived with her daughter

Charlotte Elizabeth in Worsbrough, near Barnsley. Ann and Charlotte moved into 163 Sheffield Road to care for both Mary Louisa and her newly born son. By the end of 1892 it became obvious that Mary Louisa was seriously ill. Unfortunately she was to die just over a year later on 22 May 1894 at 163 Sheffield Road. George Hamlet arranged for her to be buried in the grounds of Drumreilly Church, County Leitrim, Ireland. A headstone marks her grave engraved with the words 'Mary Louisa Willis, beloved wife of GH Willis who died May 22 1894. She is not dead but sleepeth.' Below on the same headstone is inscribed 'She is safe in her Father's House above, in the loving arms of her Saviour's love.'

It appears that George Hamlet was fortunate indeed to have found a capable retired woman, Ann Varley, with her daughter Charlotte Elizabeth who would stay on at 163 Sheffield Road, both as housekeeper and foster mother for his son, just two years old. This arrangement appears to have worked well, with Ann returning to Worsbrough in 1895. Ann died in 1901 at Worsbrough, aged 68. In the meantime, the grocery business was truly flourishing. We have a photograph of the grocery store, with George Hamlet standing in the doorway, taken around 1892 (right). The obviously prosperous look of the shop was just a forerunner to a much larger enterprise that George Hamlet would create. In this photograph we can see, hanging on hooks outside the shop, over twenty hams with more inside plus many rolls of bacon and a full side of bacon, all hanging on hooks. Advertised on the window 'Eggs 16 for a shilling', together with the slogan 'If you want good cheap eggs shop here.' No doubt the eggs came from Ireland.

Chapeltown Co-op, Station Road in the early 1900s. This was a large emporium which offered stiff competition to local independent shopkeepers. At that period the branch contained grocery, drapery, boots and butchering departments. With branches all over Barnsley this type of store was George Hamlet's major competitor.

According to the England and Wales Civil Registration Index George Hamlet, aged 28 and Charlotte Varley, aged 33, married at Wortley near High Green, in midsummer 1895. There were to be no children but it was a very happy marriage, tragically cut short when Charlotte died in 1910 after just 15 years of marriage. George Hamlet was quite devastated. Ever since it was founded and built in 1897, George Hamlet had been a regular member and supporter of St Edwards Church in Kingstone, Barnsley. He was on the sidesman register from 1902 to 1910. In memory of Charlotte he commissioned and paid for a very fine stained glass window, in the perpendicular style, featuring St Edward and the Blessed Virgin Mary. This very fine stained glass window was the first to be placed in the church, being erected in 1911 in the Lady Chapel, being dedicated on 5 June 1911. A brass plate records the dedication and George Hamlet's tribute. 'In loving memory of my wife Charlotte Elizabeth.' Present church members keep this brass plate well polished. According to the 1901 Barnsley Census register, Ann Varley was still in her old home in Worsbrough at the age of 68.

In 1910 George Hamlet's only son, Robert Thomas, was 18 years of age and again without a caring woman to support his emotional needs. There are no family records of the early life of Robert Thomas. In all probability he would have been a day pupil at a local Church of England Junior School from the age of five of six until he was enrolled into Penistone Grammar School as a boarder, probably at the age of ten, that is in 1902. In early December 1992 I visited Penistone Grammar School at the invitation of the then headmaster, Mr MA Bould. My purpose was to see what records there were of Robert Thomas Willis's attendance. We know that he was a boarder at the school at least to the age of 17 as recorded on his examination certificate. We also know that Florence Elsie Willis, in later life heard from her husband Robert Thomas that he had run away from Penistone

Grammar School, escaping from the dormitory with the help of a bed sheet, the dormitory being located above the ground floor. Arriving at 163 Sheffield Road, having walked from Penistone, Robert Thomas asserted that his father refused him entry and told him to walk back again. This story has probably been enhanced in the telling, as Charlotte would be at 163 Sheffield Road and no doubt gave Robert Thomas the chance to rest before returning to Penistone.

However, my visit to see Mr Bould revealed how difficult life could be for Penistone Grammar School boarders in the very early years of the 20th century. Mr Bould informed me that there was no record of Robert Thomas Willis having ever attended Penistone Grammar School, despite certificates of educational achievement proving that he had. What was the explanation? Mr Bould then told me that in the 19th century and early 20th century the governors of Penistone Grammar School decided on the number and fees to be paid by boarders. Penistone Grammar would have forty boys as boarders, with the governors stating how much of the fee had to be used for the care and feeding of boarders. What the governors did not know, at least officially, was that during Robert Thomas's years at Penistone he was one of approximately six boys who were not registered and whose parents paid the headmaster fees, which were not recorded. It is possible that these fees were lower than the official fees and perhaps squeezed the quality and quantity of the food supplied to the boys. Mr Bould showed me the dormitory, now in use as a general purpose room, and additionally pointed out the area of land where, under the supervision of the headmaster's wife in the early nineteen hundreds, the boys grew and tended vegetables for the table. It does appear that a boarder's life could be rather hard as Mr Bould indicated there was some history of boys running away.

The academic achievements of Robert Thomas, as certificates from the Cambridge University Local Examinations Board indicate were quite reasonable, covering Latin, Geography, Arithmetic, Geometry, Algebra, Religious Knowledge, English Language and Literature, History, French, Geometrical Drawing and Dictation. In 1909, at the age of 17, he was awarded a Second Class in the Stage 1 Examination in Inorganic Chemistry (Practical), together with a further certificate for Latin from the Cambridge University Local Examinations Board. It seems that his ambition was to be a chemist. Leaving Penistone Grammar School in 1909 it appears Robert Thomas became an apprentice to a chemist based in Barnsley, whose premises were, I believe, in or near Town End, off Peel Street, Barnsley. It appears that several attempts were made to pass the necessary examinations between 1910-1915 needed to qualify as a dispensing chemist. Florence Elsie Martin, later to be his wife, always maintained that Latin proved to be the hurdle Robert Thomas never overcame.

RT Willis, c1911

In these early years of the 20th century, prior to the First World War, the grocery business of George Hamlet continued to grow. An extension, designed by Robert Thomas, was erected behind 163 Sheffield Road as George Hamlet grew his business by supplying travelling salesmen with grocery products, which they in turn sold to small shops or households in the new mining villages which had sprung up between Barnsley and Doncaster. Thus the wholesale business was born.

As a regular member of St Edward's Church in Kingstone, the contract to supply the Christmas Fare, for members of the St Edward's congregation, was acquired by George Hamlet in November 1905. These contracts, commonly supporting what became known as 'Goose Clubs', were Christmas savings clubs, very popular at that time, until brought to an end by the First World War. We have details of George Hamlet's 1905 contract in which he agreed to supply on Friday 22 December 1905 the following provisions to the savings club members, namely 923 Russian geese at 4/6 per goose, 1263 Hungarian turkeys at 4/9 per turkey, 2700 parcels of groceries at 1/- per parcel and 2700 Christmas cakes at 6d per cake. The place of distribution was to be the Corn Exchange building at the top of Market Hill, Barnsley. Over the years delivery could be delayed by problems with the rail transport, resolved on one occasion by a last minute unloading of railway vans in Barnsley railway sidings by members of St Edward's. Undoubtedly George Hamlet made a great success of this and similar enterprises, which were to finance his business interests after 1918.

At this time a new phase in his life opened up. George Hamlet was married for the third time in 1912 to Marianne

Alice Hardy, whose father was a dentist in Doncaster and whose brother was a doctor in Wakefield before moving to London. Marianne brought two children into this world from the marriage, Monica born on 18 April 1913 and Joan born on 20 September 1915. Marianne, born in 1880 and 13 years younger than George Hamlet comfortably survived her husband, who after a very successful business life died on 26 December 1950.

By 1904 George Hamlet had so expanded his wholesale business through the use of agents drawing their supplies from 163 Sheffield Road, that he was able to acquire a fine open top touring car, as illustrated in a photograph of that time. Seated in the car (right) are George Hamlet and his son Robert Thomas in the front with Charlotte and her mother Ann on the back seat. This wholesale business prospered so well that shortly after the marriage to Marianne, a warehouse of around 2,000 square feet was acquired in Foundry Street, Barnsley, formerly a part of one of the two foundries located in Foundry Street, and closed down in the early part of the century, as more modern and larger establishments were developed in Sheffield. The new Willis premises in Foundry Street were located on the corner of Foundry Street and Wellington Street on the edge of Barnsley town centre. Documents show that by 1919 George Hamlet was handling, through these premises, single consignments of over 5 tons of imported Canadian hams which, in view of the absence of refrigeration, would have to be sold within days. These hams, known as short cut Canadian hams, were very popular with the many small South Yorkshire house shops, who cooked the hams and then sold the product to miners' families. Boiled ham and a tin of salmon were the staple treat, especially on Sundays, for working class families.

Records in the research department of Barnsley's Public Library indicate that George Hamlet left 163 Sheffield Road in 1913. The warehouse in Foundry Street was probably purchased at this time. Happily married again he continued to live in Sheffield Road in various locations before settling down, in 1915, at Willowbank, Sheffield Road. The retail business probably stayed with George Hamlet until he moved from Willowbank in 1919 to Grenfell, a brick built detached house and garden in Granville Street, Barnsley. This last location was far away from the Sheffield Road shop, being at the northern edge of Barnsley. The retail store was probably disposed of in 1920 shortly after the move from Willowbank to Granville Street. The premises did not survive as a retail store after disposal, becoming a barber's shop owned by Mr Eli Shaw. The shop and adjoining property

GH Willis warehouse, Foundry Street, Barnsley 1925. RTW on the left.

were demolished, along with all the crowded terraces and courts to the rear, shortly after World War II.

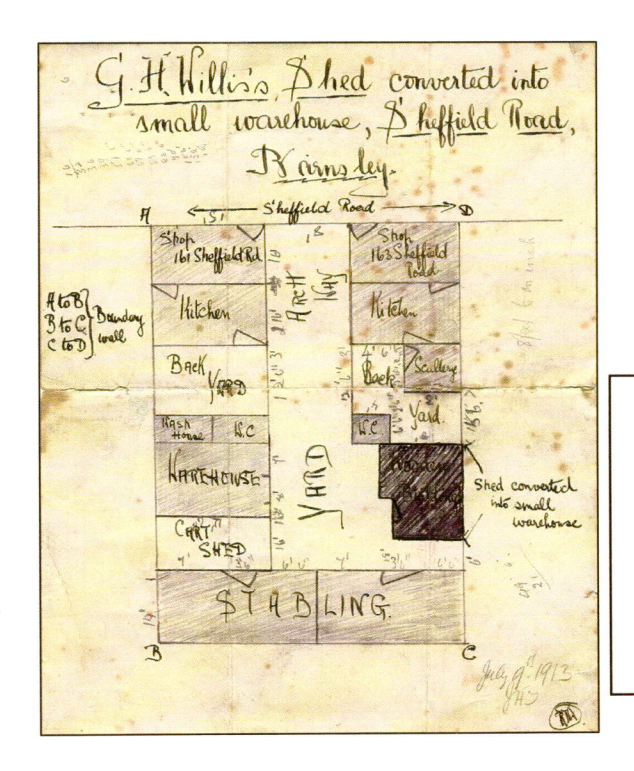

Ground plan of shed converted into small warehouse on the premises of GH Willis, Sheffield Road, Barnsley, 9 July 1913.

By the time that George Hamlet moved to Granville Street in Barnsley, he and Marianne had a new family with two daughters, Monica and Joan. Both these young ladies were sent at a very early age to Ackworth Public School as boarders. Prior to Ackworth both Monica at around age 8 and Joan at around 6 years old were boarders at The Grove, a nursery school at Malton, East Yorkshire. At Ackworth, a Quaker school, it was a strict regime with both girls feeling quite lonely. In the meantime, as mentioned earlier, George Hamlet's only son was apprenticed to a dispensing chemist in Barnsley, after leaving Penistone Grammar School in 1909 at the age of 17. In that same year Robert Thomas was also Confirmed at St Edward's, Kingstone, Barnsley where he must have been a regular attender. After leaving school he took up permanent residence with his father, firstly at 163 Sheffield Road and after at Willowbank, Sheffield Road. As far as we know, he played no part in George Hamlet's grocery business prior to enlisting at Barnsley on 18 January 1915 in the York and Lancs Regiment. Despite having left Penistone Grammar School with good academic qualifications, Robert Thomas failed to pass the final examinations necessary to become a dispensing chemist before he enlisted. He was posted to Aldershot and later to Salisbury Plain as a PT and Bayonet Fighting Instructor. Sometime in 1918 he suffered an accident when a bayonet pierced his left hand during a training exercise. At this time he held the rank of Corporal, but following the accident he was transferred to The Kings Own Yorkshire Light Infantry Training Reserve, retaining the rank of Corporal. After hospital treatment in a military casualty ward at the Royal Hospital, West Street, Sheffield, he was deemed unfit for military duty and discharged from the army on 18 November 1918, with the rank of Corporal. Returning home to Granville Street he found a very different situation as George Hamlet had truly prospered during the war, despite severe food shortages, a doubling of income tax from the pre war levels and the imposition of price controls from 1916 onwards. He was looking for investment opportunities which were initially pursued by the purchase of good quality housing in Park Grove, Barnsley.

Then the final opportunity came which was to establish, with three partners, a Malt Vinegar Brewery in Penistone in 1923. His son Robert Thomas, still unable to pass his final exams to become a dispensing chemist, agreed, after recovering from the bayonet wound to his hand, to join his father in the expanding wholesale provision business based in Foundry Street, Barnsley. Documents discovered after the death of Robert Thomas on 13 February 1955 indicate that a legally binding partnership between George Hamlet and his son was drawn up and executed in 1921. This agreement divided the net profits of the partnership, trading as GH Willis and Son of Foundry Street Barnsley, on the basis of two thirds of the annual net profits of GH Willis and Son to be paid to GH Willis and the balance of one third to be paid to RT Willis. These payments were in lieu of salary, after all expenses including business tax, depreciation and an agreed reserve to cover the cost of fixed assets and expanding stock levels in a growing business. Probably due to the lack of an independent professional accountant supervising the partnership agreement, by 1926 the partnership had fallen apart. After a court hearing the partnership was dissolved and George Hamlet agreed to allow Robert Thomas to acquire full control of the Foundry Street business. George Hamlet also agreed to avoid providing competition to his son, who in turn was required to purchase the two third share at the book value of the business over a period of years. Documents and letters from Smith and Ibberson, Solicitors in Church Street, Barnsley indicate that the final payment for the business by Robert Thomas of £300/16/8 was made on 13 May 1929.

George Hamlet was now able to concentrate on building up the malt vinegar business in Penistone. At the same time he disposed of his Foundry Street property as Robert Thomas took the wholesale provision business to fresh premises in New Street, Barnsley in July 1926. One unfortunate aftermath from the dissolution of the partnership was that father and son became totally estranged and never communicated with each other from 1929 to the time of

Top left: Penistone & Victoria Malt Vinegar Brewery, Cubley Brook.
Top right: Vats in the Brewery.
Above left: Yeast advert. Above right: 90,000 gallon vats.

George Hamlet's death in 1955. There was one exception, which we know about, when George Hamlet made a visit to his son at New Street during World War II. This visit may well have been an attempt at reconciliation which was not repeated and totally failed to heal the breach.

Moving to the domestic front, George Hamlet's son Robert Thomas took up residence at Grenfell after discharge from hospital and from the army in 1919. After his marriage to Florence Elsie Martin on 24 July 1920 he moved out to a detached stone built house off Park Grove, Barnsley. This house, owned by George Hamlet, still retains its original name of High Stile Cottage, and was given to Robert Thomas and his newly married wife rent free as a wedding present. Sometime, prior to the dissolution of the Partnership, a rent book for High Stile Cottage arrived from George Hamlet which was to precipitate the move of Robert Thomas and his family to a small bungalow, to be built and named Corrawallen, in Worsbrough Dale, Barnsley. George Hamlet's interests were now entirely focused upon developing the malt vinegar enterprise in Penistone. A new house was built in Chapel Lane, Penistone, formerly St John's Lane, into which he and Marianne with their two daughters, moved in 1927. This house with double fronted bay windows, five bedrooms, oak panelled reception areas with parquet floors, garage and greenhouse was also known as Grenfell. Its reputed cost in 1927 was between £3,000 and £5,000. Grenfell, situated on a large plot of over two acres, some of which was sold off later and containing a large conservatory plus a snooker room over the garage, demonstrated how well George Hamlet had prospered from his retail and wholesale provision business.

At the same time, after buying a major stake in the malt vinegar business, he was able to invest not only in that business, but in properties in Barnsley and Penistone. Undoubtedly he was a very successful entrepreneur.

Top: Grenfell, Granville Street, Barnsley.
Above: Grenfell, Penistone.

George Hamlet was joined in 1923 in his new enterprise by Mr Holmes of Lincoln, Mr Drabble of Conisborough and Mr Waterhouse of Nether Edge, Sheffield. These four partners acquired the larger half of the Ale and Porter Brewery, at Cubley Brook, Penistone which had been founded by Brook and Co in 1848, closing down in 1924 after selling most of the buildings in 1923 to George Hamlet and his partners. The new brewery which was to become a Malt Vinegar Brewery and was incorporated as Penistone Pure Malt Vinegar Company Limited, of Cubley Brook Brewery, Penistone. George Hamlet was appointed managing director, a position he held until he retired at the end of World War II at the age of 78. The brewery was very successful, being noted for the quality of its product, using the best English barley together with various flavours and 4-12% of acetic acid. This success owed much to the skill of Mr Wilfred Bradley, the brewer, who was later to be succeeded as brewer by his son Arthur. One of its major customers was the HP Sauce factory at Aston Cross, Birmingham.

Marianne Willis, 1924.

A Mr Jack Smith of Barnsley related to the writer his experiences of driving a steam wagon to Aston Cross every week in the 1920s with a large round tank full of malt vinegar for the HP Factory. In 1961 British Vinegar amalgamated with Penistone Malt Vinegar. By 1973 the Penistone brewery was producing almost two million gallons a year of malt vinegar with the product being sold world-wide. In December 1973 British Vinegar announced that the plant in Penistone was to close down, with all the production facilities being transferred to Middleton near Manchester. Sadly a workforce of sixty was made redundant but fortunately neither George Hamlet or his wife Marianne were around to witness the end of a business to which George Hamlet had given and gained so much.

Above: Monica, Joan and their half brother Tom (RT Willis).
Right: Monica, 1931 age 18, Grenfell, Penistone, just back from Germany.

When George Hamlet moved to Penistone in 1927 his two daughters Monica and Joan were still at Ackworth Quaker Public School near Pontefract. Monica indicated to me that she felt very lonely and unloved when away from home in a boarding school but, much to her credit, she became Head Girl and very proficient at German. Monica became a translator but soon turned to teaching which she enjoyed. Marianne had a secretarial role at the vinegar brewery, but whether part time or full time and with what responsibilities is not known.

From 1927 to 1945 George Hamlet took a keen interest in the welfare of Penistone, serving from time to time as a Councillor on the MDC and one time as its Chairman. Over the years he was the chairman of several committees, most notably the water committee and the Penistone Food Committee. He was a keen supporter of the local branch of the British Legion, being made an honorary member of the branch. He was a governor of Penistone Grammar School, a regular church attender and a freemason. Withdrawing from public life in 1945 he retired to enjoy his fine garden at Grenfell. He died after a very short illness on Boxing Day 1950 and was buried the following Friday 29 December at Eyam, the place of his birth, after a well attended funeral service at St James, Penistone. His wife Marianne sold Grenfell for around £4,500 and purchased a house at Hatch End in London. Marianne sold her shares in Penistone Malt Vinegar and helped to support her two married daughters, but she also made investments in local paper mills which lost value over the years with many of the mills going out of business. Marianne then suffered a severe car accident in 1952 when travelling north from London. This put an end to her driving causing her to move into the home of her daughter, Monica, at Bella Vista, a farm house on Hartcliff Hill on the western hills overlooking Penistone. She died peacefully on 18 July 1962. She was buried alongside George Hamlet at Eyam after a service in St James, Penistone. An interesting footnote is that the old family home Grenfell was sold in 2007 for just under £700,000.

History was to repeat itself but with a happier ending, when George Hamlet bought, as a wedding present in 1937, a large farm house named Bella Vista for his newly married daughter Monica and her husband William Horne Hoyland. After spending the working week at Charles Marsden and Company Limited, Paper Merchants in Matilda Street, Sheffield, Billy spent weekends helping the farmer who lived in a wing of Bella Vista. It was not an easy life on a remote farm which only received mains electricity in 1952 and mains water in 1960. However, Monica was able to continue her vocation as a teacher at Oxspring School besides bringing up a family. their daughter Gillian Mary was born in April 1940 but unfortunately died in 1961. A son Richard William was born on 16 November 1944 who became, in due course, a Chemistry graduate and PhD and then a lecturer at UMIST, Manchester in paper making technology. He retired in 2008. Richard married Margaret Gillian Mary Brass only to lose her to cancer leaving behind two young sons David aged 5 and James, 3.

In due course Billy Hoyland was able to acquire the Charles Marsden paper merchants business in Sheffield, which was sold after Billy's death in 1993 for £33,000. Although much of George Hamlet's inheritance had been spent or lost through some ill advised investments, Monica and Billy were able to leave Bella Vista in 1968, moving to a modern bungalow, Netherholm, in Chapel Lane, Penistone. When Monica's mother Marianne died in 1962 there was only £20,000 remaining from George Hamlet's estate. Nevertheless this was quite a considerable sum at that time to which Monica would have a share, including the shares in the Yorkshire Property and Investment Company Limited controlled by the Nicholson family. Michael Nicholson, a chartered accountant, was for many years the auditor of RT Willis and Son. Joan, Monica's sister, also inherited 160 shares from the property company. Yorkshire Properties and Investment Company who owned many independent cinemas in South Yorkshire, two of which, situated in Goldthorpe and Hillsborough, Sheffield, RT Willis and Son converted to supermarkets in the early 1980s having no knowledge of the connection with the Penistone family. Billy Hoyland also had investments in Samuel Fox, the Stocksbridge steel strip mill, which was founded by his grandfather and a partner. Billy's grandfather pulled out but the strip mill prospered to become one of the largest in Europe. It still flourishes to this day. Together with the sale of steel shares and Monica's shares in the Penistone Malt Vinegar Company Billy and Monica were able to live comfortably after their retirement. When Billy died in 1993 Monica purchased a very pleasant bungalow in 1995 not far from the site of the old vinegar brewery and giving reasonable access to local shops. Monica had many friends, was a regular attender at St James and enjoyed golf and bridge. In 2006/7 Monica was to suffer a series of accidents resulting in her subsequent transfer to a well run nursing home in Stocksbridge, organised by her son Richard. She died peacefully on 29 March 2008. (Please note, information above on investments and sale of same were related to the writer by Monica but still contain inaccuracies although giving a general picture.)

After leaving Ackworth Quaker School Joan, George Hamlet's younger daughter, was supported by him as she took up a three year training course as a Physiotherapist at

Middlesex Hospital. In 1941 Joan married Charles Francis Forster who was a research chemist with the GPO. For the first years of their marriage Joan and Charles lived in Sheffield before moving to Poole in Dorset, moving again after just twenty months to Harrow, Middlesex. They were both able to pursue their careers, Charles at the GPO and Joan as a physiotherapist. Their first daughter Carolyn Joan was born on 16 September 1942 at Grenfell in Penistone. Her sister Dorothy Elizabeth Alison (always known as Alison) was born on 23 April 1944 in Barnsley General Hospital. Carolyn has two children from her first marriage, Andrew Paul and Sarah Louise, the marriage ending in divorce in 1990 after 15 Years. Shortly after Carolyn married Sidney James Stone who tragically suddenly died in October 1998. Apart from bringing up a small family in rather difficult circumstances, Carolyn has an interesting working life, starting with the BBC as a secretary and then with Trans World Airlines. Several years then ensued as she brought up her family, before taking up a post with Kodak at Harrow, where her late husband Sidney Stone also worked. Carolyn, now retired, is happily married to Bill Nickson, living in the pleasant village of Pitsford near Northampton.

Carolyn's younger sister Alison gained a PhD at University before moving to America in the late 1960s. She has had a most distinguished career including Royal recognition with an OBE for services in fostering British links with America. Alison met her future husband, Roger Taunton-Rigby, at university. They married, moved to America bringing up four children, three boys and a girl, Jonathan, Rolf, Jason and Liev. Sadly the marriage was not to last as they divorced and Alison developed her own business which today, in 2008, is a consultancy known as Forester Biotech, based in Lincoln, Boston, Massachusetts, of which Alison is the President and Chief Executive Officer. She pays regular visits to England to see and support her mother Joan.

When Charles retired from the Post Office (Royal Mail) he had been engaged for many years in introducing new technology to the postal service, including the bar coding of postage stamps. He and Joan moved into a town house in Woodbridge, Suffolk to enjoy their retirement in this pleasant and historic area. Charles did a great deal of genealogical research of the Willis family, going back 300 years. He very kindly passed copies of this research to the writer who has found the detail to be very accurate and most helpful. Shortly after his 90th birthday Charles died, resulting in Joan leaving Woodbridge to live with her daughter Carolyn at Pitsford. Through increasing disability Joan moved into a pleasant care home nearby and died peacefully in January 2009 aged 93. No doubt, the George Hamlet story will be passed on down many generations, correcting and enlarging on the information given here.

Above left: GH Willis as a baby.
Above right: GH Willis age 16.
Left: GH Willis.
Bottom left: GH Willis age 29.
Bottom right: GH Willis on a bicycle.

Above left: GH Willis, Churchwarden, St Edward's, Kingstone, Barnsley.
Above right: Pre motor era, Nell in the shafts.
Right: GH & Marianne Willis.
Bottom left: GH & Marianne Willis.
Bottom right: GH Willis and Marianne's wedding, 1912.

Left, above left & right: GH Willis 1920s.
Bottom left: GH Willis passport photograph, 1931.
Bottom right: Outside the garage & billiard room at Grenfell.

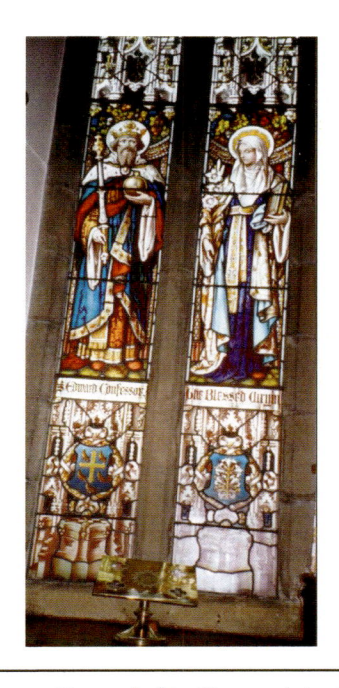

Above left: Memorial window to Charlotte Elizabeth Willis, side chapel, St Edward's Church, Barnsley.
Above right: GH Willis with Uncle Percy (Percy Chambers, brother in law), Grenfell c1937.
Below: GH Willis presenting the Willis Bowls Cup.

CHAPTER 4

HEW HORIZONS
THE IMPACT OF THE MARTINS

Prior to the coming of the railway age, in the middle of the nineteenth century most families, whether of working class or lower middle class, pursued a life style much constrained by their survival needs. Social mobility was very restricted confining most families within their immediate neighbourhood. The Willis branch were tied to the land in north Derbyshire and to the town of Eyam with its shoe making industry. The Nowells were caught up in the Industrial Revolution in Dewsbury, seeking their opportunities on the fringes of the textile industry, working as traders and processors of the waste material discarded by West Yorkshire mills. The Palframan's roots were in Bradford finding many opportunities as small builders of houses for the workers of this fast expanding city, the centre of the woollen industry. The branch of this family, whose daughter Lily married Clifford Nowell, moved from Bradford to Leeds and then to Whitby around 1902, seeing opportunities in an expanding sea-side town.

Revd William Martin, East Halton, 1930.

When I married Joan Nowell on 24 November 1945, I supplemented the cultural background of both the Willis and Nowell inheritance of two typical northern families, with an intellectual element inherited from my mother, educated within the environment of a late nineteenth century parsonage. Social mobility in the nineteenth century was largely governed by economic factors as families moved off the land to the growing industrial cities. The agricultural revolution of the eighteenth and nineteenth centuries brought crop rotation, improved farming implements, better seed stock and larger farms, all leading to much pressure on families to move off the land, as demonstrated, in its most extreme form, by the land clearances in Scotland and Ireland. Families, if they survived, moved to new lands overseas or to the factory or mining towns of the north or south Wales. The Willis and Nowell families were products of the factory town with their intellectual horizons largely focussed on their local community and church, almost certainly of the Methodist or 'low' church tradition.

The intellectual and cultural infusion into the Willis family came from Florence Elsie Martin, the daughter of the Revd William Alfred Martin, a very unassuming vicar of the Church of England. Florence Elsie experienced an education of scholarship, equipping her with fluent French and great musical ability, which generated a desire for learning within her family. Her achievement was quite remarkable as her husband, Robert Thomas, always asserted that education was corrupt and undermined the necessity, as he put it, "to earn one's living".

Florence Elsie Martin was the tenth member of a twelve children family. In the following chapter she describes the life of her parents and two of her brothers, Harold Edgar and Albert Percival. A little more detail can be given here about her father and the other children.

The Reverend William Alfred Martin owed much to the evangelist, Charles Hadden Spurgeon (1834-1892), the great Baptist preacher who drew crowds of many thousands to the Metropolitan Tabernacle, seating 6,000, in London, during the late nineteenth century. It appears that William Martin moved from Coventry to the south of England shortly after his marriage to Elizabeth Lightfoot in 1872. Apparently he was employed by the London Metropolitan Tabernacle as a supporting minister. Following the death of Charles Hadden Spurgeon in 1892 and before the Tabernacle was burnt down in 1898, William Martin was taken under the wing of Bishop Burrows, the first Bishop of Sheffield. Bishop Burrows, much impressed by William Martin's Christian faith, said to William, "come to Yorkshire and I will ordain you into the Church of England". William did not hesitate, was ordained in 1896, taking residence as a Deacon in Halifax to be followed as a Priest in Ripon in 1897. Following this he became Curate of Windhill, Yorkshire 1896-1898, Curate at All Souls, Halifax from 1898-1901 and then Curate at Lockwood, Huddersfield from 1901-1903. From there he moved to be Curate at St George's, Barnsley, (now demolished) 1903-1907 where he lived in a large detached Victorian house in Dodworth Road, Barnsley. From there he became Curate at St Bartholomew, Carbrook, Sheffield from 1907-1912 and then Vicar at Emmanuel Church (now demolished) Attercliffe, Sheffield from 1912-1924. Finally he moved to Lincolnshire to be Vicar at East Halton, near Immingham from 1924-1931.

Left:
East Halton Vicarage and St Peter's Church, East Halton taken in 1995 and 1990 respectively.

He retired, for health reasons, in 1931 to Nether Stowey, near Bridgewater in Somerset. He and his wife Elizabeth, accompanied by their daughter Edith, always known as Edie, were able to acquire a large Victorian detached family home in this pleasant village, quite secluded down an unmarked road. There was a large garden, but no electricity or gas although there was running water and a flush toilet. All communication to the outside world was by letter. The house, named Hibernia, never sported the luxury of a telephone or radio. News from the outside world was confined to the daily newspaper or news from visitors. As Florence Elsie describes, Edie stayed with them to the end.

William Alfred and Elizabeth Alice Martin, 1938.

William had a pleasant study, full of books, where he spent most of his time. Elizabeth rose late morning and was able to sit in the garden or summer house and enjoy a cup of tea. Much of the garden was given over to growing produce for the table, looked after by a kind elderly man from the village who looked for no reward, except for a little of the produce grown. Edie looked after all the finances, cooked all the meals on a paraffin stove and ran the house with some help from her sister Anne who came to Hibernia shortly after WWII. On Sundays Edie played the organ in the village church from time to time. William died on 7 March 1947 aged 90 with Elizabeth dying before him on 13 May 1943 aged 85. Both William and Elizabeth are buried in Nether Stowey church cemetery. Their gravestone reads 'Elizabeth Alice Martin the beloved wife of the Rev William Alfred Martin who ascended to be with Christ May 13 1943 aged 85. Angels bear her forth to air grief and loss. Hers is the better part, the haven of rest and pure delight. Ours the distressful storms of life, help us good Lord. In heaven they enter into rest and with rapture behold the Glory of the Lord. Also of Rev William Alfred Martin born July 6 1856, died March 7 1947, from their loving family. Lovely and pleasant in their lives and in their death they were not divided.'

Apart from what Florence Elsie recorded, we do not have detailed histories of her brothers and sisters, apart from the few notes she handed down which follow and some personal experience I can recall. Here is a list of the twelve children referred to by Florence Elsie.

The children:

Annie Harrop, 12 December 1876 - 22 November 1954.
Edith Alice, 1878 – 1976.
Frank William Ernest, 1880 - 1943, married with 4 children, 3 boys and 1 girl.
Eleanor Louise (Nell), 1882 - 1972, married Harry Pearson, no children.
Charles Haddon Spurgeon, 1884 - 1894, died of double pneumonia, age 10.
Florence Beatrice, 1886 – 1887, died in infancy of bronchitis.
Lilian Beatrice, 1888 – 1971 (Aunt Lily).
Edward Bertram, 1890 - 1950, married Emmie, 2 children Ida May (married a Swiss national and lived in Switzerland) and Barbara (married a doctor).
Harold Edgar, 1892-1971, married Gwyneth Rees, 2 children, Pat Cadier (married Ronald Cadier, two children) and Jean Harrison (married Warwick, two children Craig and Catherine, all living in Victoria, Australia).
Florence Elsie, 1894 - 1988, married with 5 children.

Albert Percival, 1896 - 1915, killed in WWI, aged 19.

Evelyn May, 1889-1971, married Thomas Marshall, 1 son Martin (Thomas Cedric Martin Marshall), deserted by her husband when her son was only 4. May never saw her husband again.

Harold Edgar Martin:
- University College, Durham, BA, 3rd class in Classics & General Literature. MA in 1917. Served as a Lieutenant, 1917-1919, in Mesopotamia under General Allenby. Lost a leg, amputated, convalescence in a military hospital in Leeds.
- 1920, Christ Church, Cambridge, BA 2nd class, Classic Tripos Part II.
- 1925 MA, University of London.
- 1925 BA 3rd class, French.
- Assistant Master, King Edward VII School, Lytham from 1925-1929. Headmaster, Royal Orphanage School, Wolverhampton 1929-1931. Returned to King Edward School in 1931.
- 1930 Bishop College, Cheshunt. Deacon & Priest, Blackburn 1931. Curate of St Paul's, Fairhaven, Diocese of Blackburn from 1931-1956.
- Lived at: 1) Henley, Clifton Drive South, St Annes, Lancs; 2) Jesmond, 12 Caryl Road, St Annes on Sea; 3) Park Court, Park Road, Burgess Hill, Sussex.
- Harold on retirement went to 10 Park Court, Burgess Hill, Sussex and left in 1968 moving to Lake View, Newmillerdam, Wakefield as a close neighbour to his sister Florence Elsie, collected from Burgess Hill by Robert and Joan in their car.

Albert Percival Martin:
- Private 12489, 8th Bn, York & Lancaster Regiment. Died aged 19, Saturday 25 September 1915. Son of the Rev William Alfred Martin, Vicar of Emmanuel Church, Sheffield. Born at Dover. Remembered with Honour, X Farm Cemetery, La Chappelle-D'Armentieres, grave C7 and also named on the Menin Gate.
- Recorded on the Commonwealth War Graves Commission Debt of Honour Register.
- X Farm Cemetery is approximately 1 km south of the village on the west side of the road to Bois-Garnier, between the road and the site of a farm.
- The village was in British hands from October 1914 until the fall of Armentieres on 10 April 1918, and it was retaken the following October. During the British occupation it was very close to the front line and the cemeteries which it contains are those made by fighting units and Field Ambulances in the earlier days of trench warfare. X Farm Cemetery was begun in April 1915 and used until June 1916, and it was sometimes called 'Wine Avenue'. It was intended to take the place of Desplanque Farm Cemetery. There are now over 100 1914-1918 war casualties commemorated in this site. The cemetery covers an area of 1,065 square metres and is enclosed by a low rubble wall.

Annie Harrop appears to have spent most of her life employed by the Mission for Seamen in Portsmouth. In 1947 she came to stay with Robert and Joan at Whitwell, having retired to Nether Stowey. She never married. Edith Alice (Edie) described by Florence Elsie as her favourite sister, devoted her whole life in support of her parents and the life of the Church community. She never married. She always attended Florence Elsie's confinements and I suspect acted, in effect, as a midwife on more than one occasion. She was extremely talented as a superb cook, household manager, piano and organ player, parish organiser and friend and counsellor to all. Edie was able to earn a little money for herself by the sale of very fine knitted garments to a drapery merchant in London. A much loved lady, who lived to the age of 98, spending her last years, after the death of Lily and Nell, with her nephew Martin Marshall and his wife Ruby in Surrey.

<u>Frank William Ernest</u> never came within the Willis orbit except during WWII when he took up residence at the Queens Hotel in Barnsley to escape the blitz. He died aged 63 in 1943.

<u>Eleanor Louise</u> (known as Auntie Nell) married Harry Pearson, a fitter at the local gas company. They lived in modest circumstances, firstly in a small terrace house in James Street, Barnsley. After his retirement they moved to a small new terrace house off Broadway, Barnsley. Harry served as a private soldier in the Boer War. They had no children. Whilst living in Barnsley Florence Elsie kept in touch with her sister, but Robert Thomas made it clear that visits to Hyland House were not to be encouraged. In 1965 Nell moved to Hibernia, Nether Stowey where she died aged 90.

Charles Hadden Spurgeon unfortunately did not have long enough to live down his name, dying of double pneumonia age 10. Florence Beatrice died in infancy in 1887. Lilian Beatrice (Aunt Lily) had an unfortunate life, apparently being sent to an institution which cared for mentally retarded individuals, as judged by Victorian standards. After the death of her parents Edie rescued her and she lived with her and Nell until she died in 1971 aged 83. Joan and I met her at Nether Stowey and found her quite normal to speak to. She was probably a victim of Victorian prejudices.

Edward Bertram joined Dunn's Hats in Manchester at an early age. A man of much energy and talent who rose to be the General Manager of Dunn's. He was able to pursue a very comfortable life style, living in a large modern house containing a full size billiard table room, garage and a large car. He sent his two daughters, Barbara and Ida, to Switzerland to be educated. He died at the comparatively young age of 60, in 1950.

Evelyn May (Auntie May) was an aunt much admired by the Willis children because of her Christmas gifts. After her husband deserted her shortly after the Great War she turned her talents to writing books for children, which she was able to have published in London. From the 1930s she was the editor of the 'Nursing Mirror', a position she held until her retirement in 1950. She retired from London to live on her own, having never re-married, to Petherton in Somerset, fairly close to her sister in Nether Stowey. She died peacefully in 1971 aged 82.

Florence Elsie took much comfort from the intellectual achievements of her brothers and sisters, as opposed to the iconoclastic attitude of Robert Thomas who took only a modest interest in the academic achievements of his children in Junior School and Grammar School. Fortunately, the Martin influence prevailed generating literary, scientific and musical pursuits, to varying degrees, in his five children.

Just prior to completing this publication our son Ian conducted some research on the parentage of William Alfred Martin. I am very grateful for the contribution as there do not appear to be any records, letters or documents relating to the early life of William Alfred in the possession of the family. here follows Ian's contribution, which he hopes to supplement in the years ahead. The great unknown is how did William Alfred break away from a family supported by the 'poor law' and arrive in London?

<u>George Martin</u> was born around 1830 and married Sarah Lester. <u>William Alfred Martin</u> was born on 6 July 1856 at Coventry. On his birth certificate his father's occupation is Stone Breaker, an occupation which was commonplace if you lived in or were supported by the workhouse. Also on this certificate it is signed 'x, the mark of Sarah Martin, mother, Gosford Street, Coventry'. It appears that she could not write and probably could not read either. Immediately off Gosford Street was Coventry workhouse.

William was born in the parish of St Michael's. In 1918 the parish church of St Michael became Coventry Cathedral. The building was destroyed in 1940 by German bombing and today stands as a ruin next to the modern rebuilt cathedral. William may have been baptised in this church. I need to study the church records which are situated at the county records office in Warwick.

In 1342 Whitefriars Carmelite monastery was found at Coventry. It was situated between the modern day Gulson Road and Gosford Road, about ½ mile east of Coventry Cathedral. The monastery was dissolved by Henry VIII in 1545 and the buildings were taken over by a local man, John Hales. In 1801 these buildings became Coventry Workhouse and continued until 1945.

I have studied the admissions and discharges records of Coventry workhouse and can find no instances of any Martin family member being resident in the workhouse. However, in the Directors' Minute books it states that outdoor relief was a regular part of the system. In return for receiving outdoor relief one of the tasks that the able-bodied had to undertake was stone breaking - normally for road making materials.

The Directors held a weekly meeting. in the minutes of the meeting held on 9 July 1856, approval was given to the appointment of Charles Holt as the new registrar of births, deaths and marriages for Coventry. His signature appears on William's birth certificate which is dated 21 July 1856.

According to the 1881 Census William Alfred Martin was living at 41 Princes Square, Stepney, which is about 1 mile due east of the Tower of London, in the parish of St George in the East. His occupation is Scripture Reader. The household comprised William, age 24, Elizabeth 23, Annie H 2 and Edith A -. The age of Annie H would indicate that she was born in 1878 or 1879; this differs from her birth date of 1876 as stated earlier in Chapter 4. Also Edith A -, would indicate that she was born in 1880 or 1881 and not 1878. To clarify this I would need to obtain copies of their birth certificates.

In the 1891 Census William Martin was living in Kent. In the 1901 Census he was living in Yorkshire.

Tracing the Martins in the earlier censuses is proving difficult. However, there is an interesting entry in the 1871 Census. William Martin does not appear in Coventry but a William Martin appears in Leamington Priors, which became Leamington Spa, and it could be the same person. The entry for 15 Printer Street reads:

Person	Relation	Age	Occupation	Where born
Sarah Wright	Head	43	Shop keeper	Coventry
Daniel Wright	Son	24	Labourer	Badby
Ruth Wright	Daughter	12	Unemployed	Whitmarsh
George Wright	Son	11	Unemployed	Leamington
Ernest Wright	Son	4		Leamington
Emma Wright	Daughter	2		Leamington
Elizabeth Wright	Daughter	3		Warwick
William Martin	Son	14	Errand boy	Coventry
Mary Martin	Daughter	10	Scholar	Coventry
John Martin	Son	8	Scholar	Coventry

Is this the same William Martin as his age and place of birth both fit? Has Sarah Martin been widowed twice? George Martin dies and she marries a Mr Wright, who also dies, and she is left as head of the household with 9 children?

Above right: Hibernia, Nether Stowey.

Right: Grandma Martin, Terry and Mary, 1932.

Above left: Cousin Pat Cadier (nee Martin) with three Martin sisters, Edith Martin, Nell Pearson and May Marshall with Marianne at the front taken in the garden at Hibernia, 1960.

CHAPTER 5

ROBERT THOMAS WILLIS 1920–1955
Overcoming a generation split

The early life of Robert Thomas is given in some detail in the chapter on his father George Hamlet. His service in the First World War is also outlined in the George Hamlet narrative. Further research will be very difficult as it is already established by visits to the National Archives at Kew that the service record of Robert Thomas was lost during the Second World War in the London blitz, when over 50% of First World War service records were lost. A more fruitful avenue for further research on the army career of Robert Thomas could possibly be found at the Kings Own Yorkshire Light Infantry museum at Doncaster Public Library. A visit to the museum of the York and Lancs Regiment, which is housed in the Rotherham Public Library, could be useful. The author has not visited either of these establishments, details of which were given to me on a visit to Kew. However, research at Kew did establish that Robert Thomas remained a PT Instructor for the full period of his service and was never posted to or served overseas.

Robert Thomas, born on 4 January 1892, and Florence Elsie Martin, born 16 August 1894, were married on 24 July 1920 at Emmanuel Church, Pitsmoor, Sheffield by the Revd William Alfred Martin, the father of Florence Elsie and the then vicar of Emmanuel Church. Florence Elsie was escorted to the church by her friend the Revd Rees of Brightside

Vicarage, Firth Park Avenue, Sheffield. As described by Florence Elsie in Chapter 6, Robert Thomas, known by all as Tom, met Florence Elsie at the home of the Gantillin family when Tom visited the family at Easter in 1919. By the end of the year Tom and Florence Elsie were engaged to be married. Tom, having failed in his ambition to become a qualified dispensing chemist, was brought into the GH Willis wholesale provision business as manager of the Foundry Street Warehouse, Barnsley in 1919. As already narrated this warehouse handled a very substantial provision trade, particularly of imported products such as bacon, ham and butter from Denmark and Canada. As George Hamlet had other ambitions, later to be realised in the founding of the Penistone Malt Vinegar Company in 1923, it was, for both George Hamlet and his son Robert Thomas, necessary to form a legal partnership.

Willis & Son Model T Ford, 1927.

When the partnership broke up in late 1925, and having agreed, through solicitors to both parties, a way ahead, the provision business in Foundry Street changed to the sole ownership of Robert Thomas, who traded as RT Willis and Son. The 'Son', George Robert Thomas, had no say in the matter being only four years old! It should be mentioned that the solicitors acting for Robert Thomas were Smith and Ibberson of Church Street, Barnsley. Robert Thomas mentioned on more than one occasion how indebted he was to the senior partner of that law firm, namely a Mr Algy Smith. Many years later the same law firm and senior partner, Mr Alun Thomas, gave much valuable advice to the writer as he too wrestled with the problems of inheritance. No doubt George Hamlet enjoyed good advice from his own solicitors who I believe were Bury and Walker of Barnsley. Speculation on the cause of the breakdown between father and son would not be in anyone's interest. The writer asked both Smith and Ibberson and Bury and Walker if any records existed. As they both stated that all records were destroyed many years ago, it would be impossible to take a balanced view of the reasons behind this rift between father and son, which was never healed in their lifetime.

It appears that during World War II, in 1943, and according to information given to me by Ernest Foster in the late 1950s, an attempt by George Hamlet to effect a reconciliation was made. In 1943 Ernest Foster was the warehouse manager at New Street when George Hamlet made an unexpected visit to New Street and asked to see his son Robert Thomas. According to Ernest Foster he had to persuade Robert Thomas to at least see his father. He left them alone in the office at New Street but had no idea what was discussed. After some time George Hamlet emerged and Robert Thomas instructed Ernest Foster to give George Hamlet a parcel of groceries and then retreated back into the office. I do not know if they spoke to each other again, which appears to be doubtful, before George Hamlet died. From December 1950 the two branches of the Willis family completely lost touch, until Monica, George Hamlet's eldest daughter, sought the help of the editor of the Barnsley

Chronicle to contact the writer, after her reading a review in the paper of the book 'No Hero, Just A Survivor'. Monica, who died peacefully on 29 March 2008, contacted me in 1999, enabling us both over the next few years, to bring both our families closer together again.

Robert Thomas had the provision business but his father still owned the Foundry Street warehouse for which a rent had to be paid, in addition to monies owed to GH Willis following the partnership termination agreement. RT Willis found the answer by purchasing the freehold of four terrace houses and the adjoining court on the corner of New Street and Joseph Street, Barnsley. These four dwellings known as 96 New Street and Nos. 1, 3 and 5 of No. 3 Court, New Street were all contained in one block with stone slated roof and cellars. They dated from the early nineteenth century and with a court behind the premises allowed room for vehicle parking and the building of outhouses. All the tenants were persuaded to leave these dwellings on the payment of a lump sum all under £50, apart from one tenant who refused to go until the full £50 was paid. With this acquisition completed in July 1926 RT Willis now had to convert these dwellings into a warehouse. A rope lift was installed, all doors facing New Street were blocked off with the only entrance to the premises from Joseph Street. Doorways were put through the house dividing walls and fixtures in which to store canned goods were created from wooden Coleman's Starch boxes. All the cellars were joined together by doorways pushed through the dividing walls, with a single trap door at street level facing into New Street through which goods from trucks or drays parked in New

Street were received. The whole building was whitewashed inside and then the stock and business moved from Foundry Street to New Street. The business was fortunate in being able to retain the services of two very loyal salesmen, a Mr Sydney Cable and a Mr Horace Brooks, both of whom were to stay until the Second World War.

Sydney Cable behind Locke Park, Barnsley, 1935.

As could be expected many customers could not understand the move to New Street from a purpose built warehouse in Foundry Street. Due to inadequate facilities at New Street over three quarters of the provision business was lost to three major competitors in Barnsley, namely firms by the name of Gaimsters who took the bacon and ham trade, with Charlesworths and Jacksons taking much of the grocery trade. Robert Thomas had a fight on his hands to survive, made far from easy by the need to pay off his debt to his father as quickly as possible. Fortunately, in 1926 J Bibby of Liverpool were looking for agents to market and distribute their speciality, namely a fish frying compound, very suitable for the fish and chip trade. This compound came in two varieties, the cheapest was marketed as Bibby's FF and the more expensive variety as Bibby's ABC Fish Fryers Compound. This Compound was distributed as a lard or dripping substitute and provided a cheaper alternative to lard, dripping or oils used by fish fryers. Robert Thomas travelled to Liverpool and secured the franchise for the Barnsley, Dearne Valley area. During the 1926 general strike and prolonged miners disputes the new product was to prove a life saver to the new Willis grocery business. Fish frying was, and still is, a cash business which ensured prompt payment to suppliers. In those early days of the late 1920s Robert Thomas was the only employee who had a car. Salesmen used the bus or a small van which was kept firmly locked up in the garage at New Street every evening and at weekends. There were no staff perks, a five and a half day working week and just one week's holiday a year, the last full week in August, Barnsley Feast week.

1926 was a very difficult year for Great Britain with widespread unrest in the working population, due to high unemployment and falling wages, culminating in a General Strike in May of that year. Largely thanks to the efforts of thousands of volunteers to keep vital services going, the strike petered out in a very short time. Unfortunately for Barnsley the troubles were not over as the miners stayed out on strike for five months, eventually drifting back to work in November. These were very difficult times in which to build a business. The New Street premises were far from ideal, boasting very few facilities. Hams were cooked in aluminium pressure pots in a gas fired oven designed to hold eight pots. The premises had just one telephone, Barnsley 375, located on the wall of a small lobby outside the entrance to a former kitchen now used as an office and store for cigarettes. The only hot water was drawn from a setpot or boiler located in another converted kitchen, and heated by an adjacent coke fire. The water supply was just one single tap in the same area as the setpot. There were fortunately two flush toilets out in the yard, which could freeze up in winter. Apart from an open grate in the office section there was no heating. Just a few years before the gas lighting had been replaced by electricity. Staffing was very modest being recruited from Foundry Street, comprising Robert Thomas, the salesmen already mentioned, a warehouse manager, a van driver and a teenage warehouse assistant. Deliveries to house shops, corner shops and fish and chip shops were by a van which could carry up to $1\frac{1}{2}$ tons (about 1500 Kg). Wages for the teenage male warehouse assistant would be 10/- (50p) a week with a salesman earning between £3-4 a week. Jobs in Barnsley were in very short supply with long queues of mainly men in shabby suits and cloth caps every week outside the employment exchange in York Street collecting the 'dole'.

When Robert Thomas joined his father in 1919, George Hamlet arranged to purchase a suitable home for the engaged couple, Tom and Elsie, which they occupied immediately after the wedding on 24 July 1920. This detached stone built house, High Stile Cottage, off Park Road, Barnsley was rented from George Hamlet at the normal market rate. A family of small children was soon on the scene, George Robert Thomas, born 20 June 1921, Florence Maisie, born 22 May 1922 and Derek Percival, born on 13 December 1924.

After his discharge from the Kings Own Yorkshire Light Infantry on 18 November 1918 and discharge from Sheffield

Royal Hospital following treatment to the wound on his left hand, Robert Thomas took up residence at 163 Sheffield Road. We can only assume that he took over the management of the retail business located there, with all the wholesale business transferred to Foundry Street. We know that prior to his marriage, Robert Thomas did not have a car or any other private transport, despite holding a driving licence from 18 December 1918. His address of 163 Sheffield Road is the address on this driving licence. Following the occupation of High Stile Cottage by Tom, as he was always known, and Elsie, the Sheffield Road business was disposed of. This shop did not survive as a grocery store, becoming a barbers shop occupied by a Mr Eli Shaw for many years.

Robert Thomas was now able to relieve George Hamlet of the management task at Foundry Street which would give George Hamlet the time to investigate and found the Penistone Malt Vinegar Company in 1923. The Partnership Agreement, already referred to, appeared to work well and amicably with Robert Thomas producing a balance sheet each financial year of the GH Willis and Son business from 1920 to 1924 inclusive. In 1925 a disagreement arose over the accuracy of the sales and profit figures of GH Willis and Son. Legal action followed in which, as related to the writer by Monica, George Hamlet's daughter, some 74 years later, ruled against George Hamlet. A legal agreement to dissolve the partnership between father and son followed. Robert Thomas, under the terms of the dissolution agreement, agreed to buy the wholesale business of GH Willis and Son over the next few years and also to move from Foundry Street to other premises.

In 1925 Tom and his family left High Stile Cottage to move to a new bungalow, Corrawallen, he had purchased in Worsbrough Dale. In 1926 Tom obtained a short term loan from the Midland Bank, Market Hill, Barnsley to provide the funds necessary to fulfil his obligations to his father and to finance his new business. A mortgage for the bungalow came from the Barnsley Building Society. Bertram Terrence Martin was born at Corrawallen on 9 May 1927. Elsie's favourite sister Edie came by train from the vicarage at East Halton to look after the family during the time Elsie was confined to bed. However, the financial pressures were so great that Tom was obliged to sell Corrawallen and clear the mortgage in late 1927 and move to a terrace house he purchased at 15 Swift Street, Barnsley. The deeds of this house were deposited at the Midland Bank to support an extension to the period in which he was to repay the loan. On 13 May 1929 the sum of £300/16/8 was paid to George Hamlet being the final payment for the wholesale provision business. The break between father and son was complete and sadly never to be repaired. In 1930 Robert Thomas paid off his loan from the Midland Bank, collected the deeds of 15 Swift Street and resolved never to borrow from a bank again or to run an overdraft. He pursued this policy successfully to the very end of his life.

From 1930 to the outbreak of the Second World War Robert Thomas, much to his credit, set about growing his business and, at the same time, moving into a better home.

A second daughter, Mary Christine, was born on 17 January 1930, completing a family of five children. In 1929 a plot of land, of approximately half an acre, was purchased in Greenfoot Lane, Barnsley. A new four bedroom brick built house was built, to be named Hyland House, at the bargain price of £500, by Potters builders from Wombwell near Barnsley. Times were hard, which enabled Robert Thomas to negotiate a very good price with the builder. There was a cellar for food storage, fittings were adequate but basic. However, thanks to Elsie it was a closely knit and caring family. There were open fireplaces in the living rooms and bedrooms, only lit when really required. Floors were covered by linoleum. Cooking facilities and hot water were provided by a multi-purpose coke fired stove in the kitchen called a 'cook an' heat'. All running costs were kept to a minimum. Elsie baked her own bread and walked into town and to the market every week, often with a pram, to ensure a good supply of fruit and vegetables. Usually it was fish on Fridays and a joint on Sundays. There was no mortgage, much to Tom's credit who kept the wholesale business quite profitable. Tom, as a father, was a little unpredictable, illustrated by the difficulty Elsie had in keeping hold of any domestic help.

In addition to her love and care for the children, Elsie's other main interest was in keeping up her French language skills and reading a weekly French newspaper 'La France'. Most fortunately Hyland House was within easy walking distance from a newly built junior school reputed to be the best in Barnsley. The headmistress, Miss Richards, took a lively interest in all the Willis children who all won scholarships to either the Boys' Grammar School or the Girls' High School. This local junior school fortunately compensated for the hostility Robert Thomas displayed towards all teachers and the current education system in the 1930s. This attitude was doubtless a reflection of his own experience. On the other hand Florence Elsie, as the mother of five children, made sure that attendance at school was never missed and that homework was completed.

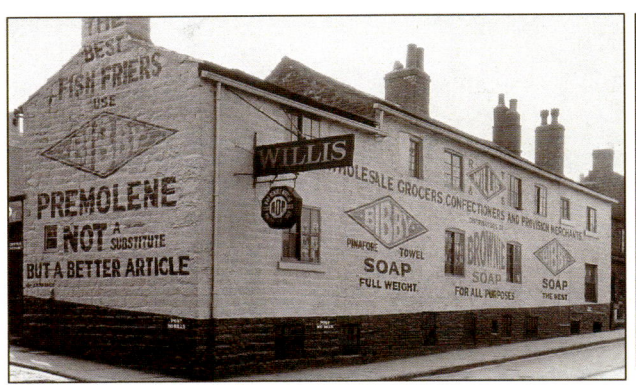

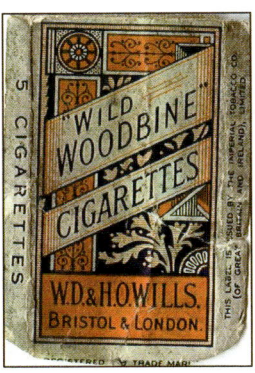

Left: New Street Warehouse, Barnsley 1938.
Right: 1930s, 5 cigarettes 2d

The 1930s were a very turbulent and for many people a very depressing period, with a world wide recession, many businesses in difficulty and high unemployment. If you had the cash it was also a time when entrepreneurs, such as Robert Thomas, would snap up opportunities. A small wholesale business, based at Chapeltown between Barnsley and Sheffield, came on the market. It was a perfect fit to the RT Willis and Son business with a complementary product range of pre packed sundries, such as syrup, split peas, pearl barley, hair pins, combs and all manner of carded sundries, prepared on the premises. Robert Thomas paid £2,614/11/8 for the business, including a custom built freehold warehouse plus stock and goodwill. This business, traded under the name of MK Senior, with a staff of two salesmen, a van driver and six ladies who pre packed a wide range of products, was always profitable. As already reported, this enterprise was transferred to the expanding warehouse facilities in New Street, Barnsley in the early 1960s, with the Chapeltown warehouse sold to Jehovah's Witnesses.

Staff Party, Barnsley Baths, Racecommon Road, 1938.
RT Willis centre front with his family.

The next opportunity came when Robert Thomas purchased for £700 all the machinery, stock, vehicles and goodwill of the mineral water manufacturing business from the liquidators of the Barnsley and District Grocers Company

Ltd. An additional sum of approximately £500 was paid for the mineral water premises located in Foundry Street, situated just 300 yards from the RT Willis New Street premises. This small business with a staff of a manager, two driver salesmen and two female assistants was always profitable until overtaken by changing consumer demand resulting in its closure in the 1960s. In 1938 another small wholesale grocery business came on the market, namely Ashton Brothers of Station Road, Eckington, south of Sheffield. Robert Thomas acquired this business in 1938 for probably no more than £1,500. This business, which had spare storage capacity in its warehouse, proved to be very useful as Robert Thomas purchased the canned goods stock of wholesalers in liquidation at auctions in 1938/39, later to be sold at high margins in 1940 as rationing of basic foods was introduced. The Second World War brought in regulations and the need to register your food inventory and customers if you wished to continue to supply shops with rationed products. This was a world of red tape in which Robert Thomas was not prepared to participate. He was rescued by his daughter Maisie who was to devote the rest of her life to the detailed work required to comply with food supply regulations. Additionally during the war she took on the role of salesman, necessary to keep contact with customers as men departed to the war. There is no individual in the Willis family who gave so much to ensure future generations had a profitable business to come back to, if that was their wish. Maisie died on 14 September 1949 from valvular heart disease, much aggravated by sheer exhaustion during and immediately after the Second World War. Just a little footnote to mention that Robert Thomas and Maisie were quite mobile during the war as they were able to draw on 1000 gallons of petrol in two 500 gallon storage tanks at New Street which Robert Thomas installed in 1937 with a view to selling petrol retail. These tanks were filled just prior to rationing.

Left: T Sandford behind Locke Park, Barnsley in a Bedford van, 1939.
Below: Commer 1½ ton delivery van, 1938.

The Robert Thomas business story during the post war period has already been narrated. However, we should note that when the Foundry Street provision business was transferred to New Street in 1926 the turnover fell to approximately £300 a week, or to around £20,000 a week at 2008 values. In 1949 a slow recovery was taking place from the shortages of the war years and after. The turnover at New Street, excluding all the pre war acquisitions, was at this time a modest £65,161, for the year, equivalent to almost £4 million annual turnover in 2008.

On the purely social side, Robert Thomas was probably at his most relaxed in the few years before the outbreak of the Second World War, illustrated by his sponsorship of an annual staff party in January 1938 and 1939, comprising a supper, dance and entertainment at the Baths Hall, Barnsley. During this period he was also elevated to be the Grand Master of Thalia Lodge of Freemasons. This lodge was the national actors lodge of which Robert Thomas became a member, sponsored by Bertram Mills, of national circus fame, who wintered with his circus in Doncaster. Thalia Lodge met at the Cumberland Hotel, off Oxford Street, London. Other social activities included the founding of the Limes Golf Club, Staincross, Barnsley in the early 1930s where Robert Thomas was the Treasurer during the pre war period. However, his favourite haunt was the pavilion of Barnsley Cricket Club, Shaw Lane, Barnsley where alcohol was available to members until the early hours of the morning. At this venue the 'gentlemen' of Barnsley gathered to enjoy a pint of Barnsley Bitter, gossip and play dominoes.

Family life, already touched on, always saw father treated with much caution. Holidays pre 1939 were usually confined to August with mother and children taken to East Halton, Acaster Selby or Nether Stowey. Father would return to Barnsley coming back two to four weeks later to pick up the family. During the post war period, father enjoyed growing tomatoes in his greenhouse and the nightly visit to Shaw Lane. The children were all going their own way, much saddened by Maisie's death in September 1949. In 1954 as he was moving house to Dodworth, Robert Thomas was losing energy and in obviously poor health. He struggled on, working at home, reluctantly letting go in late 1954 and dying of lung cancer in Sheffield Royal Hospital on 13 February 1955. What cannot be denied is that he created the foundation on which his children and grandchildren built their own careers. In 2006 another chapter closed with the sale of the New Street site, occupied by short term tenants since 1991, to SI Investments of Manchester, with a view for development into shops, offices or housing. The whole site was demolished in early 2009.

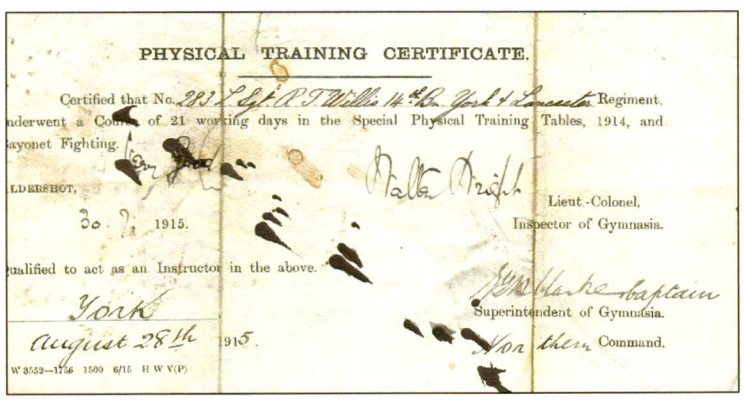

Above: RT Willis Physical Training Certificate, 1915.
Left: Salisbury Plain, PT Instructors, 28 August 1915, RT Willis centre front.

RT Willis, 17 July 1950.

Florence Elsie Willis at Hyland House, 1940.

An Unsung Hero of World War II

A tribute to a remarkable young woman who, as already mentioned in Chapter 5, saved the Robert Thomas Willis business from total collapse.

We should record that Florence Maisie Willis, always known as Maisie, born at High Stile Cottage on 22 May 1922, was a very remarkable lady. Attending Barnsley Girls' High School from 1933 to 1938 she achieved great academic success, despite being absent from the High School for many months due to the onset of rheumatic fever, resulting in incurable, by 1930s' standards, valvular disease of the heart. Apart from excelling academically, she took an active part in school activities particularly netball. Knowing her father's unwillingness to pay university fees, she was encouraged by the school to sit the Civil Service exam. Maisie passed the exam without any difficulty, but before acceptance had to submit to a full medical examination. After the examination she was interviewed by the doctor in charge who informed her that, much to his regret, she was severely disabled with severe valvular disease of the heart. He advised her to return home and for the rest of her life not to undertake any active employment. To Maisie, a young lady of very high spirits, this was a severe blow indeed, particularly as she had not been informed after recovery from rheumatic fever that she was so disabled.

Father was very supportive and said to his daughter, "Don't worry, just come down to the office in New Street for three or four hours each day, helping me in a secretarial role". Maisie was anxious to earn a little money so readily agreed to father's suggestion. Little did Maisie realise that within 12 months, with war declared against Germany, she would be confronted with a secretarial task far more demanding than any civil servant job.

Robert Thomas had ready cash. His view of the war was to buy all the food products he could find at that time, store and sell at a later date when shortages pushed up the price. As described elsewhere, this policy was so successful that Hyland House, Sheffield Road, Birdwell, three miles from Barnsley, was bought for approximately £3,500 in 1943, with Hyland House, Greenfoot Lane, being disposed of at the same time. As Maisie narrated after the war, Robert Thomas saw no need to register as a supplier of food products due to be rationed. He suggested that, as he had ready cash, he would go across to Ireland, a neutral country, and find sufficient products to keep him in business. The firm's leading salesman, Horace Brooks, left to work for a London wholesaler. At the age on only 18 Maisie took the salesman's role, filled in all the necessary registration forms for customers still loyal to RT Willis and Son and took on all the associated paperwork. From 1940 to 1947 Maisie, with a small car, converted to commercial use, worked full time six days a week. With the move to Birdwell and profits assured by Maisie's efforts, Robert Thomas lost all his interest in business growth expecting his two oldest sons to run the business for him, provided he kept ultimate control. He had no idea that the whole organisation depended on Maisie, who living at Hyland House was additionally was the prime factor in keeping the family together. Maisie was always the person the younger generation turned to for help or advice in those war years.

Maisie was leading an exhausting life both at work and outside with gardening, church activities and as a leader of the Worsbrough Church Girl Guide group. The end was the inevitable physical collapse in 1947, followed by several months nursing care by mother, the end coming on 14 September 1949 at the age of 27. Maisie gave all, for family, for the RT Willis business and for the Church community at Worsbrough. Never to be forgotten will be the sight of the Girl Guides weeping as she was laid to rest.

CHAPTER 6

FLORENCE ELSIE WILLIS
16 August 1894 – 2 July 1988
Reflections on her life, written in her own words at 'Greenways' 1983-1988

Except where duplications occur, these reflections have not been edited or amended.

I was born at 4 Deburgh Terrace, Deburgh Hill, Dover. My birthday is August 16th and I was born in 1894. May was born in Yorkshire on January 17th 1890. My father, Revd WA Martin was born in Coventry. Spurgeon helped him to study to become a priest in the Church of England. He went to college in London, with Spurgeon's help. My mother was born in Runcorn, Cheshire and came from a farming family. My mother's maiden name was Lightfoot, Elizabeth Alice Lightfoot. My mother always called my father Willy, my father always called my mother 'my dear'.

I remember going on a picnic in a wood near Dover. We had a black pram with us in which was my brother Percy. I could not see him as the pram was too high. I insisted on carrying all the parcels. I became very tired while in the wood. My father carried me the rest of the way home. I would be 3 years old. My mother filled the pram with plants which she had dug up out of the woods. She loved plants and flowers and was a great gardener. My brother Percy would be about 8 months old. He was born on 14 December 1897. He must have slept all the time in the pram. I never heard him cry once. I remember this walk most vividly.

My father, William Alfred Martin, was born on 6 July 1856 and died, aged 90, on 7 March 1947. My mother, Elizabeth Alice Lightfoot, was born in 1857 and died, aged 85, on 13 May 1943. At that time they were living at Hibernia, Nether Stowey, near Bridgewater, Somerset. My favourite sister Edie was looking after them. When my parents died my sister May's only son Thomas Cedric Martin Marshall and his wife Ruby looked after her and took her to their home until she died. Edie was the 2nd child of my parents. My parents had 12 children. I was the 10th child. The 11th child was called Albert Percival (Percy). He was killed at Amiens, France in WWI in 1915, he was only 20. My sister May, the youngest child, was deserted by her husband when her only son Thomas Cedric Martin Marshall, was only 4 years old. He never saw his father again. It was Martin and Ruby, his wife, who looked after Edie until she died. Martin still writes to me regularly. They are a splendid couple. They have two daughters, both married and each of them has a son. The Revd William Alfred Martin (aged 21) married Elizabeth Alice Lightfoot (aged 19) in 1872. I do not know how they met. Victorian parents were very reticent towards their children.

My family had always lived in a town or city, although they loved the country. My father was a clergyman. We left Dover, where I was born, for Halifax, then Huddersfield. When I was about 8 years old we went for a holiday to Appleton, a small village about 8 miles from York. Here we met an elderly lady called Miss Chipperfield. She ran a village school at Acaster on the banks of the River Ouse. She became very friendly with my parents. She suggested I should go to her school and live with her. I was longing to go to school so I thought this would be marvellous. It was arranged that I should go to live with her for 3 years. She was very strict and often I was unhappy. But all the farmers in the village were very kind. I regularly spent every Saturday at one or other farms.

Right: The Dame School, Acaster Selby, c1870.

Below: The School House, Acaster Selby.

I lived with Auntie (adopted) Chipperfield at her school in Acaster, 2 miles from Appleton and 4 miles from Bolton Percy, for 3 years (aged 10-13). Aunt Chipperfield was the Headmistress and only teacher. The school was on the high banks of the River Ouse, which flowed on to York. Every morning before school started (after our meagre breakfast – 1 slice of bread and butter and 1 cup of tea) I used to walk to Jackson's farm, the end farm at the end of the village. Opposite the River Ouse was Selby. At this farm Mrs Jackson gave me a pint of skimmed milk. This I took back, being careful not to spill it, to the school. Then before school started at 9am I had to put our daily rice pudding in the oven – 2 small tablespoons of rice and a smaller one of sugar. This pudding cooked slowly in the oven (a fire oven of course) and was quite delicious. It helped to satisfy me after our meagre dinner of one slice of cold brisket and a few potatoes, all from the garden, which Arthur Jarrett looked after, and which he himself had planted. The garden had a few trees full of apples. I was not allowed to touch them as Auntie sold the whole crop to a local farmer.

Every Saturday morning all the farmers went to York in their horse drawn carriages to sell their produce at the fair or market. At the Jackson's farm Annie Jackson always stayed at home to tend to the poultry and milk the cows. Annie used to invite me every Saturday to spend the day with her. Aunt Chipperfield always let me go. I used to enjoy myself very much. The food was delicious and I was always given a glass of creamy milk. Annie used to give me a second glass full. Every Thursday, after school, I went to the Jackson's farm to get our 1lb of butter, which had to last us a full week. I used to love to turn the handle of the churn and hear the cream go flip-flop. The 1lb of butter used to cost $\frac{1}{2}$d.

Farmers at Acaster Selby were the Jacksons, the Gavigants, Mr Eglin (housekeeper Miss Sinclair), Mr Precious (unmarried, living with his sister and a very old grandmother) and Mr & Mrs Mills. Mr Eglin and Miss Sinclair later married, she was a marvellous cook. Arthur Jarrett lived with Aunt Chipperfield from being a young boy. He became sexton, bell ringer and grave digger at Acaster Church, 4 miles from Bolton Percy. Lady Dawson, Nunappleton Hall, Bolton Percy. Lady Dawson played the organ on Sunday afternoon at Acaster Church. Lady Dawson invited all my children to tea on the lawn at Nunappleton Hall when I stayed with Arthur Jarrett and the children on holiday in the 1930s. Auntie Chipperfield had died and Arthur provided holiday accommodation. I lived at Acaster for 3 years. I then went to the High School in Sheffield for 2 years. After that May and I went to the Clergy Daughters' School, Clifton, Bristol.

Horace Montague Dalton was the organist at St Bartholomew's Church, near Attercliffe, Sheffield, where my father was curate. We became great friends, although he was a fully grown man and I was a girl totally ignorant of sex. He never abused my fascination for him in any way. My parents knew nothing about this friendship. I visited his rooms every afternoon when coming home from school. I was heartbroken when I knew I had to go to boarding school in Bristol. He gave me a gold locket with his face on one side and my face on the other side. I dare not let my parents see this gold locket. I hid it under my blouse when it was round my neck. But before going to boarding school I was forced to destroy it. My mother took me and May to Sheffield Midland Station and put us on the train which would go direct to Bristol, where one of the teachers from the school would meet us. My brother Harold also came to the station to say goodbye. Just as the train started going Harold shouted 'who is Horace?' I was furious but mother never heard him. I had left, for a few minutes, one of Horace's letters on my dressing table. Harold had walked into my bedroom and read it.

The Clergy Daughters' School, Brandon Hill, Bristol was where I met Gwendoline Knapp. My friend was in the same class as me at St Brandons. Her brother George Knapp was a very nice young man, a few months younger than me, training to be an engineer. I wonder what happened to him in the 1914-1918 war. His sister Gwendoline told me he would be building bridges. His father was vicar at Rodbourne Church, near Swindon. He had caught a lot of butterflies. He had preserved them and showed me his beautiful collection. George and I used to go cycling for miles. How I loved it. The weather was always marvellous. One day I barged into a man straying on the road. I knocked his hat off. I could do nothing but giggle. I was only 16. George was my first boyfriend.

Miss Palmer was Headmistress at the Clergy Daughters' School. Sometimes, because the school was situated at the top of a road called Brandon Hill it was called St Brandons. Right opposite was Cabot Tower. Miss Hooper was a very kind lady who invited me and May to her house when we had a day's holiday once a month. We used to have a delicious dinner where the waiter stood behind our chairs. Miss Carver lived with her as her companion. If it was a beautiful day we often went for a drive in an open carriage. Other times we were taken to the zoo in the afternoon. Miss Carver used to come and call for us at the school and take us back after tea as we were never allowed to go out alone. Miss Hooper lived in a beautiful house which I think was called Harley Place. Every Christmas Miss Hooper gave us a present. I particularly remember a sewing kit which I kept and used for years. We used to drive over the suspension bridge.

I was there for 3 years and did well in French, German and English Literature. I was now 18 years old. My Bristol school offered me a job at a school in Ostend, Belgium. I was to teach English and of course I learnt French and never spoke any English in the full year I was there. I enjoyed this experience very much in the school at Villa Aurora, 104 Boulevard van Jegham, Ostend. This was from September 1913 to 28 July 1914. I had only been home a week when Belgium was invaded by the Germans. Madame Giar, head of Ostend School, escaped on the last boat to England with her two sisters, Mlle Laura (teacher) and Mlle Martha (cook/housekeeper). Gwen Groome, a doctor's daughter, was at the school in Ostend at the same time I was there. We became great friends. In 1914 when we went back to Dover she invited me to stay with her at their country home in Ramsgate, Kent. She had an elder sister called Irene, and a younger brother called George. They were staying at their country house on the coast. They were exceedingly kind to me. I had absolutely no money of my own at all. Whenever we went anywhere, and we went somewhere every day, they always paid for me and just took it for granted. I had a wonderful month's holiday. Adele Klocke, who lived in

Cologne, was the German teacher at the school in Ostend. We became great friends but always spoke French together. I wonder what happened to her with the Germans suddenly invading Belgium.

My great French friend, Madame Brougham, I got to know after the First World War. She lived at 5 Rue le Bastarde, Rennes, Isle-et-Vilaine. We went on a wonderful holiday together and toured Norway, from east right across to the west, finishing at Bergen on the west coast. Our interesting journey was from Oslo to Bergen and was a wonderful experience for me. We always spoke French together. I learnt French fluently when I was in the school at Ostend. I made great friends with a family who lived in Dixmunde, their daughter was called Melanie. Melanie and her parents were very fond of 'les huitres' (oysters). After leaving Ostend in 1914 I became a nursery governess to Canon Hayes' three young daughters. Canon Ambrose Hayes was the vicar of a church at Parkgate, near Rotherham. His wife was called Annie Hayes.

I was there for two years but as the war continued I became restless, resigned and decided to become a hospital nurse. I was accepted at Sheffield Royal Hospital. I also nursed for a short time at a fever hospital. While at Sheffield Fever Hospital (Lodge Moor) I also nursed patients with the killer disease of flu which was raging all over the country in July 1918. I was in a ward full of patients of all ages, including tiny babies. Patients were dying every day. It was very sad but I had no fear of catching anything. I kept quite well and never caught anything and never had a day off. I finished up by becoming a Sister and stayed there until just before my marriage on 24 July 1920 to Robert Thomas Willis. Mary Dunsmoor and I were great friends when we were both training to be nurses at Sheffield Royal Hospital, West Street. I became a Sister on a men's medical ward, where I stayed until I married. Mary went to Dumfriesshire where she became a District Nurse.

My future husband did not want to get married until we had a house. I quite agreed as I detested his stepmother Marianne Willis. Sooner than I expected my husband's father bought us a house called High Stile Cottage, 2 Park Avenue, Park Grove, Barnsley. Tom had to pay his father rent for it. It was called High Stile Cottage because when it was first built one had to climb over a stile to enter the garden. I was used to stiles because when I lived at Acaster every farm field was separated by stiles instead of a simple gate. I was often teased about this address as everyone thought it meant 'style' which has a totally different meaning – namely fashion. I, Florence Elsie Martin,

High Stile Cottage, Park Avenue, Barnsley, 2007. There was no front porch or conservatory in 1921-1926.

married Robert Thomas Willis on 24 July 1920. We were married by my father, Revd William Alfred Martin at

Emmanuel Church, Pitsmoor, Sheffield where father was the vicar. Robert and Maisie, my two children were baptised in Emmanuel Church, Pitsmoor, Sheffield. Derek, Terence and Mary were baptised at East Halton Church, Lincolnshire where my father had moved to be the vicar.

Mrs Gantillin was a great friend of the Martin family. Ulric, her only son, gained his degree at Keeble College, Oxford. He lived with his mother and taught my husband, Tom, Latin but he never passed his exam to be a chemist because he always failed in Latin. Mrs Gantillin had one daughter, Innes, who was rather an invalid and died in her early forties. She was very tall. I liked her very much. When she stayed with my parents I had to share her bed (a double one). Ulric had a great friend, Gerard Taglis, whose father was vicar of Denby Dale. My husband Tom, who had just been demobbed, came to see his old tutor Ulric while I was staying with the Gantillin family. It was Easter 1919, when I had a few days holiday from night duty at Sheffield Royal Hospital. He used to come every evening. Mrs Gantillin said it was love at first sight. After a holiday I returned to the Royal and later to my home in Pitsmoor, at the top of Catherine Street in Sheffield. As a Sister at this time I had every weekend off duty. From then on I stayed at our Pitsmoor house every weekend and met Tom, who came by bus from Barnsley.

Corrawallen, Carigallen, Country Leitrim, Eire was the home of Tom's mother, Mary Louisa Hyland. She died from emphysema at Corrawallen on 22 May 1894 when Tom was just over two years old. Tom had two uncles at Corrawallen, George (*William?*) and Tom Hyland. Aunt Prairie was the wife of one of them. She had a daughter, Yvonne, who married a local farmer. They had two daughters who both died young while still children. They also had a son, Cedric. Cedric's wife was called Katherine or Kathy (*Cassie?*). They had four children, one girl and three boys, the oldest was called Prairie. Katherine was not popular with the rest of the family. They ran the Post Office at Corrawallen which also had a useful grocers shop. It was also the centre to which local farmers brought produce and eggs for export to the UK. Tom and I spent a holiday with them in the late 1940s.

Florence Elsie Martin & Robert Thomas Willis, engaged.

Joan and Monica were Tom's half sisters, whose mother was Marianne Willis. She was the third wife of Tom's father. His second wife, Charlotte Varley, who died in 1910, was childless. Marianne was very disappointed that she never had a son, she had several miscarriages – every time it was a girl. She wanted to get rid of Tom so that she could rule the business. Marianne was very unkind to me and often made me cry. She was jealous that I had three sons and two daughters. She never gave any of them anything.

(Footnote: This was Florence Elsie's perception, written when in her 80s and could well be much overstated)

Hibernia,
Nether Stowey,
Somerset, 2000.

My father retired on 16 September 1931 from his East Halton living which he took up on 16 May 1924. East Halton, near Immingham, had a population of approximately 700, supporting St Peter's, a fine medieval church. My parents went to live at Hibernia, Nether Stowey, near Bridgwater, Somerset. One went on the bus to Bridgwater which on return turned right into the village from the main road. The bus then went on to Minehead. When I was there every summer in the late 1930s we went to Minehead for a picnic. My favourite sister Edie always went with us to help me look after the children. Terry did not like the sea very much, it made him too cold. Edie and I quickly dried him and put on his clothes, then he happily built sand castles in the lovely soft sand. Mary loved the sea, we had a job to get her out of the water. She became very sunburned but she did not seem to mind and never complained.

A few notes written by Florence Elsie, after the death of her husband Tom on 13 February 1955:

The Rev Clarence Moore was the Vicar of Dodworth where I lived when I became a widow. He was very popular with all the church members. His widowed mother lived with him, she was very difficult to please. His wife had deserted him. I could never understand anyone leaving such a saintly man. I admired him and liked him very much.

Mr Totty, a retired miner, used to chop my wood for my fire. He also looked after my garden. I only paid him £1 a week. He would not accept any more. He often brought me things from his own garden, like vegetables and very often rhubarb, which I liked very much. I made many friends at Dodworth Church. Miss Kinder – also all the family. Mr Payne was the church organist, he was a brilliant musician. He could play anything by ear and could also read music straight off. They were quite a delightful family. He was also an expert cobbler, I bought all my shoes from him. They had four sons and no daughters. I became very friendly with one of the sons called Eric. He often visited me and did little repairs in my house.

Hyland House, Keresforth Road, Dodworth, Barnsley was sold for £5,000 on 26 June 1963, Florence Elsie taking up residence in a bungalow in Mosbrough, near Sheffield, at her son Derek's suggestion. This move left Florence Elsie without Yorkshire friends, so she moved to Lake View, Ashton Court, Newmillerdam, near Wakefield in 1967 into a pleasant apartment. Florence Elsie was very proud of her language skills, maintaining complete fluency in speaking French all her life. In these later years she also took up the study of Russian and German, becoming particularly good at reading Russian. Florence Elsie continues:-

At Newmillerdam house martins used to come about March, but then fly away in a flock at the end of September. I expect they went to a warmer country like Africa to escape our English winter. Every March a flock of wild geese would come in the field opposite the back window of my flat. There were eleven of them, six all white, like swans, and five of them white with dark grey wings. There were also coots and two white swans on the lake. When the swans had young (cygnets) they would not let the other chicks come near them. There was also a great crested grebe on the dam, very beautiful. The Canada geese used to come on the dam, very beautiful birds.

Mr Grimme of Grimsby was a very charming man who called once a week at Newmillerdam with his lorry full of delicious raw fish. He had been a fisherman in his young days, like his father before him. He used to go down to the beach about 3am to wait for the fishermen to come in from the sea with their catch of fish. Therefore nothing could be more fresh than his fish. He also brought crabs for those customers who liked them. My friend Mrs Proctor, who had always been kind to me when I lived in Ashton Court, Newmillerdam, always bought crabs from him as well as lovely fresh haddock. Sheila Clements was also very kind.

I had 2 operations when I was about 40 years old. First, appendicitis and peritonitis. The following year a second operation for a prolapse. Both operations performed successfully. On 5 November 1987 I had a bad fall and fell on my back. I broke the femur on my right side. I was in hospital until 1 December but am now back in my room at

Greenways, Emley, newly decorated and with a new carpet. Fortunately I had no pain at any time.

We can add a few footnotes to these memories of Florence Elsie Willis. To enlarge a little on the short life of her brother Albert Percival, we have a valuable archive inherited from this brother of Florence Elsie, in the shape of an original second edition of 'Scouting for Boys' by Robert Baden Powell, published in 1909. The first edition was published in 1908. This book was given to me by grandfather Martin on a family visit to Nether Stowey in 1932. I was a keen Scouter becoming a patrol leader of the 5th Barnsley Boy Scouts based at Old Town, Barnsley, only leaving when dispatched by father in 1938 to his small warehouse in Eckington, south of Sheffield. General Lord Baden Powell came to prominence during the Boer War for his defence of Mafeking. He retired from the army in 1910. In 1935, along with other members of the 5th Barnsley troop, I took part in a march-past, at which Baden Powell took the salute, on Pontefract racecourse.

We should also enlarge a little on the Irish connection. Following Tom's mother's death in Corrawallen, George Hamlet employed Charlotte Varley to look after his baby son, Robert Thomas, born on 4 January 1892. According to the 1891 census, Charlotte Varley was already living in the house on Sheffield Road, Barnsley along with her mother Anne, which also contained the grocery store. Situated close to the corner of Park Road and Sheffield Road, Barnsley this house with its grocery shop must have been a cramped and difficult environment for George Hamlet's first wife, fresh from the open country of Ireland.

St Mary's Churchyard, Worsbrough, grave of Maisie, Tom and Elsie Willis.

CHAPTER 7

THE NOWELL AND PALFRAMAN FAMILY HISTORY FROM 1750

We open the history of the Nowell and Palframan families with Benjamin Nowell, born in 1750. We do not known who Benjamin married but he had a son George, born in 1773. George Nowell married Martha Radcliffe on 1 January 1787. They had five children – John, born 1793, George, born 1796, William, born 1798, Jacob, born 1803 and Grace, born in 1805. Jacob married Mary Chadwick on 13 April 1823. They had seven children – Mary Ann, Sarah, John, William, Joseph, Benjamin and Jacob.

By the time of the Census in 1871 Mary Nowell (née Chadwick) is living at Churwell between Morley and Leeds with her son Jacob Nowell, born in 1839 at Hunslet. Jacob is listed as head of the house. He was married on 31 July 1859 to Harriet Hawkhead, born in 1837. Also living at Churwell is their daughter Elizabeth Ann born 1860, John Chadwick born 1861, daughter Alice born 1863, their son Jacob born 1868, daughter Miriam born 1870 and son Benjamin born 1873. Living there as well is Mary's son and Jacob's brother John, born in 1829. Mary Nowell died at Churwell in December 1874, aged 77.

Some time prior to 1871 Jacob and Harriet Nowell had lived in another house in Churwell with their children Elizabeth Ann and John Chadwick. Before the Census conducted in

1881 Jacob and Harriet had moved to 19 Co-operative Street, Morley near Leeds. At that time there was also living with them their daughter Alice and sons John Chadwick and Benjamin, together with Elizabeth Ann and her husband Fred Woods, born 1861 at Bramley near Leeds. At the time of the 1881 census, their daughter Eliza, who was born that year, was added to the family. Jacob is listed as being a woollen rag grinder in the 1881 census, and as head of the household. It also appears that Jacob and Harriet had another son, Orlando, who is not listed in the 1881 census.

We now focus on John Chadwick Nowell (pictured left c1920), Joan's grandfather, who married Florence Annie Smith, born in 1866 in Leeds, on 6 February 1892. They had three children – Clifford, born 11 March 1893, Harold, born 1896 and Marjorie born on 14 July 1904.

According to the census of 1891 and that of 1901 John Chadwick, prior to his marriage in 1892, was living at home with his mother Harriet, who was now a widow. By 1901 John Chadwick and Florence Annie were living in Armley, Leeds with his mother Harriet and 2 children, Clifford (Joan's father) and Harold, together with two boarders, Ernest Mays, born in Peterborough in 1882 and Walter Smith, born in Leeds in 1875. John Chadwick Nowell's occupation in 1891 was listed as a cloth worker – wool. In 1901 he is listed as a woollen rag merchant. John Chadwick had a musical talent as a player of the cello.

John Chadwick Nowell and his wife Florence Annie lived in Bramley, Leeds during the 1920s with Marjorie the last to leave home marrying Clifford Cox, born 25 July 1895, in Armley, Leeds, in 1927. A year or two later John Chadwick retired and moved with his wife to Trinity Road, Cleethorpes to live near his daughter Marjorie. He died during WWII, probably in 1943.

Marjorie married Clifford Cox when she was 23 at Armley Parish Church. Clifford was a musician who played the violin during silent films on the pier at Cleethorpes and on the liner the Mauritania. He also played the xylophone. During the 1930s Marjorie Cox owned a small fabric retail shop in St Peter's Avenue, Cleethorpes with herself, Clifford and the children living over the shop. After WWII Marjorie and Clifford were living at Lindum Road, Cleethorpes. Clifford was another casualty of the Great War where he lost a leg.

It is interesting to note that Marjorie and Clifford Cox had three daughters, all of whom ultimately broke away from the North. Janet, the oldest daughter married Edwin Harvey at St Peter's, Cleethorpes. Edwin did his National Service shortly after WWII and, having acquired good qualifications, worked at Fisons, Immingham. Some year later he and Janet moved south with Edwin becoming a production manager at British Leyland in Longbridge, Birmingham. They later moved to Swindon with Edwin becoming a senior manager for the

Japanese car industry, then expanding production in Swindon.

Judy, Janet's younger sister, became a Queen Alexandra nurse, marring Wally Maxwell who was to pursue a successful naval career, retiring as a Commander RN and earning an OBE for services in Saudi Arabia. They, with their naval connections, reside in Plymouth. Helen, the youngest of Marjorie's three daughters lives and works with her second husband in Virginia, USA. Marjorie retired to Highworth, Swindon to be near her daughter Janet during the closing years of her life, her husband Clifford having died many years earlier.

Harold Nowell, Clifford Nowell's younger brother, also enlisted around 1916 and served in the Royal Army Service Corps. He was married to Doris who was a driver in WWI. After WWI Harold worked for Motor Union Insurance, City Square, Leeds. He and Doris had one son, Brian. During WWII, Harold joined the Observer Corps in a Leeds suburb.

Moving back to the centre of our family history, around 1919 in Whitby, Clifford Nowell married Lily Palframan (right), whose family lived in Chubb Hill, Whitby. The marriage was at 8am, probably in the Presbyterian Church near Chubb Hill. Clifford was born in Dewsbury, the location is unknown as his mother, Florence Annie, loved moving house. Clifford left school at 14 and moved into the Rag Trade. He enlisted in the King's Own Yorkshire Light Infantry as a driver, probably in late 1915 or 1916. He served in France and was discharged in 1919. After discharge from the army in 1919 Clifford (right) was living with his parents in Whitkirk, near Crossgates in Leeds. During the 1920s and 30s Clifford, self taught in French and German which helped him to keep his employment, worked for his father's export business in Belgium, France and Germany. When John Chadwick retired to Cleethorpes around 1928 he left to Clifford Nowell, the oldest son, his rag business in Huddersfield Road, Dewsbury. Clifford quickly disposed of this rag business left to him by his father and worked from home as a commission agent for various Dewsbury and District companies who sold and processed rags.

John Palframan married Susan Marshall in 1853 and resided in Bradford. John Palframan was born in Pontefract in 1833. Susan Marshall was born in Bradford, also in 1833. There were five daughters and three sons. Joan Nowell's direct ancestor was Albert Palframan, born in Bradford in 1855 where the family resided. William, born in 1854 was the oldest followed by Albert and Martin in 1860. All the boys attended school.

Albert Palframan married Alice Bolton about 1877 and resided at 14 Woodsley Grove in Leeds, later moving to

Bradford. They had ten children, five daughters and five sons, one, Martin, dying shortly after birth. In 1901 the family were living at Ruswarp, near Whitby. One daughter, Lily, born in 1894, was to be the mother of Joan Nowell and her sisters Dorothy and Marjorie. Albert was a house builder from Bradford on a fairly modest scale. By 1890 the family were resident in Whitby, Albert seeing opportunities in an expanding seaside town.

Albert Palframan, according to the 1881 census, was still resident in Leeds and is listed as head of house with his wife Alice. The children living with them in 1881 were Joseph Bolton, born 1878, Susan born 1879 and Martha, born 1881, all probably born in Leeds. The 1891 census states that Albert and Alice had more children – Albert Marshall, born 1884, Alice, born 1886 who later emigrated to Canada, Harold Atkinson, born 1890, Annie, born 1892, Lily (Joan's mother) and Norman, born 1898. Albert's unmarried sister Sarah, born in 1862, was now living with Albert and Alice. Harold, who never married, always lived at the family home. Alice, married in Canada, had two sons Bert and Lennie. Bert was in the Canadian Air Force in WWII and was stationed for a time in the UK (Drem).

When Albert Palframan and his family first arrived in Whitby, around 1890, they lived in the Railways Cottage in George Street, Whitby where Lily was born. In 1899 the family owned and lived in 'Leesholm', run later as a boarding house, until the family moved to Chubb Hill, Whitby just before WWI. Lily went to Cliff Street School, Whitby, prior to attending Scarborough Grammar School, travelling from

Whitby daily by train. At that time it would be a fee paying school. Doubtless Lily's education set the standard for her daughters to be achievers at the Wheelwright Grammar School for Girls, Dewsbury. At this time Lily's brothers, Albert, Joseph, Harold and Norman would also be residing at Chubb Hill. The house was a semi detached of Victorian vintage. At the top right of a small cul-de-sac on the left at the top of Chubb Hill

Leesholm, Whitby pre WWI (left) and in 2001 (right).

We know that Albert Palframan employed his son Joseph Bolton Palframan in the Whitby building business. Joe and his wife Gertrude, who had married in 1928, had five children – Joseph Burnett, Robert, Alice, Alan and Kenneth. Joe and his wife and their five children lived at 13 Well Close Terrace on the West Cliff at Whitby. By 1937 the building business was known as Albert Palframan and Son, with a warehouse/builders yard in Whitby. Albert senior died during World War II.

In 1909 Susan and Martha Palframan were running the boarding house 'Leesholm' at 9 Bagdale, Whitby. Albert, their father, also resided at this address in 1909 together with other children, including his son Harold who we met in later years.

By 1928 Albert Palframan, with an interest in a warehouse and factory, and his son Harold resided at 'Meggen, in Whitepoint Road, Whitby. Subsequent research reveals that Albert Marshall Palframan, the brother of Lily, was killed in France in 1916. He was buried near Amiens, France. He was a private soldier in the Northumberland Fusiliers. His name appears on a memorial plaque in St Mary's on the Cliff, Whitby. One of Lily's other brothers Norman was the Stationmaster at Levisham on the Pickering Line. Lilian King, Norman's wife came from a railway family. Her father was Stationmaster at Goathland on the Pickering Line and later Stationmaster at Kirbymoorside. Lilian went to school in Whitby by train.

Clifford Nowell and Lily Palframan, c1919.

When Clifford Nowell married Lily Palframan in Whitby in 1919 two families, of different occupations were brought together. The Palframans from Bradford, then Leeds and finally Whitby, were an artisan family who became builders of distinction in Whitby. The final family residence, built by Albert Palframan, in the early 1920s and named 'Meggen', was at 6 Whitepoint Road, Whitby. In 2007 it was observed that the house had been converted into flats. The Palframan connection brought another side of life in the early part of the twentieth century, to the Nowell family, with their unique shoddy trade based in Dewsbury. These were real Yorkshire roots.

Lily Palframan, prior to her marriage to Clifford, worked in a Leeds bank filling the place in the bank normally reserved for men who had enlisted during the 1914-1918 war. When Lily met Clifford she was probably in lodgings having come from Whitby during WWI. Their first home was a stone built terraced house in Leeds Road, Dewsbury, followed by a detached house at 'Lealholm', 14 Moorend Lane, Dewsbury around 1925. Moorend Lane (pictured above in 2006) was a newly built 3 bedroom house with a separate bathroom, of brick construction, surrounded by fields.

Clifford and Lily's first child was Joan, born in Whitby at the family home in Chubb Hill on 23 September 1921, followed by Dorothy on 2 December 1924 and Marjorie Alice on 8 January 1927.

Lily found living in Moorend Lane quite difficult due to the steep hill on which number 14 was located. Lily had contracted rheumatic fever when very young, leaving her with valvular disease of the heart. In July 1939 Joan was on a weeks holiday with a friend, Joyce Speeden, in Morecambe, to find on her return that her mother was very poorly at Meggen in Whitby. Albert Palframan, who built Meggen, was still very much in charge with various family members staying from time to time. Lily died on the weekend immediately following Joan's return from holiday. Clifford had departed for Whitby before Joan returned from Morecambe. The funeral was held at Whitby cemetery with the burial in the Palframan grave. The headstone marks the death of Alice (Lily's mother) in 1918, Albert (Lily's brother killed in France) in 1916, Susan who died in India in 1919, Albert (Lily's father) in 1942 and Lily in 1939. The location of the Palframan headstone is at the north end of the cemetery.

l-r Joan, Marjorie, Dorothy, c1932.

We should note that at the outbreak of WWII, Clifford Nowell became a uniformed senior air raid warden covering Dewsbury Moor, in charge of a team of volunteer uniformed wardens. He continued with this duty, despite his wife's death, throughout the war.

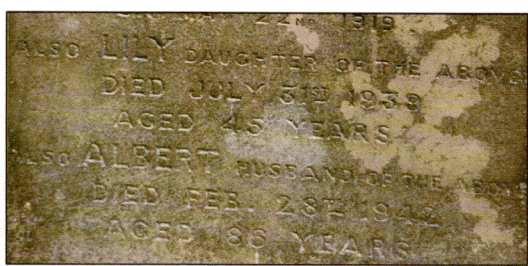

Lily, Joan's mother, who died on 30 July 1939, is commemorated at the bottom of a headstone (above and left) in Whitby cemetery. Lily's early death was a severe blow to the family. Joan, the oldest, had been working at Dewsbury Town Hall since 1937, with Dorothy and Marjorie still at school. Clifford's export business for local textile companies had dried up. He could not afford a house keeper employing instead Mrs Linwood, a neighbour, to assist with general household duties. Fortunately, Clifford was able to find a post at RT Secker and Son, Gedham Mill Sheds at Ossett, West Yorkshire as a general manager with responsibility to keep the Secker shoddy business in as good a shape as possible, until the two sons returned from the war. Clifford, a regular attender at the Dewsbury Rag Exchange, was well able to carry out these duties. He stayed as a manager with Seckers until he retired around 1960. During this time Seckers moved into a mill at Healey, Dewsbury. The Secker business flourished quite well all this time. In 1941 Clifford resolved his immediate domestic problems by marrying Elizabeth Ackroyd with whom he had a daughter Suzanne, born in 1943. After his retirement from Seckers, Clifford died peacefully at Moorend Lane in 1973.

On 26 July 1948, Joan and I with two small children, Catherine and Ian, travelled in our small Austin van to Whitby to stay as guests of Auntie Pat (Martha) and her husband David Braithwaite at 'Meggen' in Whitepoint Road. Auntie Pat, a sister of Lily, Joan's mother and daughter of Albert, was suffering from Parkinson's but being well looked after by her husband with a lady Nelly who did the cooking. Whilst in Whitby we visited Harold, another son of Albert, who cultivated a smallholding by the River Esk at Ruswarp. Harold, a bachelor, died a few years later leaving Joan a small legacy of £300 in his will. As a footnote I should report that I was able to identify the date we visited Whitby as it was the same day that Freddie Mills won the World Light Heavyweight Championship at the White City in London, which we listened to that day on the radio.

Apart from Morrie, who was a granddaughter of Albert and daughter of Susan, another sister of Joan's mother Lily, we lost all contact with the Palframans on the death of Harold. Morrie who died in 2005 in York surrounded by her family, married Tony Callan during WWll. Joan was the only bridesmaid, with the wedding taking place at Ugthorpe, near Whitby. They spent most of their married life in North

Shields, moving to York on Tony's retirement as a Junior School teacher. Tony and Morrie had five children, Frances Mary, Moira, Joe, Teresa and Margaret. Margaret was killed by a bike in a road accident in York. Moira lives in London with the other three offspring living in York as I write in 2007. We should also note that Alice, a sister of Susan, Morrie's mother, married Bert Hughes and emigrated to Canada. They had two sons, Bert and Lennie. As previously mentioned, Bert came over to England in WWII as a member of the Royal Canadian Air Force. Lily, Joan's mother, was the youngest daughter of Albert and Alice, the other sisters being Susan, the oldest, Alice, Martha (Pat) and Annie.

A life devoted to nursing and caring for others

In February 2004 Joan's sister Marjorie outlined her interesting life for inclusion in this family history. Some items previously mentioned are included.

Marjorie Alice Nowell was born on 8 January 1927, the youngest daughter of Lily and Clifford Nowell at 14 Moorend Lane, Dewsbury. Father's occupation at the time was a 'Textile Agent' with mother a housewife (prior occupation as a Bank Clerk). Lily was educated at Whitby Junior School and Scarborough Grammar School. Lily was the 12th child of a family of 13 (one died aged 3 and one died in infancy). Grandfather's occupation was house building with a part share in a Timber Merchants. Clifford and Lily were born in 1893. Two other sisters, Susan and Martha, ran a boarding house. Clifford was denied Grammar School by his mother and had to leave school at 14. He possibly worked for his father, John Chadwick Nowell who was married to Florence Annie Smith. Clifford was the oldest of three children, Clifford, Harold and Marjorie. John Chadwick and Clifford had a rag picking warehouse in Dewsbury creating shoddy. Clifford was born in Central Street, Dewsbury, but his mother liked moving house.

Joan lived in Leeds Road up to the age of 5 when the family moved to Moorend Lane which Clifford bought new. Clifford became a manager for Seckers in Dewsbury, the two Secker sons being in the army. Clifford attended the Rag Exchange in the basement of Dewsbury Town Hall. Clifford taught himself French and German.

Marjorie's first school was Moor Council School, then to Wheelwright Grammar School which she left at 17 in 1944 to work in a war time nursery. She left here to take up Nursery Nurse training for 15-18 months at Rugby in Warwickshire where she gained her certificate. She then went to a nursery in Limpsfield, Surrey where she was not happy and was rescued by Clifford. She then joined the staff in a day nursery in Hillingdon, Middlesex. From here she went to Hillingdon General Hospital in 1948 for three years and qualified as a SRN. From there to St Giles Hospital, Camberwell for Part 1 Midwifery and then to the Lewisham Hospital for Part 2 and qualified around 1952.

All the Nowell children went to Sunday School, twice on Sundays and additionally twice to the Methodist Chapel. Clifford taught a young men's Bible class. Their mother Lily had rheumatic fever as a child.

The Matron at Hillingdon Day Nursery had an active relationship with God through Jesus Christ. When midwifery training was complete overseas called but where was not revealed, so what followed was two years at Bible College – Ridgland Bible College, Bexley, Kent. Fees were paid by a legacy from Harold, Lily's brother.

In 1954 Marjorie did one year's night duty as an SRN at Bermondsey Medical Mission. She resigned and went to a Christian Guest House in Brighton for a week to 'find out'. One night she heard a 'voice' telling her to apply to OMF – the Overseas Missionary Fellowship (previously the China Inland Mission). She sent for an application form the next day and in March 1955 went to Newington Green for preparation. In October 1955 she disembarked at Singapore from the SS Corfu, after a very comfortable voyage, with about 20 members of OMF all destined for the Singapore International HQ. They were all then sent to different countries in SE Asia. At Singapore Marjorie discovered she had diabetes which was diagnosed at Singapore General Hospital so she had to stay in Singapore to be stabilised. The question now arose as to whether she should go home. Clifford was very concerned. Dr Christopher Maddox on the OMF Council in Singapore said, "let her go forward into Thailand and I will take the responsibility for her".

In April 1956 Marjorie moved up to Bangkok to undertake Thai language studies. After approximately 3 months she moved to Uthai to continue language studies and to work with leprosy patients with a fellow missionary, Barbara Morgan.

In August 1956 Marjorie moved to Manorom Hospital 150 miles north of Bangkok where she did nursing and midwifery, remaining there for seven years until 1963. From here she moved south to Saiburi on the coast near the Malayan border where she became a teacher of Nurse Aides who were all ladies, mostly Thai but with some Malay. She stayed there for fourteen years with leave home every three years or so at OMF cost. The missionaries only received modest sums according to the support the Mission was receiving. Marjorie had to prepare and write her own lectures in Thai for the Nurse Aids. There were no Thai textbooks at that time. The students trained for three years and studied in their spare time while they worked in the OMF hospital.

In 1978 Marjorie came home to the UK and worked in the office of the OMF in Sevenoaks as a general assistant until retirement in 1985. She had worked for OMF for 30 years. On her retirement she became a friend of Cornford House, a residential home owned by the OMF at that time. Marjorie lived with Naomi Kelly, the widow of the Revd Leslie Kelly, who the Home Director of OMF knew was seeking a companion in 1978. She stayed with Naomi until 1991 when she moved into a flat at Cornford House. Cornford House was later sold to Ernie Graham and is now run as a rest and nursing home. Marjorie was very happy and satisfied to help and support the residents of Cornford House. Marjorie fractured her leg in a severe fall in the grounds of Cornford House just before Christmas 2006. After a short illness Marjorie died peacefully in hospital in Tunbridge Wells in November 2008.

PHOTOGRAPHS FROM THE NOWELL/PALFRAMAN FAMILY ARCHIVE

Left top: Back l-r Alice, Albert, Grandfather, Grandma, Martha (Pat); Front l-r Harold, Nannie, Joe, Norman, Susan, Lily.

Left below: Back l-r Susan, Alice; Front l-r Lily, Martha (Pat), Nannie.

Right: Susan (Morrie's mum), who married William Perkins. Morrie was their only child. Susan died in India when Morrie was 2 and Morrie was brought to England by her Ayah (nanny) to be placed under the guardianship of Martha and her husband David Braithwaite, a tailor, resident in Whitby.

Left: Front l-r Florence Nowell, Marjorie, Joan;
Back l-r Dorothy, Annie Palframan, Lily Nowell, Bramley, Leeds c1930.
Below: l-r Marjorie, Joan, Dorothy.

Left:
Back l-r Lillian Jessop, Miss Moseley, Marjorie Blackburn;
Centre l-r Annie Humphries, ?, Mrs Gladys Blackburn;
Front l-r Dorothy, Marjorie, Joan.

Above: Beach at Whitby, August 1928, Albert Palframan, Clifford Nowell, Lily Nowell, Marjorie, Morrie Perkins, Dorothy, Joan and the pram!

Right: Clifford Nowell, c1930.

Below: Back l-r Mrs Pickering, Lily Nowell, Mrs Hebden, Mrs Blackburn, ?, Mrs Walker. Front Joan (left) and Muriel Humphries, 1930s.

Above left: Back l-r Lily Nowell, Annie Palframan, David Braithwaite; Front Albert Palframan, Martha Braithwaite.

Above right: Dorothy in her early 20s.

Below: Bingley Training College, front left Raymond Crofts, Joan; Back left Jimmy Nowell (no relation).

Above: Air Raid Wardens 1942, centre back Betty; middle row 2nd from left Jenny Booth, 3rd from right Betty Booth (sisters), 4th from left Clifford Nowell; centre front Frank Swift.

Below left: Morrie's wedding, c1942, back l-r Clifford Nowell, ?, ?, Priest, ?, Mary Noble, Peter Noble;
front l-r David Braithwaite, Morrie Callan, Tony Callan, Joan Nowell, Mrs Callan.
Below right: Morrie and Tony Callan.

Left : Morrie and Tony Callan.
Above: l-r Peter Noble, Morrie Callan, Tony Callan, Joan Nowell.

Above: Joan Nowell, 1945;

Right: Invitation to Audrey Lee's 21st birthday celebration, 1944

Mr. & Mrs. Lee
request the company of

Miss J. Nowell

on the occasion of the 21st Birthday of their daughter
Audrey Mary
at Ravensthorpe Parochial Hall,
on Saturday, 8th April, 1944 at 5 p.m.

612 Huddersfield Road,
Ravensthorpe.   R.S.V.P.

Top left: Clifford Nowell, 1945.
Top right: Betty and Clifford Nowell.
Above left: Suzanne, 1945.
Above right: Suzanne and Dad, 1947.

Left: Suzanne, c1948; Suzanne, college student, 1960.
Right: Marjorie, Camberwell, 1955 (top); Marjorie on home leave from Thailand, 1960.

Above left, clockwise: Marjorie, Suzanne, Joan, Dorothy, 1976.
Above right: Clifford Nowell, 1976.
Below: l-r Suzanne, Dorothy, Joan, Marjorie, 1976.

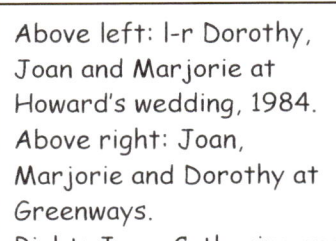

Above left: l-r Dorothy, Joan and Marjorie at Howard's wedding, 1984.
Above right: Joan, Marjorie and Dorothy at Greenways.
Right: Joan, Catherine and Marjorie at Igtham Moat, Kent

Left and above: Marjorie & Suzanne; Claude & Suzanne, Pembury, c1994.

Above right: Marjorie and Dorothy, November 2005.

Above left: Morrie Callan, 2004.

Right: Marjorie, November 2005.

Below: Claude and Suzanne, Morocco 2006.

CHAPTER 8

THE ROBERT WILLIS STORY 1921-1946
Early Days

Florence Elsie Willis, a nursing sister at the Royal Hospital, West Street, Sheffield married Robert Thomas Willis, a partner in the wholesale grocery business of George Hamlet Willis, of Foundry Street, Barnsley at Emmanuel Church, Attercliffe, Sheffield on 24 July 1920. Robert Thomas, always known as Tom, was given possession of a small stone built detached house, owned by his father, known as High Stile Cottage, situated at the bottom of Locke Avenue, Barnsley. This location, provided rent free, was a wedding gift to the newly married couple from Tom's father, George Hamlet. Mother in later years recalled the shock they suffered when a year later, shortly after I was born, the rent book arrived. Tom was determined to move out as soon as possible! As relations with his father inevitably became more strained, Tom built a small three bedroom bungalow in open country between Worsbrough Dale and Kendray, Barnsley naming the new home 'Corrawallen', after the birth place and home of his mother who died in Ireland in 1892 just over two years after Tom's birth. Tom and Elsie moved to Corrawallen in 1925 with their first three children, George Robert Thomas, Florence Maisie and Derek Percival.

I was born at High Stile Cottage on 20 June 1921. In all her confinements mother was able to call upon her unmarried and older sister Edith for help. Edith, always known as Edie, was

Above: GRTW aged 11½ months, May 1922.
Below: GRTW 2yrs 8 months, Maisie 1 year 9 months, February 1924.

in charge of their father's household, a large Victorian vicarage in the Diocese of Sheffield. Mother's father who married the couple at Emmanuel Church was ordained by Dr Burrows the Bishop of Sheffield. I and my subsequent brothers and sisters were brought into the world to live in a household in which the atmosphere would be marked by an enduring conflict between commercial ends and the higher educational and Christian commitments of mother. Despite the tensions Elsie never really faltered. In their own separate ways, mother and father were totally loyal and devoted to each other. At the age of five and now living at Corrawallen in Worsbrough Dale, I was enrolled at Worsbrough Dale Junior School. My memory recalls the long walk, about a mile, to the school and the tall Victorian classrooms. There were no school meals, just an hour to walk home and back at mid-day. One incident still stands out when I was knocked down by a motor cycle as I crossed the road. For a few days the driver was a regular visitor bringing chocolate as I recovered from cuts and bruises. No police report or insurance claims were made in those days! Anyway, father was far too engrossed in establishing his own wholesale grocery business in old cottages in New Street,

Barnsley, to worry about minor cuts and bruises suffered by his oldest child! At the time, I was quite unaware of the break between Tom and his father George Hamlet.

At the age of five or six one was also unaware of the chaotic conditions in many parts of the world. Mussolini had established himself as the fascist dictator of Italy; Hitler was out of jail in Germany but very vocal in pushing forward the Nazi party agenda. Nearer home the mutual tolerance between the working class and the middle class had fractured, resulting in The General Strike on 5 May 1926. The General Strike lasted just a week but the miners' strike dragged on for six months, ending in early November. I was to learn later that father's memory of this strike and his struggle to survive in business, in a mining environment was to colour his attitude towards both his customers and to his work force to the end of his days. It could be summed up as a very hard nosed Yorkshire business culture of watching every penny, charging as much as the market would bear and wasting nothing. A good example of this philosophy, which he practised in the 1926-1939 period, was to remove all spare wheels from his commercial vehicles, which ensured that drivers repaired their own punctures if they wanted to get home! Very many years later, he was to pursue this policy when his daughter, Maisie, got into difficulties with a car she was unable to start, with a rather unfortunate impact upon Maisie's health.

A good life at Corrawallen was suddenly shattered in 1927 by our abrupt departure, much to mother's distress, to live at 15 Swift Street, Barnsley. For some reason, father had lost the temporary use of a car and together with an increasing depression in the coal mining villages, which he served in the Barnsley area, a move to a cheaper and more convenient location was essential. The house was a two up and two down terrace house, with a cellar and kitchen extension into the back yard, commonly known as a tunnel back design. This Victorian house was just large enough to accommodate a family with three children, soon to be five. The year was early 1927. I now had to walk to St Mary's Junior School, affiliated to and near the parish church of St Mary's, in the centre of Barnsley. This was another Victorian establishment with very tall classrooms, crowded classes of 50 pupils and teaching which made little impact. A few years later this school was swept away to make room for Barnsley's central fire station. Very shortly after moving to Swift Street my brother Terry was born, on 9 May 1927, to be followed by Mary on 17 January 1930.

15 Swift Street, Barnsley, 2007. In 1928-31 there was no front hedge or door canopy, windows were Victorian sash.

Despite the General Depression of the 1930s and under increased pressure for more bedroom accommodation,

Left: GRTW 7, Maisie 6, 1928.
Above: Derek, age 5.

Above: Terry 15m, Derek 3, 1927.

father put together enough money to persuade a Barnsley builder, Potters, to build him a detached house in open country in Greenfoot Lane, just inside the north west side of Barnsley. The price paid for a four bedroom detached house with cellar and a large garden was £600. We moved from Swift Street, now a family of five children, to Greenfoot Lane in 1930. This move proved to be of enormous benefit to all the children as we all went to a new Junior School, opened about two years before, at Wilthorpe, just a short walk away. The headmistress, Miss Richards, was first class and recruited excellent teachers. I had two years at this school, with a truly excellent teacher, Miss Stone, in the final year. Mother's influence in encouraging the reading of Victorian classics such as Lorna Doone by Richard D Blackmore must have played a big part as Miss Stone sent me to sit for the Carnelly Scholarship, which sponsored a university place every year and was open to Barnsley boys of eleven, later won by my brother Terry. I subsequently learnt that I came out at number five. To follow was the eleven plus scholarship exam which I passed without difficulty. Sent home on the morning the results came out, father was still in bed. Mother called up to say, "Bobbie has won a scholarship". I always remember the reply, "A good job, I wouldn't have paid for him anyway". There was, however, a price to pay. Father was already trading as R T Willis and Son, which meant I was earmarked for the business. From the day of entering Barnsley Holgate Grammar School, Saturday mornings belonged to father's business in New Street. The wages were 2d (1p), dependent upon arriving at the warehouse in New Street, Barnsley by 8.30am and leaving at 1pm, when the establishment closed down until 8.30am the following Monday. Travel to the warehouse was by bus, with mother providing the bus fare. I was to remember these long hours in later years when I established the core working week, after I assumed control of the Willis business in 1955, as being from 8am to 5pm, with an hour for lunch and an early finish on Fridays making a 39 hour week. After 1955 there was no working on Saturdays except by the management giving extra to build up the business and the staff who worked flexible shifts in the office and warehouse. I was to learn a great deal about worker attitudes and practices as I spent those schoolday years with warehouse operatives who, at that time, were

Hyland House, Greenfoot Lane, Barnsley built in 1930 (garden wall, porch & front gable are post war additions.

working an eight and a half hour day in the week plus four and a half hours on Saturday. There were no holidays except one week in the last full week of August (Barnsley Feast Week) together with two days off at Christmas, plus one day at Easter (Easter Monday). Stock taking always took place on New Year's Day followed by a retreat to the local pub, from which I always escaped.

For me Barnsley Holgate Grammar School, due to a series of circumstances, including a whole term off through scarlet fever in the first year, was to be a disappointment. However, I have always been grateful that the move to Greenfoot Lane, near Wilthorpe Junior School, ensured that I was able to develop my interest in history to the full and acquire good reading and basic mathematical ability.

We must remember that the house built by father in the 1930s, whilst having many benefits for the children, was for mother's working environment no better than general conditions at the beginning of the century. There was no central heating, no gas, no domestic appliances, apart from a Ewbank carpet cleaner – just a coke fired oven to cook in and open fires for heating. My sister Maisie probably paid the ultimate price, contracting rheumatic fever resulting in her early death at the age of 27. Housekeeping money was always in short supply, with mother in the early years pushing a pram to Barnsley market once a week and then walking back, an overall distance of over 2 miles, fortunately mostly on reasonably flat roads.

Family Life in the 1930s

RT Willis with l-r Maisie 7, Derek 4½, Terry 2, GRTW 8, 1929.

School days passed without the five Willis children really appreciating the suffering and poverty which was all around them as the Wall Street crash of 1929 heralded a decade of lower living standards, particularly in the north, with unemployment rising to over 25% in many Yorkshire mining towns and villages. I well remember the crash of the airship R101 on 5 October 1930 shortly after I had moved to Wilthorpe Junior School. Moving to Barnsley Holgate Grammar School in 1932 established a way of life which was certainly more affluent than the vast majority of the working class in Barnsley. Unemployment was steadily rising, many miners were only able to work three days a week for a wage of around ten shillings a day. Unemployment pay, always called 'the dole', was 17/- (85p) a week for men and 15/- (75p) a week for women. Yes, we had a radio, which mother always referred to as the 'wireless'. Listening to the radio over these years key events registered, such as the Japanese invasion of Manchuria and China, the formation of the National Government in October 1931 after Britain came off the Gold Standard and the Pound was devalued by 30%. Wages for many workers fell, with some members of the armed forces earning as little as 25/- (£1.25) a week.

How did father cope with the declining purchasing power of the working class, who were the customers of the multitude of small house shops and corner shops he supplied? There is no record of perhaps father's most important business decision of his life, which was to enter into a contract with J Bibby and Son of Liverpool who would supply and market for father, as a local supplier, a fish frying compound manufactured by Bibbys in Liverpool. The J Bibby factory was an offshoot of the then famous Bibby Shipping Line, with its headquarters in Liverpool. The compound supplied produced tasty fish and chips and was marginally cheaper than conventional frying fats, with the added advantage of being of a consistent quality. Why was it so important to the Willis business? Quite simply, father ceased to trade with many grocers at this time who could not pay their bills. Debt collecting was a time consuming and distressing business. Father recruited two salesmen from Brooke Bond Tea who had been made redundant. In those days it was not really redundancy, you were simply paid one week's wages in lieu of notice. These two salesmen had just one objective, call on every fish and chip shop within a prescribed area, as defined in the Bibby contract, and sell the Bibby Fish Frying Compound. There were two variants, the standard product known as Bibby's FF (Frying Fat) and a higher quality compound known as Bibby's ABC. How do you save a business when a large number of your old grocery customers are losing theirs? The answer was quite simple, sell a product which is always paid for by ready cash. Traditionally 'fish and chips' has always been a cash up front business, right to the present day. On the other hand, the small grocery store and corner shop had always been a source of credit to the neighbouring working class families. If you fell on hard times credit or 'tick' was available. As a mining family you would never go to a bank for a loan. Most working class families were too poor and without the necessary assets to secure a loan, but the local shopkeeper knew you would pay for essentials when you could. The 1930s' depression reduced the ability of the local grocer to sustain many local communities, but father could always be sure to be paid by the fish and chip shop owner, who was providing a ready cooked nutritious food product at a very low price. Another great advantage to a supplier of Bibby Frying Compound was that once a fish and chip shop converted to this new frying medium, it was virtually impossible to go back to dripping or lard as these products were generally less economical in use than the new compound. It could be truthfully stated that the fish and chip shop was largely responsible in averting starvation or semi starvation in many poor families at this time. A fish and chip supper cost from 4d(2p) to 6d ($2\frac{1}{2}$p) and children could get a bottle of milk at school for 1d ($\frac{1}{2}$p). Father's cash flow was assured. His competition was the dripping manufacturer which, despite the variable quality, the majority of fish fryers continued to use. However, enough fish and chip shops took to the new Bibby product to give the Willis business increasing prosperity up to the outbreak of the Second World War.

Top left: l-r Derek, Maisie, Mary and Terry, 1933.
Top right: Derek and Maisie.
Above left: GRTW age 12, 1933.
Above right: Masie age 11 and Mary age 3, 1933.
Left: Derek, Mary and Terry with Harry Chapman, 1933.

Above: RT Willis with, back l-r Barbara (cousin), Maisie, GRTW and front l-r Derek, Mary, Terry.
Right: Maisie and GRTW, 1930s.

Father was always an enigma to his children. He was always respectful to mother but he never had any intention of doing any household chores, such as lighting a fire, making a bed or washing up. His normal time of rising in a morning was between 10am and 11am, back for lunch around 2pm and then back to the warehouse until around 6pm. Most evenings he was away to meet up with his 'cronies', all local business people or managers of local establishments. It was always the same venues that he attended, the Three Cranes Hotel in Queen Street, Barnsley or Barnsley Cricket Club's licensed premises in Shaw Lane being the most popular. There was certainly no difficulty in having your pint of beer until the early hours. Father was not a heavy drinker by any means, but he enjoyed the company. He had always owned a car, which in later years improved in quality as he prospered, but arriving home any time after midnight rendered an early start the next day impossible. The pattern did change for special events, such as holiday journeys or at Christmas, but there is no doubt that this pattern of life took its toll on mother who, mostly unaided, had to keep the household routine going. Cleaning ladies came and went, often staying for only a few weeks, frightened off by father.

Father's experience at Penistone Grammar School had made him very prejudiced against the education system. Mother more than made up for his indifference, particularly by her enthusiasm for the French language. For years we had the French magazine 'La France' delivered to the house. Father's routine resulted in the children very much doing their own thing, but within a strict disciplinary regime. Despite father having a car, mother walked to Barnsley at least once a week to shop for fruit and vegetables in the market and for fish at the Co-op in Market Street. On this weekly journey she was usually pushing a large pram containing my younger sister Mary. I joined the local Scout group, 5th Barnsley, affiliated to St Paul's Church in Old Town, a working class neighbourhood of terraced housing, about a quarter of a mile from our house in Greenfoot Lane. Mother found the money for the Scout uniform as I stayed with this troop for over five years, eventually becoming a patrol leader. The other saving refuge for me, as a young teenager, was the YMCA in Barnsley and the Public Library. Chess in the YMCA with Ron Wainwright, later to be killed at Dunkirk, and reading history and exploration books in the library was always absorbing and enjoyable. Mother and the children were left even more to their own devices during the August summer holidays. Father took us in the early 1930s to Acaster Selby, where we stayed in the old school house occupied by an old Martin family friend, Arthur Jarrett, who now lived on his own.

Acaster Selby is situated on the west bank of the River Ouse, near Bolton Percy and about six miles from York. The form of travel on holiday in the family car was, for many years, a Standard 10 saloon, with mother nursing Mary, the baby, in front plus three children on the back seat with me sitting on a large square biscuit tin in the well between front and back seats. The biscuit tin on long journeys contained the picnic. On a luggage rack attached to the back of the car was a large trunk containing clothes etc for say three weeks. The trunk was secured by the washing line on the rack. The children were commanded to keep an eye on it through the rear window!

Acaster Selby was a small farming community with around six tenanted farms and a small row of terraced cottages, fronting onto a village road from Bolton Percy, which ended at the gates of Nun Appleton Hall, an eighteenth century stately home then owned and occupied by Sir Benjamin Dawson, of the Dawson textile empire, and his wife Lady Dawson. Just outside the estate gates and adjacent to the old school house was the village church, with a weekly Sunday service conducted by the curate from Bolton Percy, attended by just six or seven worshippers, with Lady Dawson playing the organ. When the family were staying at the school house on holiday, we all attended the service with myself acting as organ blower. This was a village without mains water or electricity. Earth closets and oil lamps were the order of the day. I always remember that the earth closet adjacent to the kitchen, at the school house, was a two seater without any partition! It was a very small community with no shop or pub but I soon found a good friend in a local farmer, Mr Cammidge, who had served in the 1914-1918 war as a driver with the Royal Horse Artillery. I worked in his fields hoeing and helping with the harvest. It was a mixed farm of 160 acres which, during the summer, employed a couple of Irish labourers who slept in the fields or in the stackyard. Mrs Cammidge fed them on bread, cheese and tea. I enjoyed these holidays, particularly the occasional trip to York with Arthur on a borrowed cycle. The cycle would be left in an alley in York for the day, no lock required as it was sure to be there on our return. The attraction of York was the stamp dealers shop near the Minster. Where was father during this time? As soon as were we established at Acaster Selby and he had paid Arthur the agreed sum for our stay, he was off to Barnsley, back to work and his old haunts, and then back to collect us three or four weeks later. During World War II, the Cammidge farm became an RAF airfield, Acaster to be restored back to agricultural use after the war.

Left above: RT Willis and Mary.
Right above: l-r Derek, Terry, GRTW, Maisie and Mary.

Holidays before the Acaster forays would be a boarding house in varied locations, Filey and Aberdovey in North Wales spring to mind. In the later 1930s on two or three occasions we followed the Acaster Selby routine in being left by father for three weeks or so, but this time at 'Hibernia' in Nether Stowey near Bridgwater, Somerset. Grandfather Martin had retired to Nether Stowey from his last 'living' as an Anglican vicar at East Halton, near Immingham, north Lincolnshire. I was usually sent to sleep next door at Rose Cottage, a large Victorian house owned by Captain Kelly, a Merchant Navy captain, who had a very kind wife and allowed one or two of us to sleep in their family dormitory. These were good holidays as we caught various buses and explored the Quantock Hills, picking bilberries which Aunt Edie, who baked delightful pies, enhanced with Devonshire cream. 'Hibernia' had flushing toilets, but all cooking and lighting came from oil. Electricity did not arrive until after World War II and if you required a telephone, just after the war, you had to wait and then pay for the line and pole to be installed.

Back home in the winter months, mother encouraged indoor activities such as charades or performing short plays founded on extracts from Shakespeare or of historic events such as the death of Nelson in which we all took part. Saving pocket money to buy Hornby model trains or Meccano parts was another passion.

As already mentioned, the Greenfoot Lane home had a large garden of about two thirds of an acre, all grass surrounded by a fence and privet hedge. All father ever did in the early years was to cut the hedge. The grass was just left to grow. When I reached my early teens, mother and I decided we would try to create a proper garden. We acquired a small hand lawn mower and a few basic tools. I constructed a wheel barrow. Across the lane from our house, always called 'Hyland House', a name taken from father's mother's maiden name, was an old farm house, known as Tinker's Farm, recently purchased by the local authority as part of a house building scheme. This farm house had a large garden which had been abandoned for many years. Mother and I decided to build a large herbaceous border, using plants from this abandoned garden across the lane. We moved lupins, delphiniums, rhododendrons and various shrubs, by means of our home made wheelbarrow (the barrow wheel had fortunately been left by the house builders, otherwise a wheelbarrow would have been impossible).

One day father considered I was taking over his garden. It was a Sunday, he exploded in fury and inflicted several blows on my head as punishment. This assault I never forgot, but it was part of the make up of a person who had suffered severely when young. He ran away from Penistone Grammar School, then a boarding school for some scholars, and walked all the way to his home in Sheffield Road, Barnsley only, according to mother, to be told by his father George Hamlet to walk back. He never forgot this episode which he related to mother. Anyway a garden at Hyland House was established by mother and myself which father, after I left home improved by planting fruit trees and taking over the grass cutting with a better machine!

School Days and After

In September 1932 I was enrolled in Barnsley and District Holgate Grammar School, an establishment of some 650 boys under the headmastership of Arthur John Schooling MA, described by RH Greenland in his history of the school as 'a distinguished man of upright character, who ruled over the ever expanding school with inflexible courage'. His 'inflexible courage' was to result in the infliction of three strokes of the cane as I bent over, as commanded, in his study not many weeks after entering the school. It was an unjust punishment for a misdemeanour which was committed by the boy seated in the desk immediately in front of me. He did not own up and allowed the teacher to think it was me. This misfortune rankled for many years. The school was a 15th century foundation with roots going back to 1370 AD and before. The school provided a good classical and basic scientific education, with University or a good position in local government or commerce being the ultimate goal. Perhaps the most important lesson, for me, was that ambitious goals could not be achieved without application, good planning and hard work. Unfortunately, much of the hard work, for example in trying to master compulsory Latin, was quite a chore. In contrast, most of the further education work I undertook after leaving school was enjoyable and fulfilling.

I was bitterly disappointed that after five years at the Grammar School and obtaining a reasonable School Certificate, I failed to qualify for an automatic entry into a university despite obtaining two distinctions in the

Matriculation exams. Seven subjects were taken in this exam which included compulsory Latin, for which I had no natural inclination. Much time and effort was spent in trying to come to terms with this subject, all to no avail, resulting in a total failure in the exam. My start at the school had been far from auspicious which threw me into a period of disenchantment with all study, except the reading of history and biographies. Firstly, as already mentioned, I was wrongly picked out by the form master in my first term in form IIA. The result was summary dispatch to the head with no explanation asked for. Many tears and three strokes of the cane followed. More serious was the loss of attendance in the Spring term due to Scarlet Fever, resulting in isolation in Kendray Hospital, Barnsley. The food in the hospital was so sparse that on returning home after about six weeks isolation, I can well remember eating a whole loaf of bread and butter. No account was taken of my absence through sickness, or any help offered prior to the year end exams. The inevitable result was that in the following term I was dispatched to form IIIB, a lower grade class than I had aspired to. The result was two years of minimum application. I was not encouraged by father who was just looking forward to the day when I left and joined his business. Mother, with her hands full with the three youngest children, did her best to be interested, but without father's support it was impossible for her to become involved with the school or the teachers. My attitude changed in the last two years, but it was too late to achieve initial ambitions.

I was not the only one to suffer from illness in early teens. My sister, Maisie, with whom I became particularly close, contracted rheumatic fever a year or so after winning a scholarship to Barnsley Girls High School. Maisie was certainly highly intelligent, and despite never making a complete recovery from rheumatic fever, entered and passed the Civil Service exam at the age of 16. She was then provisionally accepted into the Civil Service, subject to a medical examination. The result was a complete set back for Maisie. The advice from the doctors, who examined her, was to 'go home, do as little physical work as possible, and enjoy the life around you'. The end result was that Maisie kept father's business going during WWII, organised and worked in the garden and ran a Guide Group. The inevitable result was fatal heart strain and death at the age of 27. My debt to Maisie will emerge as we recount the years just prior to and during WWII.

Barnsley Chronicle, August 2001. Maisie back row 2nd from right, Class 5A, Barnsley Girls' High School, 1937.

Sport figured quite large at the Grammar School. I was not a particularly skilful football player only managing to reach the dizzy height of playing for Locke House under XIV eleven as a left back or left half. I tried my hand at rugby union without making any impact whatsoever. One sport I did enjoy and with some success was cross country running. I was always pleased that the school taught me to swim as a few years previously I fell into the Dearne/Calder canal after our dog, Nigger, which I had foolishly thrown in during a Sunday walk, and nearly drowned. Unable to swim at that time, Maisie, who was with me on the walk, saved my life. The canal under the '39 steps' where this episode took place was well over six feet deep. Maisie had the presence of mind to grab a long twig which I clung to and clambered out. Needless to say, I was not exactly greeted with much acclaim on arrival back at Hyland House. Unlike one or two boys who suffered from bullying at school, this was an experience which, thankfully, escaped me. Friendships came and went, but were difficult to cultivate as weekends were prescribed by Saturday morning attendance at the Willis warehouse with Sunday morning taken up by compulsory church attendance. Maisie and I walked on our own to and from St Mary's Parish Church in the centre of Barnsley. Many Sunday afternoons were spent at the Limes Golf Club at Staincross to act as father's caddy. After the experience of a six mile walk around eighteen holes and then the wait in the car park for at least an hour or more, whilst father enjoyed the pleasure of the 19th hole, I resolved never to set foot on a golf course again.

A highlight of attendance at the New Street warehouse on Saturday morning was that a Barnsley Football Club hero was the landlord of the public house, known as the Commercial

Inn, immediately opposite the warehouse in Joseph Street. A sign of the times in Barnsley in the 1930s was well illustrated by the lack of a telephone in this pub. Orders to Barnsley Brewery were made by the one and only telephone in the warehouse opposite. The Exchange number being Barnsley 375. My interest in Barnsley Football Club was encouraged by my use of father's season ticket when Barnsley were playing away from home. Father had a Stand ticket which he only used when he attended home matches for the first team. I attended on several Saturday afternoons, when the first team were away, to watch the second team who played in the Midland League. The landlord of the Commercial Inn was Jimmy Moore, who earned a very modest living despite having been a member of the Barnsley FC team who won the FA Cup in 1912. Barnsley played West Bromwich Albion FC in the final at the Crystal Palace stadium, in front of a crowd of 60,000. Jimmy Moore was on the left wing as 'outside left'. The result was a draw of 0-0 on 20 April 1912, a Saturday. The replay was four days later on Thursday 24 April 1912 at Bramall Lane, Sheffield in front of a crowd of 38,555. It was a hot day. After 90 minutes the score was still 0-0. In extra time, after 118 minutes of play, Harry Tynell, the outside right, scored the winning goal. The captain of the winning team was Archibald Taylor at left back. I was rescued by the only real friend I made at school, Ron Wainwright, who introduced me to the YMCA in Eldon Street, Barnsley and the challenge of chess. We spent many hours in the YMCA after school playing chess together or watching some of the very talented older players. After leaving school Ron joined the Territorial Army as a cadet. He was killed at Dunkirk. His name is on the WWII memorial in the Assembly Hall at the Grammar School. All the ex students, lost in World War II, have their names recalled on 11 November each year, when the school stops all work to remember them.

Above left: back l-r GRTW, Harry Chapman, Maisie; front l-r Terry, Mary, Derek.
Above right: Derek, late 1930s.
Left: Maisie, Stratford, 1941.

Leaving school in July 1937 father agreed to pay £5 to allow me to accompany a group of students from my old school, led by Dr Andrews, my old form master in my second year, to visit the World Exhibition in Paris. Dr Andrews was a very supportive teacher who organised the trip by rail and ferry from Newhaven to Dieppe, staying at a Paris Pension. The Exhibition was fascinating and it could be said was the start of the many journeys across the world I made in later years. The Exhibition reflected national characteristics at the time with the German and Russian pavilions looking across at each other in a very challenging fashion. It was certainly a portent of what was to come a few years later. The British pavilion did not boast in any way over our national or historic achievements as an industrial nation, as did most of the other participating countries, particularly the German and Russian. The British pavilion reflected the British weekend with the emphasis upon sport and outdoor activity, including most leisure pursuits outside work. On return from Paris mother was anxious that I had a good holiday before starting work and that it would be a good opportunity to give Maisie a holiday as well. Off we went by car to Stratford upon Avon. Father found a boarding house where the lady in charge undertook to provide two rooms, one each for Maisie and I. He gave us sufficient money to eat out and to attend the Shakespeare Theatre, which is exactly what we did. A week later father returned and home we went. Maisie and I had such a good time that the experiment was repeated again in Keswick in the Lake District. Maisie, at this time, was fit enough to walk to the top of Scafell, which is what we did. Back home I was kitted out with a 50/- (£2.50) suit from the 'Fifty Shilling Tailors'; Burton's suits cost £3 or more! I was allowed to buy a cycle on which to go to work. In September 1937 I earned my first salary of 10/- (50p) a week, most of which I was allowed to keep provided I opened a deposit account with the Midland Bank, Market Hill, Barnsley.

In the 1930s all work in a warehouse was manual, until fork lift trucks appeared in the 1960s. I was soon initiated into the technique of cutting up a side of bacon, preparing bacon rolls from the middle cut and hams for the cooker, a gas fired steam pressure oven. Hams were boned, placed into aluminium pots, cooked and then trimmed, removing skin and surplus fat prior to the application of bread crumbs. Whilst the main income for the business came from the supply of Bibby compounds to fish fryers, the three salesmen then employed also called upon small grocers concentrated in the Dearne valley from Stairfoot, Barnsley through to Wombwell, Wath, Mexborough and South Elmsall. If in work, miners would treat their family to boiled ham or a tin of John West salmon on Sundays. At least, handling bacon gave me a most useful skill, namely the ability to sharpen a carving knife on a wet stone or steel, a skill still in demand from the family today!

I soon discovered that father's business was run on very rudimentary lines. Firstly, the book keeping system was virtually non existent with control maintained by the simple expedient of destroying all copy invoices once that account was paid. The cash or cheques were banked daily. Father paid all the bills on receipt and in many cases deducted $2\frac{1}{2}\%$ discount for prompt payment whether authorised or not. All expense invoices received and paid were saved and all cash payments, such as bus fares and postage stamps, recorded in a diary. On New Year's Day each year, stock was taken, valued and together with the expense documents, sales records and the bank statements taken to an accountant, Jack Sampson, who although unqualified, prepared a balance sheet and a profit and loss statement. Father, as a sole trader, and with his accountant's help, submitted these documents to the Inland Revenue for tax purposes. In practical terms, the business, although employing many people, was run as a small shop on similar lines to George Hamlet's grocery shop in Sheffield Road, Barnsley in the 1890s!

1938, Cyril & Ethel Garrett, Blackpool.

What was I to make of this system which depended entirely on everybody's honesty? I enrolled at Barnsley Technical College to sit the Grocer's Institute Certification Exam and also to take a two year course in touch typing and general office procedure. After twelve months all this study was to be interrupted when father purchased another small wholesale grocery business in Station Road, Eckington, south of Sheffield in late 1938. I was dispatched to live in lodgings in Eckington to take up the post of warehouse manager at the age of 17. I was very fortunate as my lodgings at 41 Station Road, Eckington, with a miner and his wife were excellent. By name of Ethel and Cyril Garrett they provided excellent care for 25/- (£1.25) a week. At the time Cyril was working three days a week underground at Renishaw colliery. They were thankful for the extra income. I had a room of my own in this two up two down terrace house with outside loo, and soon learnt the joys of plain but plentiful food, kippers, sausages, vegetable from Cyril's allotment and home baked bread.

Being the warehouse manager sounds rather grand. The reality was I had just two female assistants plus the delivery driver to supervise. All the heavy lifting, loading and unloading fell to me but the freedom from parental authority was very pleasing. The remaining staff were the manager, an ex naval rating, Tom Sandford, who also acted as a salesman with a small Austin van, together with Ted Collinson the other salesman who used a cycle to visit local shops within a 5-6 mile radius. Orders were collected, my team and I assembled them for delivery, Tom Sandford prepared the invoices which went out with the goods. Our main stock in trade was sugar, butter, prepacked margarine, cooking fats such as Bibby's Trex and various cuts of bacon supplemented by canned beans, peas, tomatoes and canned fruit from the USA. We also prepacked dried fruits such as currants from Greece and sultanas from the USA. Two staples we also prepacked were flour

l-r Horace Brooks, Tom Sandford, Harry Chapman and Tom Willis, New Street warehouse unloading gantry, c1937.

supplied by Smiths flour mill in Worksop and sugar supplied by Tate and Lyle. It was all very small scale, with low overheads in an old building which had originally been built as a local brewery in the early 19th century. I arrived in Eckington in September 1938. Twelve months later all was to change as war was declared on Monday 3 September 1939 and rationing gradually came about.

In 1939 father declared that he wouldn't bother to register the business to trade in rationed goods. Instead he would rely upon unrationed products. Not for the last time, Maisie came to the rescue and processed all the necessary application forms, having persuaded father that this was the most sensible course of action. Without her foresight the Willis business of food wholesaling would have disappeared very quickly. However, father had one major asset. He had cash which enabled him to buy much extra stock for both Barnsley and Eckington. The government were also disposing of old army food reserves which were not suitable for the expanding armed forces. About 500 wooden cases of canned corned beef hash arrived at the Eckington warehouse for which father paid about 2d (1p) a can. There were 24 cans in a case. Twelve months later he sold the whole consignment to a Chesterfield Market trader for £1 a case. The outside of these wooden cases was embossed 'Army & Navy Canteen Board, Salonika 1919', eventually to be sold on Chesterfield Market for 1/3 (6p) a can but not rationed! John West salmon, also stockpiled, was sold for four or five times the original cost. What was the end result? Father bought a new house in extensive grounds on Sheffield Road near Birdwell, Barnsley. This was a large detached dormer bungalow, complete with billiard room, detached garage, large greenhouse and terraced garden. This purchase was made in 1942 when I was then in Southern Rhodesia (Zimbabwe) training to be an RAF pilot.

Left: Mr & Mrs Bob Ballantine, Bulawayo, 1942.
Right: Maisie, Florence Elsie, Terry, Mary, Derek, RT Willis, GRTW, 1941.

From September 1939 and through the early months of the war changes in the Willis wholesale business were gradual as imported products fell away and the rationing of basic foodstuffs, such as sugar and fats, came in. Again father's fortunes were enhanced as the Ministry of Food offered to pay for the emergency storage at the Eckington warehouse of prepacked margarine, chiefly Stork and Echo, a Van Den Bergh's product. The Eckington warehouse was chosen for this task as it was reasonably close to Sheffield and not likely to suffer bombing from the air. Soon I was handling and rotating hundreds of these boxes held to replace stock lost in the blitz. However, for me it was time to volunteer for active service. I called at the Cutlers Hall in the autumn of 1940, shortly after the Battle of Britain, on my way home to spend the weekend at Hyland House. My first inclination was to enlist in the Navy. The recruiting Petty Officer said there were only vacancies for certain skills such as electrical engineering. He did suggest I went upstairs to the RAF desk. I had already seen the press advertisements for aircrew and had determined that if I failed to enlist in the Navy, aircrew was the next option. Brief details of education and current job were taken down. I was then asked what role in aircrew would I like to apply for. No question, first choice was to be a pilot. The rest of the story has already been published in 'No Hero, Just A Survivor', so we must move on to the year 1946 and my return to the Willis food wholesaling enterprise.

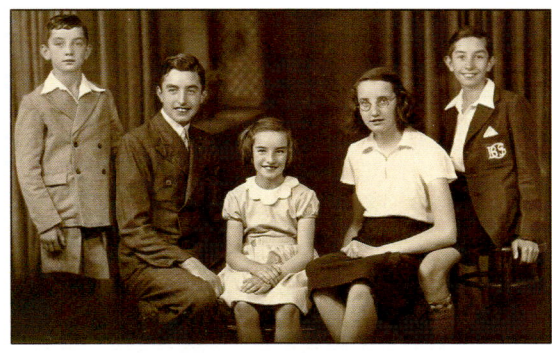

Left above: l-r Terry 11, GRTW 17, Mary 8, Maisie 16, Derek 13, 1938.

Left below: l-r May Marshall, Terry, Maisie, Mary, c1945.

Above left: Robert, outside King Farouk's Palace, Cairo, November 1943.
Above right: Tommy Thompson and Indian bearer, Ranchi, Bihar State, December 1944.

Below: Joan and Robert, age 21.

Above left: Hyland House, Sheffield Road, Birdwell.
Above right: Joan.
Left and below: Robert & Joan on their wedding day, 24 November 1945.
L-r Stan Perrett, RT Willis, Florence Elsie Willis, Tommy Thompson, Robert, Joan, Clifford Nowell, Derek, Terry.

CHAPTER 9

POST WAR RECONCILIATION AND HEALING

Although fully covered in my book 'No Hero, Just A Survivor', my RAF career from 1940 to 1946 has to be brought in here as the publication of this book had quite unforeseen, but very happy, consequences. After completing pilot training in Southern Rhodesia (Zimbabwe), South Africa and the UK, I was posted to 47 Squadron RAF, a torpedo carrying squadron based, in November 1943, in the Western Desert, near Tobruck, Libya. From November 1943 to July 1945, on this Squadron, I completed two operational tours, one based at Gambut in Libya and the second based in India and Burma, before being flown back to the UK in July 1945, to act as a Mosquito flying instructor. After demobilisation on 4 June 1946, adjustment and concentration on family life and the family business pushed the wartime experiences into the far background of one's mind.

However, as would be expected, I kept up an annual correspondence, usually around Christmas, with two old 47 Squadron friends, Bill Powell DFC and his navigator, Maurice Jones. Shortly after the end of WWII, Bill, along with other RAF colleagues, founded a 47 Squadron Old Boys' Association, which met annually for dinner in London. In 1960 I told Bill that I would become a member of this 47 Squadron Old Boys' Association and attend the annual dinner. Eventually, in the late 1990s, 47 Squadron, based at Lyneham in Wiltshire, and now a transport squadron flying Hercules, agreed to take over the original Old Boys' Association and encourage new members from the post war period. The annual 'get togethers' are now over a weekend at the Squadron base in Lyneham. This 47 Old Boys' Association sparked off the inspiration to write and publish my own RAF story in 1996, under the title 'No hero, Just A survivor', with copies deposited in the British Library in London and the Bodleian Library in Oxford, the National Library in Wales and Eire.

After the death of George Hamlet Willis in 1950, all communication with the Penistone based family ceased. However, as outlined in Chapter 3, George Hamlet's eldest daughter read the review of my book in the Barnsley Chronicle and was determined, at the age of 84, to restore contact with the family of her half brother Robert Thomas. Through the medium of the sub-editor of the Barnsley Chronicle contact was established resulting in a very happy relationship with Monica, her younger sister Joan and Joan's husband Charles Forster. Much material in this book emanated from research by Charles, who passed it on to me in 2004.

In early 2001 another surprise was to come, due to the publication of my RAF history. With the fall of the Berlin Wall in 1989 and the subsequent release by the Russian government of the Luftwaffe records covering operations in the Mediterranean, British researchers were able to check Luftwaffe activities against the RAF records of the Mediterranean conflict. Squadron Leader Chris Goss, of the

Top: Arado 196 over Heliopolis, Athens, November 1943.
Above: UFR Karl Steinbrecher (right) with his navigator Lt Eberhard Ahrends.

historical section of the RAF, phoned me to say that my book had been checked against the German records and found to be accurate in all respects except that I had mistakenly identified an Italian Cant 506B for a German Heinkel 115, both aircraft being of similar design. Chris Goss then went on to say that the present German government supported and encouraged reconciliation between old adversaries. Chris had discovered, with the assistance of German researchers, that the pilot of an Arado 196, sunk by me in the Aegean (Eastern Mediterranean) on 4 December 1943, had survived the war. His name was Karl Steinbrecher and he was living with his wife Gunda near Nuremberg. Chris asked whether I would like to make contact to which I readily agreed. Letters were exchanged resulting in a very emotional meeting taking place between Karl and I as he stepped out of the train at Wakefield station on 21 June 2002. Karl, with his wife Gunda, were accompanied by Karl's brother in law, Fritz Hartmann and his wife Madlen. Fritz could speak fluent English. They all stayed at the Cedar Court Hotel, just a few miles from Emley, for the next three days, visiting us at Greenways and exchanging wartime experiences. The highlight of the visit was the presentation by Karl of his Luftwaffe silver gilt wings to me on the steps of the Cedar Court Hotel (pictured right). As in the RAF, pilot's wings were awarded in the Luftwaffe on graduation as a pilot. An exchange visit was made to Karl's home in Spardorf where it soon became clear that the whole Steinbrecher family were very grateful that as Karl evacuated his sinking Arado and climbed into a dinghy no attempt was made to kill him or his navigator, as I flew low over the dinghy to observe the situation. Karl died in September 2005, aged 83.

Healing and reconciliation, whether it be in families or after the tragedy of wars, are at the very centre of the Christian faith which has sustained Joan and myself all our lives. Our faith has suffered many ups and downs, either from our commitment to St Mary's at Worsbrough or to our attendance at St Michael's, Emley, over the past thirty eight years. With our outside activities much reduced in recent years, the community at St Michael's has been very supportive and much appreciated.

Above left: Greenways, June 2002, l-r Madlen Hartmann, Fritz Hartmann, Joan, Gunda Steinbrecher, Karl Steinbrecher.

Above right: Karl and Robert, Spardorf, Germany, 20 May 2003.

Below: St Michael's Church, Emley.

CHAPTER 10

THE FAMILY BUSINESS 1946-1955
Return to the Family Business

It was not an easy choice to return to a family business, created by my father, who had parted from his own father in very acrimonious circumstances. The war had taken its toll. From its peak in 1938 the business had been held together by the discipline of rationed supplies, sufficient to pay the salaries of the staff still employed, but its very survival had largely fallen upon my sister, Maisie. It was with mixed feelings that I agreed to return to the business in June 1946, after father promised a true partnership. This was a promise which was never properly fulfilled, causing much tension in the years ahead.

With an 'above average' assessment as a Mosquito pilot, the Chief Flying Instructor at Middleton St George, Wing Commander 'Black' Smith DFC*, was rather keen that I stayed in the RAF and that I accepted his posting to the Central Flying School at Little Rissington, in order to obtain full qualification as a flying instructor. Three times I was placed on the posting list, three times I went to the Adjutant's office to request that I be taken off as I was due for demob, which I was committed to pursue. Personal motives to refuse the Little Rissington posting were quite mixed but the overriding consideration was Joan's welfare. She was expecting our first child in August. Another factor which weighed heavily was the thought that my luck may run out. With several hazardous experiences behind me, I had really had my fill of flying. I was ambitious too. What could I make of the family business and would father prove to be too difficult to work with? So the die was cast. I left the RAF on 3 June 1946. Three days later on 6 June I was in the Eckington warehouse with a view to growing the business. All thoughts of enjoying a long paid leave to September went out of the window when father explained that, such was the state of the business at Eckington, he had only communicated with the manager, Tom Sandford, by letter or telephone over the past six months.

Catching a bus to Eckington on Wednesday 5 June, I called at my old landlady in Station Road, who immediately offered Joan and myself temporary accommodation. The next day I interviewed Tom Sandford who admitted having paid little attention to the business for several months. His wife had left him to live with their older son and he was quite happy to leave. By Friday 7 June I was in charge of a staff of just four people, which comprised two female warehouse assistants, one lorry driver, Herbert Naylor, and one salesman, Ted Collinson, a WWl veteran who won the Military Medal on the Western Front. It was back to Hyland House to rescue Joan and to take up residence in the one spare bedroom in Ethel and Cyril Garrett's two up and two down terrace house at 41 Station Road. We were lucky, in spotting an advertisement in the weekend press and agreeing to buy, two days later, a new semi-detached house at Whitwell, six miles from Eckington, on the road to Worksop. The house, just completed, had been left at the foundation stage in 1940 when all house building ceased. We drove to view the property in our small company van to see a small three bedroom semi-detached house with a living room and kitchen plus bathroom downstairs, and three bedrooms, two double and one single, upstairs. There was a small garden to front and rear with an unmade drive and room for a garage. The ground floor you stood on was pitch as timber was in short supply. The asking price was £1,000. I had saved over £600 in the RAF, Joan had a legacy from her Uncle Harold, who had recently died. Father lent me £100 (which he later waived) and we were home and dry. We were to stay there from June 1946 until November 1948, during which time I concreted the drive, mixing the sand and cement by hand, erected a garage from redundant air raid shelter material and grew vegetables in the garden. The location of the house was on an unmade road, called Sunnyside. However, it was a good start as we began to put a home together.

Very soon Joan was back at Hyland House awaiting the birth of our first child, a daughter Catherine, born at St Helens Hospital Maternity Wing in Barnsley on 30 August 1946. The maternity wing had been adapted from the workhouse of the 1920/30 era. Mother was very good in helping Joan who suffered from a breast abscess, prior to discharge, which the hospital refused to treat. Doctor Potter, the family doctor, was called to Hyland House and came to the rescue, lancing the abscess with a safety razor blade he carried in his waistcoat pocket – suitably sterilised! Catherine was thriving and Joan was soon back at our home in Whitwell. Incidentally, Doctor Potter was a senior surgeon at this time at the Beckett Hospital in Barnsley.

What of the business? I was paid £7 per week, double the average wage at the time for a male employee. The two female assistants, one of whom, Gladys Roberts, had been there since pre-war days, were paid £2/10/- (£2.50) or £2 per week. We depended very heavily upon a weekly delivery of supplies from the main warehouse in Barnsley, which came by a 30cwt capacity van. I soon realised that the priority had to be the purchase and then the selling of unrationed products, such as patent medicines, flour (to be rationed two years later), cigarettes and canned peas from the nearby canning factory owned by Ashtons, a local family. It was hard work, calling on small grocers and house shops in all the villages within an eight to ten miles radius of the warehouse. All the orders were written out by hand. There was no price list or list of products. You remembered the price, quoted it to the prospective customer, transcribed the order, if any, into the order book, to be deposited at the warehouse for the two assistants to assemble. At the end of each day, I collected the assembled order sheets from the warehouse, including those of Ted Collinson, took them home and after tea made up the invoices incurring many twelve to fourteen hour days.

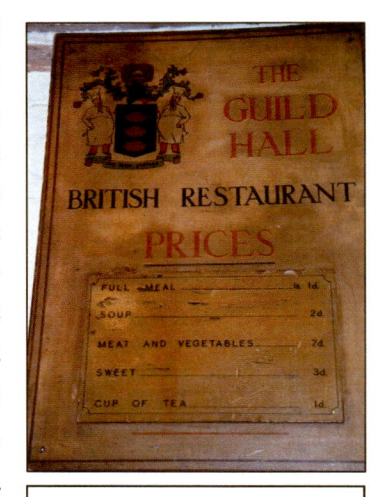

British Restaurant, Guild Hall, Barnsley, 1947. Full meal 1/1; Soup 2d; Meat & vegetables 7d; Sweet 3d; Cup of tea 1d.

Payment would be the following week when I called for the next order and explained what was available. It was hard work but you certainly became very familiar with working people serving a predominately mining community.

The most difficult time over these years was coping with the 1946/47 winter, reported to be the worst weather for over 100 years. After the first night of heavy snow, I was unable to drive on the road to work from Whitwell. The only solution was to walk the six miles. I returned later that day in the 30cwt delivery van driven by Herbert Naylor, weighed down with sacks of dried peas and washing soda to give the van a grip on the road. There were no snow ploughs, but fortunately very little traffic. You used a shovel to dig yourself out if you were stuck. Herbert Naylor and I worked together for six weeks collecting and delivering orders. Trade was good and fortunately we had enough petrol, which was still rationed, to see us through. How Maisie at Barnsley coped, with a heart condition, I can't imagine. Fortunately, late in 1948, my brother Derek was demobbed from the RAF, where he had served as a radar mechanic, and was able to take over from me at Eckington. The house at Whitwell was quickly sold and again Joan and I were lucky enough to find a new semi-detached house, just completed, at 101 Worsbrough Road, Birdwell, Barnsley. We were to stay there for nearly twenty three years, never moving as we conserved our resources in the years ahead. Paying £1,300 for this new house, without taking out a mortgage and having sold our Whitwell house, we moved in on 8 November 1948. It was a wet day. The drive to the front door was red shale which was trailed into the house much to Joan's great concern. Top priority was to pay for the drive to be concreted! The house was in traditional 1930's style with two reception rooms, kitchen and three bedrooms, one of which could just take a single bed. As the family grew we were able to push out the downstairs walls at the back and front of the house, build a garage at the side with a large additional bedroom on top. The challenge of New Street lay ahead as Maisie's health declined and I assumed her duties and tried to alert father that when rationing came to an end, competition would return. Were we equipped to survive?

The post war challenge – personal and business – six years of frustration.

After two years at the Eckington warehouse I was getting nowhere. It was difficult to look forward as one crisis in the country seemed to follow another. With the abrupt ending of Lend Lease by the United States government, in many respects the fruits of victory seemed far away. Not generally realised, but all too evident with the continued rationing of food and petrol, the country had spent all its currency reserves and was in effect dependent upon the goodwill of the United States if it was to grow into a thriving industrial nation again, able to pay its way. Everybody appeared so drab. Football crowds were virtually all men in grey mackintoshes and grey cloth caps. No colour or fashion to be seen. How were we ever going to break out and create a thriving and enterprising community in town, city and countryside? I moved to Birdwell hoping to make a difference, but father proved to be a very difficult person and virtually impossible to convince that change was the only way forward.

It was with mixed feelings that I took up my new duties at New Street where father controlled, with a very tight hand, all policies covering such items as suppliers, pricing policy, customer credit, all expenditure, wage rates, conditions of work and all future policies. Asking him to adjust some of these policies over the next few years was to result in a very considerable strain upon our mutual relationship

In 1942 father had sold Hyland House in Greenfoot Lane, Barnsley and moved into a large dormer bungalow in Sheffield Road, between Worsbrough Dale and Birdwell, approximately 500 yards from the outskirts of Birdwell. It was a well appointed house, built just prior to WWII with parquet floors in the two large reception rooms and entrance hall. The upstairs dormer section was the billiard room, complete with a $\frac{3}{4}$ size billiard table and a large alcove suitable to act as a spare bedroom. The surrounding grounds were landscaped with a tennis lawn to the front, a greenhouse to the rear and a terraced garden facing west and containing a small orchard. Father found the location much to his liking, as he employed a gardener, extended the greenhouse and cultivated tomatoes. This house too was also named Hyland House. The sale of surplus stocks, often purchased at auctions of distressed grocery businesses, had provided substantial funds to finance this more affluent lifestyle. Perhaps his most fortunate acquisition was the purchase of a soft drinks plant and business on 3 October 1934 on the liquidation of Barnsley and District Grocers Ltd who, at that time, owned this soft drinks establishment.

Throughout the war the Ministry of Food ensured that sufficient raw materials, including sugar, were available to keep soft drink manufacturing at pre war levels. For the general population a bottle of 'pop' was a morale booster, equally important to keeping the flow of beer from the brewery to the pub. Owing to the rapid growth of the armed forces, and the associated expanding spending power, both 'pop' and beer were often in short supply. The result was that for well over ten years father could sell everything he could acquire without any real sales effort. The consequence was that his ambition died, attendance at the warehouse in New Street was now just between mid-day and 3pm, then an extended lunch at home, with perhaps a weekly visit to his establishment in Chapeltown. In the case of Eckington visits were made every three months. Ambition had died so how could it be stimulated? I was to find this to be a virtually impossible task.

Mother also had her problems. She was soon to discover that the kitchen in the new house was badly designed with an open fire, an oven at the side and supplemented by an electric cooker. There was no gas, no central heating and all clothes washing, food storage and other domestic equipment was in the cellar kitchen. Access to the cellar kitchen was from the kitchen down a steep flight of stone stairs. This part of the house had been built for use by domestic help but father was always reluctant to employ any domestic help, so mother was down in the cellar kitchen, doing the household chores and more than once fell down the cellar steps. She was a tough lady, but eventually the strain began to tell. Mother was much relieved when father, in late 1953, agreed to sell Hyland House, Birdwell and move to a more modern dwelling in Keresforth Road, Dodworth, just before he became ill with lung cancer.

Both Maisie and Mary lived at home, Maisie with her own little van on rounds of visits to small corner grocery stores from Monday to Thursday and Mary off to Barnsley Girls High School on the bus, which stopped outside the house. In 1948, Mary departed for University College, London, graduating 3 years later with a BA in English. My first duty on arriving at work in Barnsley was to take over the shop calling rounds from Maisie who was showing many signs of strain and exhaustion aggravated by her heart problem. Father was now in complete control. Maisie went down to the office in New Street, Barnsley, with father at around 11am and came back with him for lunch at Hyland House three or four hours later. At this time father was running, for his own use, a 10hp Standard saloon of pre war vintage. This car was operated under a 'C' licence category (Commercial use) which enhanced its allocation of petrol during the rationing period, which was in force at that time in 1948. The 'C' licence for this car was justified by the removal of windows and the rear seats, these windows being replaced by stout linoleum. Petrol rationing was in force for 10 years before ending on 30 May 1950. It is interesting to note that throughout this period father was always able to drive home daily from the office and go out in the evening to late night sessions with his friends gathered in one or two pubs or at Barnsley Cricket Club, where licensing hours were ignored for favoured customers.

Where did the extra petrol needed come from? In 1937 father had two petrol pumps installed at the New Street premises, each serviced by a separate 500 gallon underground storage tank. Prior to petrol rationing being imposed in early 1940 these tanks were filled up leaving 1000 gallons of petrol reserved exclusively for father's use during the whole course of the war and after. When petrol rationing ended in 1950 father purchased, over the next few years, three new saloon cars, all large family models, starting with a Hudson Terraplane, an import from America, then an Armstrong Siddeley family saloon, and in 1954 an Austin Princess. Due to the parlous state of the business finances after father's death in February 1955 the Austin Princess was quickly disposed of. As head of the business, such as it was, after swingeing death duties, Joan and I managed with a small Austin van as transport during the late 1950s.

During the years 1949 to 1954 it became increasingly difficult to see where the family business was going. It was quickly apparent to my untrained eye that there were no professional skills in the enterprise, no proper accounting system, no business plan or marketing plan. Above all the premises of all the individual enterprises which father had put together, pre war, were in a very poor state of repair and even at that time totally out of date. When father died in 1955, I am often reminded of the remark I made at that time to a local joiner, Alf Hatfield, who was also an undertaker. It was a sunny spring morning, I was sitting outside on the loading gantry at New Street when Alf came into the yard to report on arrangements for father's funeral.

As our discussion ended standing in the yard, I turned to Alf and said with some despair, "What do I do with this lot?" The answer he came up with was to build a small wooden office in the yard which would at least provide space for two clerical staff and myself, so that some system of control could be put in place for the business. Fortunately, at that time, planning consent was not required.

Moving to Birdwell in 1948 did provide one clear advantage for our family, namely we had a very good Junior School within easy walking distance, some excellent teachers and a good headmaster, Mr Anderson. All our four children were able to go to this school from where they progressed to Grammar/High School and then to University. During these austere post war years, we had much to be grateful for. Our third child Andrew was born on 25 March 1951. I had a secure job with a reasonable salary, enabling Joan to devote herself to the children and for the two of us to put together a comfortable home. The problems were outside the home as it became increasingly difficult to adapt the business to post war conditions when father, after the death of my sister Maisie, failed to carry out his promises, made in 1946. This promise was that he would create a partnership or a private limited company in which all his children would have a share, depending on individual circumstances. No early decisions could be made as my brother Derek was still in the RAF, having been sent to Egypt, prior to his demobilisation in 1947. The issue was further complicated as it became increasingly clear that Maisie should cease all work due to her heart problems. This she was reluctant to do, wishing to lead as normal a life as possible. From a personal point of view, with a very young family, I was not eager to pursue thoughts of the future, on a personal basis, until I had time to settle down in a new role at the New Street establishment.

All was to change as Maisie became increasingly frail, with mother far more concerned about her health than father, who encouraged her to continue working on a part time basis. This could not last. Maisie was obliged to retire from work in early 1949, spending that summer sitting in the sun when the weather allowed. As the summer came to a close Maisie became bed fast and beyond medical help. She died peacefully on 14 September 1949, just 27 years old and probably the most talented member of the family. Without her support at father's side, from 1940, the whole Willis enterprise would have faded away. Maisie was laid to rest in the St Mary's Church cemetery, Worsbrough Village. It was a very moving occasion, with many of the local Girl Guide troop, which Maisie had led all through the war years, openly weeping.

Apart from the known ability of father to pay all our suppliers promptly, neither my brother Derek, at Eckington, or I had any idea about the financial strength of the business. It was an enterprise of small units, New Street and the Mineral Water

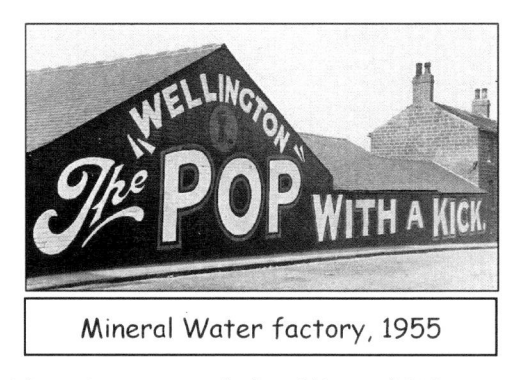

Mineral Water factory, 1955

factory in Foundry Street, Barnsley, MK Seniors, Chapeltown and Eckington, a wholesale grocery warehouse. We traded under three names – RT Willis and Son, Barnsley District Grocers (the mineral water arm) and MK Senior, who were pre packing specialists of sundry grocery products, based in Chapeltown, near Sheffield. With the rationing of petrol, flour, sugar and sweets coming to an end in 1949/50 customers would soon fall away unless we provided good consistent service at a competitive price. For personal and historic reasons, father refused to deal with major international food companies, such as Lever Brothers, Proctor and Gamble, Kellogg's or Mars. The crunch was to come in 1953/54 when father became increasingly difficult to deal with and with his health deteriorating, the whole situation became well nigh impossible to handle. His staff became very restless as he decreed that one week's holiday, the last full week in August, was the only paid holiday available and that Saturday mornings, Good Friday and New Year's Day were normal work days.

New regulations were coming in, such as pay roll taxes, value added taxes and the need to keep proper records of general running expenses. Father recruited his first secretarial assistance, Elsie Hall, who later married the New Street warehouse manager, Ernest Foster, following the death of his first wife. The staffing levels at New Street comprised a warehouse manager, two assistants, one delivery van driver and two salesmen. I was one of the salesmen! The Mineral Water factory comprised one manager, two female assistants and two sales/delivery drivers. The MK Senior business comprised one female supervisor, four female assistants, one delivery driver and one manager/salesman. The Eckington business comprised one manager/salesman who was my brother Derek, one other salesman, who used a cycle to visit shops in local villages, one delivery driver and two female warehouse assistants. In all the total staff numbers for the four branches were 24 people plus father. The wholesale enterprise was too small scale and diverse a business to survive in the competitive challenges ahead. Very little was to change until father's death on 13 February 1955. I did take some action with an eye to the future of which perhaps the most important was to enrol on an Accountancy correspondence course. Father's death in 1955, due to the work pressure at the time, prevented me from taking the interim exams, but at least I was able to understand the principles of double entry bookkeeping, bank reconciliation and trial balances. This skill was to prove invaluable for the rest of my life, in all forms of commercial and voluntary activities.

In 1951 an immediate and major problem arose which was the total inadequacy of the New Street premises which comprised a terrace of four houses, taken over by father on the dissolution of his partnership with his own father and described elsewhere. The building comprised cellars, a stone flagged ground floor and a wooden second floor. The buildings were early 19th century vintage, with outside toilets, two of which remained, and only one inside cold tap. All hot water depended on being heated in a set pot over a coke fire. The four terrace houses had been connected by making open doorways in the dividing walls in the cellar and the two floors. A rope lift was installed, with the lift shaft protected from anybody falling in, when the lift was at the top floor, by a flimsy thin plank lifted out when the lift was at the ground floor. The upper floor lift shaft was protected by flimsy wooden doors. Safety precautions were unheard of! Action was precipitated when a floor slab on the ground floor gave way as I walked along it, being unceremoniously dumped in the cellar! Father called in a local builder who, on examining the building, pronounced it to be in imminent danger of falling down into New Street! The solution was to erect an internal steel frame throughout the building on which to support the ground and first floors plus the roof. All the steel girders used were second hand, recovered from demolished buildings in Liverpool. However, most of the weight of loaded floors and the roof on the outer walls was removed. It must have been a reasonably satisfactory job as the building in New Street has only just been demolished as I write! Whilst this work was progressing and on advice from the builder, I persuaded father to part with a little more cash and replace the stone tiled roof with corrugated asbestos sheets which remain to this day. I was given a severe lecture that he was not prepared to spend any more money on the building, not even to have a modern hot water supply!

We were in the early 1950s and although conditions were, by modern standards, very unhygienic at work, I was able to come home in my small Austin van for lunch each day. In the evenings I would empty my cash bag on the sitting room carpet and with Joan's help count all the money and balance it with the receipts given. The small shops we called on paid cash, no cheques. Father banked the takings the next day.

Change was in the air as the Inland Revenue requested proper accounts, or at least reasonable records from the small traders who were our customers. I had the unfortunate experience of knowing two such small traders who committed suicide, unable to cope with these outside pressures.

Life revolved around the children, attendance at St Mary's Worsbrough on Sundays and prior to 1950 the annual one week's holiday in a boarding house on the east coast for which father lent us his car. We were also able to visit Joan's father and stepmother in Moorend Lane, Dewsbury on occasional weekends, or go into Sheffield for household needs. We had a small garden, kept in reasonable order with Joan very keen to have plenty of spring bulbs in the front windows. Moving ahead a little, the Revd Leonard Greensides the vicar at Worsbrough, newly appointed in 1961, asked me to be his Churchwarden. I carried out the duty for several years, working on various projects, particularly ecumenical work before resigning due to sheer pressure of work. I did, however, hold the Chairmanship of the main St Mary's charity, the Robinson Bequest, for over 30 years, not resigning until travel from home at Emley to Worsbrough, particularly in the evening became impossible.

From 1946 to 1955 we lived through very worrying events. We still remember the winter of 1946/47 when roads were blocked for most of January and February 1947 by very heavy snowfalls. We had power cuts, no gritting lorries, but somehow we managed to keep supplies going to our small shop customers. On 30 June 1947 food rationing was cut back to wartime austerity levels as a severe dollar shortage forced the Labour government to impose a new economy drive. Russia tightened its grip upon Eastern Europe culminating in the Berlin Air Lift from September 1948 to May 1949. India was partitioned accompanied by horrific massacres. The Arabs, Jews and British fought over Palestine. The United Nations and NATO were established and then in June 1950 the Korean war broke out and within weeks Britain was sending troops to support the multi-national force mustered to prevent the fall of South Korea to a Communist dictatorship. For Joan and myself this was an anxious time as I was a Class A reservist. Fortunately, the Allies, with the support of the United Nations, were able to defeat the North Koreans, with the border between the two Koreas stabilised in July 1953 and peace declared. Like many other anxious reservists our services were not required. By 1955 the Vietnam war was looming where the eventual outcome was to be rather different to the Korean peace agreement.

In early 1954, after much fruitless discussion with father over the future of the business, Joan and I arranged to meet him and my mother at Hyland House, Birdwell one evening shortly before the move to a new home in Dodworth, Barnsley. The meeting ended with me declaring that I was leaving the business forthwith. Father was so shocked that on the following day at the New Street warehouse he said he would consult his solicitor immediately and establish a clear path for the future. I stayed on to await events. Another meeting was held at Hyland House where he declared that he had created a trust for the benefit of mother, but that effective control of the business would pass to myself and

Derek. When I asked for a copy of the Trust deed he firmly declined. At the same time, he announced that he had abdominal pains and requested that I took him to see two specialists in Barnsley, to whom his doctor, Dr Potter, had referred him. This I did over the next couple of weeks. The two consultants declared that nothing serious could be diagnosed and that they couldn't find anything to worry about. It was the summer of 1954; father declared that a holiday at Thornton le Dale with mother would pick him up. He went on this holiday and came back to say that he was feeling worse. He and mother had only just moved into another house in Dodworth, Barnsley having sold the Birdwell residence. This new home was a much more modern house than the Birdwell residence. It was a detached house, more compact with modern fittings, good central heating, no cellar kitchen and a smaller garden. Mother was very pleased. Father never had the opportunity to enjoy his new abode as he found it increasingly difficult to rise in the morning and have a meal. He transferred all his vital office work home, from where he paid the suppliers, whilst I took up his other duties such as paying the staff, seeing suppliers and paying in or cashing the necessary cheques. Something had to be done as his was the only cheque signature. I visited his solicitor, Alun Thomas, who remains a friend to this day. We saw father together in bed, in the late summer of 1954 where Alun persuaded him to sign a power of attorney in my name. From that day father took no further part in the business, dying from lung cancer in Sheffield Royal Hospital on 13 February 1955, with myself, Derek and mother in attendance. A sad end and not one that I would have wished, but it probably saved the business. A new chapter was about to open.

Before moving on it is only proper to remember that there were many reasons why father, Robert Thomas Willis, had such entrenched attitudes. We must remember, as related in the George Hamlet Willis story, that Robert Thomas suffered a very difficult and in many emotional ways a rather harsh early life. Despite all, he could, on occasion, be surprisingly generous in many small ways to his family. It was very sad to see him fade away at home and finally in Sheffield Royal Hospital in his early sixties. Mother loved and respected him to the end.

CHAPTER 11

REFLECTIONS ON A CHANGING SOCIAL SCENE AND FAMILY LIFE

When Joan and I married in November 1945 we were quite anxious to have a small family. Joan's ambition, at that time, was a family of four children, which was a goal we ultimately achieved. In January 1946 we knew our first child was on the way. As mentioned previously, I was a Mosquito Flying Instructor at RAF Middleton St George, now Teeside Airport, near Darlington. There were no married quarters on the RAF station, but we quickly found comfortable rooms in a typical 1930s' semi detached house in Yarm Road, Darlington. The occupant was a middle aged spinster, Florrie Suttill, who had lost both her parents. This lady installed us in the front bedroom and the front room downstairs. Florrie lived on her own and had no employment. She was a Plymouth Brethren and reasonably easy to get on with, particularly important as Joan had to share the kitchen with her. She apparently had only one living relative, a sister, married to a chef, who visited Florrie from time to time. Occasionally, if time allowed, we had a short weekend break at Hyland House, Birdwell. We were fortunate in receiving a lift to Birdwell by a car owned by Duncan Swale, a fellow flying instructor, whose home was in Chesterfield. His parents owned the well known department store, of that name, in Chesterfield, later to disappear during town centre development.

Post war preoccupation, for the great majority of the many thousands being demobbed in 1946/47, was job prospects. As mentioned earlier, I had the good fortune to be offered a long term career in the RAF. As I pondered the future I often said to Joan that perhaps my luck would run out. This was one consideration, but on the other hand the RAF, at that time, was not an easy environment in which to bring up a family, especially with a baby already on the way. Father wanted me back and made many promises of partnership with himself and Maisie, which unfortunately was later to bring about tension and conflict. The job was there, manager of the small Eckington business. The problem we faced was where to live. Homes were in very short supply but as with so many other veterans returning to civilian life, Joan and I moved to my parents' house, in Birdwell, on my discharge from the RAF in early June 1946. Father intimated that the Eckington business was in crisis. I was to go over as quickly as possible, fire the manager Tom Sandford, a long standing employee, who over the years of the war only attended the business when he felt like it. I had one week's leave at Hyland House before going over to Eckington in a pre war Standard 10 motor car. I saw Tom Sandford in the small warehouse office and told him that his employment was terminated forthwith. He was living on his own, his wife had left him to go and live with their son, a policeman in Sheffield. He said he was happy to go. Shortly afterwards I went to his home in Southgate, Eckington to return some of his personal effects left in the office. The house was virtually stripped of all furniture, he was sitting on a chair, feeding a mouse with a piece of cheese, as the mouse popped out of its mouse hole in the skirting board, from time to time. In many ways he was a human tragedy, he drank too much, had violent arguments with his wife, but in his prime was very capable. He was fired after 20 years service with RT Willis with just one months pay.

Moving to our new home in Whitwell we named the house Comely Bank after the tenement block occupied by Bob Archer and his wife who were very kind to Joan and I in Edinburgh during our courtship in 1945. I travelled to work in an Austin A40 van. Petrol was still rationed, but we had enough to go occasionally to Barnsley or Dewsbury. Arrangements were made for Joan to retreat to Hyland House when our first child was due. It is interesting to remember that most families in the early post war years counted every penny, particularly if they were creating a new home after the upheaval of the war years. All our furniture was utility, but at least it was well made and sturdy. After a search we managed to acquire a small radio under the brand name of 'Pilot Radio'. We listened to the troubles in Palestine, still with us, the great loss of life in India as the country was partitioned, and the news of tighter rationing than prevailed during the war years. I was visiting shops and offering just three of most items we had in stock. For instance, our quota of corn flakes was just 24 packets a month to go around about 100 small grocery (corner) shops in the Eckington to Chesterfield area.

1947 opened with much industrial unrest with unofficial strikes by dock workers and road haulage workers. February brought the great snow and freezing conditions which were to last until Easter. Main roads were blocked overnight. The

Great North Road was closed with 10 foot drifts. Coal could not be moved from the pithead. One by one the country's coalfired power stations closed down. Workplaces and homes turned to candle light. We had a six month old baby, Catherine, but fortunately we had enough coal in stock to keep us warm. Our one delivery van driver, Herbert Naylor, loaded his van with sacks of dried peas to give him a grip on the icy roads. For six weeks he ferried me around as we travelled to our customers, delivered and sold what we could spare for an individual shop, made out the bill and collected the cash in payment. It was all very simple, basic arithmetic – no electronic calculators – just add up the bill and collect the cash! Our delivery van was a far cry from today's articulated lorries, being designed as a four wheel van to carry a maximum load of $1\frac{1}{2}$ tons (1524kg).

Later in 1947 food rations were cut still further and many towns witnessed food queues, especially for meat, with the ration for tinned meat (corned beef etc.) cut to two pence worth per person per week. The problem was a shortage of dollars. The United States granted the government a modest dollar loan, but all lend lease supplies, as in WWII, had been suspended. The war had stripped us of all our assets as a nation. On 3 June 1947 George Marshall, the American Secretary of State, proposed the Marshall Plan, designed to assist Europe to rebuild after the ravages of war. With the Marshall Plan yet to come, Prime Minister Attlee announced an austerity plan, in September 1947, to cut government costs and to cope with the present crisis. It was to take 9 years from the end of the war to see the end of all food rationing, announced on 3 July 1954.

Hyland House, Birdwell, 4 September 1949.

In June 1948 the Berlin blockade, cutting off the city from West Germany, was imposed by Soviet forces. The RAF flew in food and fuel round the clock to beat the blockade. Would I be called up as a Reservist? By September 1948, 895 Allied planes a day were flying to Berlin. Amidst all the worry we enjoyed listening to the radio commentary on the 1948 London Olympics. On 12 May 1949 the Berlin blockade came to an end and clothes rationing was abandoned. At this time, due to my sister Maisie's failing health, Joan and I sold our house in Whitwell and moved to 101 Worsbrough Road, Birdwell. We now had two children, the second Ian born on 27 November 1947 in a private nursing home in Worksop. We were to live at 101 Worsbrough Road for the next 22 years. Then the fear of being called up came again as the government stated that reservists may be needed due to the outbreak of the Korean War in June 1950.

Holidays with our growing family were for the next few years confined to boarding houses in Filey, Bridlington or Scarborough and that was restricted to just one week in

August. Father lent us his car for holidays as my day to day transport was still a small Austin van which I had to garage at Hyland House, ten minutes walk from Worsbrough Road. It was not until 30 May 1950 that petrol rationing ended. We were fortunate to be close to a well run and enterprising Junior School under Mr Anderson, who laid the groundwork for all our children to move into higher education and eventual graduation from university. Catherine set a high target achieving a first class honours degree at Newcastle University in Botany. By today's 21st century standards we were an austere household. Catherine was on her own in a very small, single bed size bedroom with the three boys, before the fourth bedroom was built, together in bunk beds in the third bedroom. Television had arrived after the war. Father had a set at Hyland House but we did not indulge. For special events, such as the coronation of Queen Elizabeth we went to Moorend Lane and watched with Joan's Dad, Auntie Betty and their daughter Suzanne.

In the early 1950s we certainly lived within our means. We had no mortgage, no overdraft, some savings later to be spent in share investment in the new fledgling company RT Willis Limited as described in Chapter 8. As at the warehouse in Barnsley, we had no electronic equipment of any kind but we lived well with the traditional roast on Sundays and fish on Fridays. Fresh fruit and vegetables came twice a week from the village store, via a small flat bottomed truck, which called at the house offering choice. We collected the meat from Mrs Thorley, the local butcher in Chapel Street, Birdwell. Groceries were purchased from the warehouse.

Andrew was born on 25 March 1951 in Pindar Oaks private nursing home, Sheffield Road, Barnsley. Six years later on 22 March 1957, Howard was born in the same nursing home. After Andrew's birth Joan had some domestic help as we still have to this day. One advantage in working at the business of RT Willis, in which I was trying to play a positive role, was that with father ruling out any growth or modernisation, Joan and I, along with three children, could get away at weekends, usually Saturday, to shop or in the summer to watch a little cricket. On 6th May 1954 Roger Bannister broke the four minute mile barrier. We still remember listening to the commentary on the radio. When the Revd Isaac Perry, of St Mary's Worsbrough, retired he was succeeded by the Revd Leonard Greensides. For several years under Mr Perry I had been a member of the PCC. Leonard Greensides invited me to be a Churchwarden, a duty I carried out for many years until sheer pressure of work obliged me to resign.

From the 1950s to the end of the Cold War, we had to live with the threat of the atom bomb. Now it is the fear of terrorist attack. In 1955 the pace of life dramatically changed. Churchill retired as Prime Minister, father died and family holidays, apart from odd weekends, were out for the next five years. In 1956 we suffered, as a country, the fiasco of the Suez Canal invasion. At the other end of the scale, and far more important in its impact, was the arrival of Elvis Presley. The cultural revolution was under way with the swinging sixties just around the corner. It is easy to forget that Joan, apart from bringing up the family, helped enormously in keeping the business afloat after 1955, acting as wages clerk for many years. I still remember Joan calculating wages in bed, in Pindar Oaks nursing home, shortly after Howard was born. From the 1960s our children easily took up the cultural changes talking place in society. Over the years all fashion changed, no longer boys in short trousers in senior school. Women's fashions brought in style, colour and variety. Men discarded ties and took up with American style jeans. Out went the old Lyons corner tea houses. In came fast food outlets. Sport changed, football became more entertaining, faster and highly skilful.

In October 1962 the world stepped back from the nuclear brink as Russia retreated from its ambitions in Cuba. Despite all these anxieties from post war rationing and the threat of nuclear obliteration, Joan and I kept our Christian faith intact through St Mary's Church at Worsbrough. As already mentioned, sheer pressure and work overload obliged me to resign as Churchwarden as I struggled with the impact of father's death and the resulting death duties. For many years our church attendance was spasmodic until in the late 1960s we became regular attenders at St Mary's once again. Our children attended Sunday School to a varying degree, with Catherine probably the best attender by far. The boys all tasted the Boy Scout experience, with Andrew staying the course as a Venture Scout. I was guilty of giving them little time or attention in these activities, although we did visit the boys in scout camps. As the 1960s and 1970s gave us a little more time for holidays, Joan planned these as tours of Scotland. We saw most of Scotland including the Outer Hebrides and Orkney, staying in good quality B&Bs. New roads were being built, the country was being opened up. We generally had a great time, cooking midday meals with a Primus stove. Our children were growing up in an age very different from the austerity, unemployment blight and the grey depressing world of the 1930s. The 1960s belonged to Elvis Presley, then the Beatles. Many good films, such as David Lean's Dr Zhivago, with Julie Christie and Omar Sharif, were seen as and when we could.

Shortly after father's death in 1955, Terry in Oxford arranged for mother to have a new piano in her new home, Hyland House in Dodworth Road, Barnsley. We were very pleased to receive mother's old piano as we were anxious that all the children learnt to play the piano and study music, if that was their inclination. As one would expect, there was a varied level of aptitude, with Catherine excelling. Joan still plays the piano which I enjoy listening to. Books have always been a feature of our establishment, many housed to this day in a Minty antique bookcase, bought in 1950, along with our utility furniture. This much prized bookcase was purchased second hand from Jay's furniture store in Peel Street, Barnsley. Despite the pressures at work, from around 1970 and onwards, we indulged in more adventurous holidays. Scotland was reached by putting the car on the sleeper train from York to Inverness. Sadly this sleeper train service no longer runs. The crowning experience was our Golden Wedding round the world tour, in early 1995. We took in Singapore, Australia, New Zealand and the USA (California). We were largely able to stay with friends and relations on this journey which covered five weeks. From the late sixties we had been to Spain, Majorca all more than once, several times to Canada starting in 1982 visiting the

Baker family in Ontario, a Cosmos tour of eastern USA in 1993 and many times to Holland when Catherine and Chris were living there. In this period we also fitted in Norway, Sweden, France, Germany, Italy (Venice), Northern Ireland, Eire, Austria, Rhodes and Kenya to stay with Catherine and Chris in Mombasa in 1997. In many of these locations, which we visited more than once, we were privileged to enjoy wonderful hospitality from our many overseas friends and relations.

From 1966, when we won the World Cup at Wembley, beating Germany 4-2, to the end of the Tony Blair reign in Downing Street, we had to cope with national anxieties nearer home. In 1980 we had a bomb scare from the sighting of a possible IRA bomb in our store in Gleadless, Sheffield. The army bomb disposal squad were called in and, using a robot, removed the object which turned out to be harmless. 1971 brought in decimal currency, followed in December 1973 by the three day working week and power cuts. There was severe industrial unrest with strikes in the coalfields, on the railways and in power stations. We had to learn to cope with this upheaval and rising inflation, partly caused by huge oil price increases of Middle East oil (OPEC). 1979 brought more local anxiety with the 'winter of discontent'. We then had to endure a year long miners' strike which badly affected our business objectives. However, like most families, we made the best of our opportunities, watched our family grow up over the years and have homes and families of their own. It is great to be able to look back and count our blessings.

We have enjoyed 38 years in Emley. It is a village much transformed from its old mining village profile to a thriving commuter village with many local activities, in which we partake as much as possible. A great variety of activity is centred upon St Michael's Church, just a short distance away from Greenways. Following extensive internal alterations, St Michael's has embraced community activity as well as keeping intact its main role as a place of worship. As regular attenders at St Michael's we have been able to make many new friends, who, along with our family, offer great support as we enjoy, as far as possible, the limitations of advancing years.

With declining physical ability, we have adapted Greenways to our changing needs. The garden, the product of much help by friends over the years, has been reshaped to reduce day to day maintenance, without losing its colour and variety. The house has been reordered with all day to day activities on the ground floor. The whole environment embracing the garden, books, pictures, memorabilia and other day to day diversions such as mobile phones, the radio and TV plus computers, makes for a life in which we can feel at home in today's society. Keeping up to date with all the changes of the 21st century, together with understanding and appreciating the achievements and ambitions of our family, certainly adds spice to life. Those thoughts are perhaps the main reason why this family history has been written.

CHAPTER 12

ENTERPRISE, GROWTH AND AMBITION 1955-1981
Meeting the Challenge of Survival

Following father's death on Sunday 13 February 1955, I was in unknown territory. Apart from being assured by father that Derek, my brother, and I would have complete control over the RT Willis business, when he retired or died, we had really no idea how suppliers and the bank would react. After my confrontation with father in early 1954, he, as already mentioned, consulted the senior partner at Smith and Ibberson, solicitors in Church Street, Barnsley. The senior partner, Mr Algy Smith, drew up a will creating a Trust of the business assets with myself and Derek as executors having full powers to maintain the business providing that all profit after tax be passed to my mother, Florence Elsie Willis. Included in the assets of the Trust was the house, Hyland House, Dodworth, Barnsley, that father purchased for himself and mother in early 1954. This home was valued at his death at £3,500, with the balance of all the business properties in four locations being valued at only £5,150. Some time before father's death I realised that, until probate was granted to the executors of father's estate, it could be very difficult to obtain credit from suppliers and support from the bank to clear cheques under the 'power of attorney' authority. Very fortunately, the business was quite liquid at this time, which was not unexpected knowing how loath father had been to spend money, even on essential repairs. For several weeks prior to father's death, I paid off creditors the moment their invoice arrived for goods delivered. Despite taking this action, at the date of death the business was still in credit at the Midland Bank, Market Hill, Barnsley. On Monday 14 February I was in the Bank Manager's office. Mr Hagar, the manager, was most helpful and agreed to clear all cheques submitted for clearance until probate had been granted, provided I maintained, at all times, a credit balance of £5,000 (approx. £70,000 in 1991 money). This constraint was not too difficult to maintain as, despite paying creditors several weeks before their account was due, at the date of death we were in credit at the bank to the tune of £5,747.

In many ways it is difficult to appreciate how low key father's funeral was, with mainly immediate family present at the funeral service, held at St Mary's Church, Worsbrough, and the subsequent burial in a double plot in Worsbrough cemetery alongside his daughter Maisie.

With the immediate crisis resolved, I was soon to realise that an even greater challenge lay ahead, namely finding the liquid funds to pay death duties and father's income tax and surtax liabilities. Probate was granted and the accountants, J Sampson and Son of Barnsley, employed by father for many years past, were asked to prepare the Estate accounts and to agree the figures with the Inland Revenue. The total business assets were valued at £29,405 (approx. £420,000 at 1991 prices), with a very heavy tax liability of £10,964 of which £2,368 could be paid out of father's personal savings. The balance of £8,596 would have to come from the business. The failure of father to plan a proper succession by his two sons resulted in this liability reducing the net assets of the business to £20,809. This tax burden could have been substantially reduced if father had agreed to form a private limited liability company and had allocated shares to his wife and children. Previously he had promised to pursue this course when I discussed rejoining the business in 1946. My hand was weak at the time as I did not relish the thought of continuing as a flying instructor as a married man, already with our first child and Joan ambitious to have more children in the future. The chief flying instructor, Wing Commander Irving Smith, affectionately known as 'Black' Smith, at Middleton St George in early 1946, made three attempts to persuade me to agree to a posting to the Central Flying School at Little Rissington, and progressing on to take up a permanent commission. He certainly considered that I was suitable material, with an above average rating as a Mosquito pilot.

However, I now had responsibility for a business valued at £20,809 or, taking inflation into account, valued at approximately £300,000 at 1991 prices, with a totally unsuitable management and trading structure to meet the new competition as wartime controls and rationing were progressively abolished. It was a very demanding challenge indeed. Could the business survive? As a footnote, and looking back, it is difficult to understand why father was not prepared to put his trust in his two sons who were to be his successors. It was only by finding a Huddersfield Building Society pass book, amongst his papers at Hyland House, that we, his executors, learnt for the first time where his personal savings were located. Were there other savings which were never located?

What was clear, rapid action was required. To understand the changes and developments of the business over the next few years it is necessary to take a snapshot of the social scene at that time and in particular the part played by the grocery trade. In 1956 the Stationery Office published 'Britain: an official handbook' which, in a chapter on 'The National Economy', set out in stark detail the personal income and living standards of all employed people, in all sectors, whether a skilled or unskilled worker, whether an employer or whether in receipt of any form of income. We find that 63% of the entire group, comprising approximately 16 million people, were in receipt of less than £125 a year, (equivalent to £2.50 per week). 27%, approximately 7 million, were in receipt of between £125 and £249 a year, i.e. a maximum of £5 per week. At the time of father's death in early 1955 salesmen and lorry drivers would be paid between £3.50 (£3/10/- in 1955 currency) and £4 per week. My own salary was £10 per week. Approximately 70% of a person's income was spent on food, drink, tobacco, rent, rates, light, heat, household goods and clothing. The average paid holiday was just one full week plus Christmas, Easter, Whitsuntide, August and New Year Bank holidays. Bank charges including interest on borrowed money were in the range of 4%, which was considered high at the time, but would soon rise further as there was another spectre on the horizon, namely inflation. As import controls were eased and rationing progressively abolished, prices started to rise at an increased pace from the relatively very modest inflationary pressures of the war years. Inevitably the government came under increasing pressure from strike action in various sectors of the economy, resulting in the declaration on 31 May 1955 of a State of Emergency to deal with the dock strike. This dock strike, which caused us much anxiety over our supplies, was to last nearly six weeks, ending on 1 July 1955. Less than two years earlier, in July 1953, the Korean War ended much to my relief. Despite the end of the Berlin blockade on 12 May 1949, the Cold War was very much a part of life, but with little time to think about it, and with unemployment levels at an all time low of under 200,000, the small staff at R T Willis and Son enthusiastically supported all the changes we were to implement during the next few years. In 1955 I was the only employee, apart from my brother Derek, to own a car. As the years went by and car ownership increased this was surely an indicator of a general increase in prosperity.

In February 1955 the imperative was to secure some working capital, having been stripped of liquid funds by death duties and father's arrears of income tax. Mr Hagar, the manager at the Midland Bank in Market Hill, Barnsley proved to be very helpful indeed. Without hesitation he advanced £6,000 (equal to approx. £85,000 in 1991 money) to the business to be secured by a mortgage on the property of the business, excluding Hyland House, after probate was completed. Working capital was secure, albeit at an interest rate of 4%, giving me time to decide upon the way forward. Our customer base of small family owned grocery shops and fish and chip outlets, with the latter already moving to other suppliers who could offer alternative and cheaper frying mediums, together with a comprehensive inventory of fresh fish, wrapping papers and other sundries, as the Willis business had made no attempt to develop the fish frying market in the post war years, relying entirely on its exclusive franchise to sell J Bibby products in the territory between Barnsley and Doncaster. Following changes in the J Bibby company structure this franchise was terminated around 1950. There was only one option available, namely to let the fish frying business wither away and to concentrate all resources in developing a comprehensive wholesale grocery business in line with the slow but steady rise in the general standard of living now taking place.

Maurice Galloway & GRTW at a Willis Trade Show, 1955, visited by Roy Mason (later Lord Mason), the newly elected MP for Barnsley, and his wife.

There was no local self service, but over the next few years Sainsburys and other large grocery multiples in the London area were to increasingly adopt this format. It is difficult to realise that in 1955 the grocery trade in South Yorkshire was largely based upon the small shop format, with the Co-op, Meadow Dairies, Lipton and the Home and Colonial multiple chains setting the standards. Every region also had its locally based multiple chains, generally family owned. The balance of grocery supplies to the home was provided by independent, family owned, small grocery shops situated in all urban areas, virtually on every corner of a main street in a built up area. This was the Willis market, which in 1955 was just over 50% of the total grocery market. Little did we realise in 1955 that within 45 years the share of the market, enjoyed by the family owned independent grocery retailer, would be under 10%. However, at this time there was a large market for us to attack, although we were but one amongst hundreds of grocery wholesalers in the country as a whole. Many of these wholesalers were very large enterprises with extensive sales forces. Unless we widened our appeal with a wider range of grocery products, including imports from the USA, Canada, Australia and New Zealand now becoming available, we were doomed to failure. One of our first actions was to contact the local representatives of Lever Brothers, Proctor and Gamble, Tate and Lyle and Nestlé, all companies with which father had refused to do business. As there were three other wholesale grocers in Barnsley at the time, namely Gaimsters, Charlesworths and Amblers, it was imperative that, at least, we matched their range of products. A young salesman, Alastair Grant, came from Lever Brothers, as a representative for Batchelors Peas, a Lever subsidiary. He was most helpful giving us an introduction to all the other Lever companies which brought into our inventory such products as Stork and Echo margarine, Lux toilet soap and Gibbs toothpaste. Alistair Grant eventually moved on, later becoming Sir Alistair Grant, Chairman of Safeway. We kept in touch throughout his life, through the medium of various trade bodies. One factor in our favour, as we developed these new sources of supply, was that we had a good credit record, which was going to stand us in good stead over the years.

It was all hard work, obliging me to hire an ex retired employee, Bill Dickinson from Worsbrough Bridge, to call upon my own customers for the next few months. Going home for lunch was now a thing of the past. Joan and I, with our young family of three children, soon to be four in March 1957, were unable to enjoy any family holiday longer than a snatched week for the next few years. Starting work at the office by 8am or before and arriving back home any time between 6pm to 9pm, together with Saturday morning also at work was the standard routine until retirement! However there was some flexibility with the odd day off for family events and better holidays.

New products coming into our inventory gave me the opportunity to purchase these products through the medium of a limited liability company in which, hopefully, we could accumulate assets without increasing the assets of father's original business. My brother Derek and I were now acting as Trustees of RT Willis, trading as RT Willis and Son, with a view to ultimately incorporating all the Trust assets into a new limited liability company. Our new company was registered as RT Willis & Son Limited on 14 November 1956. For the next few years the new company, acting as a broker for the Trustees, expanded its range selling on all its products, at a very low margin to cover costs, to the original RT Willis & Son administered by Derek and myself.

Having acquired sufficient working capital from the bank, we now took stock of our situation as a very small wholesale company with sales in the year to December 1954 of £242,942 and net profit of £5,439, a margin of 2.24%. As the years went by we would count ourselves fortunate if we achieved a net margin of 1%, which was the industry norm. It was quite easy to see what were our immediate problems. The Barnsley warehouse of converted housing was totally inadequate. There was no proper financial control, as father refused to introduce double entry book-keeping. The Barnsley warehouse was located at the edge of run down terraced housing, scheduled to be demolished by the local authority. We had four lots of premises, two in Barnsley, one in Chapeltown north of Sheffield and one at Eckington, south of Sheffield. They were all in a poor state of repair.

New Street warehouse, with land above cleared for expansion in Joseph Street, 1955/56.

The question soon arose as to where were all our new products to be warehoused. In the summer of 1955, I had the old lean-to garage in the New Street yard demolished and commissioned a temporary wooden office, sufficient to provide space for myself and up to three clerical staff, with a small telephone switchboard to replace the one and only wall telephone outside father's old office in the main building. Father's office was then converted into warehouse space. As previously noted, this New Street warehouse was created from four terraced working class houses, totally unsuitable to store large quantities of canned goods. The cellars were cleared out, father's Austin Sheerline car was disposed of enabling us to use the garage at Hyland House, Dodworth, for the warehousing of newly imported Australian canned fruit. I spent many an hour unloading and loading this product at Hyland House until our first proper warehouse extension was built, adjacent to the original warehouse, on land leased to us by the Borough Council at the end of 1956. I negotiated a design and build contract with Finlans of Liverpool, for a 6,000 square foot portal frame building, at an overall cost of approximately £3,000, together with a 100 year lease from the Borough Council at a very modest rent, subject to review every 25 years. As the years went by, 100 year leases soon became a memory as inflation developed and we expanded further

The Reception at New Street, 1956.

onto council land, previously covered by early Victorian working class terraces, immediately to the rear of our New Street premises. It was all very well to solve the problem of space for the time being, but much more important was the need to establish proper financial controls and to introduce into the business professional staff who could develop the opportunities arising from the end of all food rationing and the greater expectations from the general public.

We were soon to reap the consequences of a lack of financial controls when my brother Derek discovered that his one and only salesman at Eckington, a Mr Eric Scott, had defrauded the company of £3,807 between September 1954 and September 1956. The monies the business lost, through inadequate accounting procedures throughout the business were later estimated to have been approximately £6,000 (or the equivalent of £90,000 forty years later). It was a heavy blow to sustain at this time. Derek had to take over all Eric Scott's customer base until he found a replacement. In the meantime, I spent much of the winter of 1956/57 in travelling to Eckington and accompanying an Inspector Fraser, from Renishaw police station, as Scott's customers were interviewed and the level of fraud established. In June 1957 Scott was sentenced to 12 months imprisonment after pleading guilty to all charges. The judge in sentencing Scott at the Quarter Sessions in Derby severely criticised the firm for lack of supervision, rudimentary accounting practices and for Scott's inadequate salary of £9/10/- a week (equal to approximately £140 per week forty years later). We were undoubtedly paying low salaries, which was another area of reform required. As one would expect, the staff in the business were certainly looking for better conditions of work now that Derek and I had full responsibility. The first reform was to grant all the staff two weeks paid holiday plus paid Bank holidays at Christmas, New Year, Easter and in August. Previously the only paid Bank holiday had been Christmas Day and Boxing Day, plus one week's paid holiday in August. Hours of work were adjusted to an eight and a half hour day, plus one hour for lunch, with no Saturday working unless paid overtime. Pressure was such that to finish at 5.30pm for myself was a luxury I was never in a position to enjoy. However, from 1956 until the business was sold in 1991, salaries were always in line with the industry norm and for office staff in line with local authority rates of pay. As the years went by warehouse hours were reduced to 39, office hours to 37. Many years later, when Trades Unions were recognised salaries were never a major issue.

We were indeed fortunate to be able to keep all our staff at this time with the country, in 1955/56, enjoying full employment. The clerical staff at New Street, which was in effect the Head Office, comprised just one lady, Elsie Foster. To enable me to reform our accounting procedures I recruited a Secretary for the day to day correspondence and as an administration assistant. An advertisement was placed in the Barnsley Chronicle and the local Ministry of Labour informed. We had just one response, a young lady just out of school who came along with her father. This was Dorothy Hill, who proved to be an absolute winner, staying with us until she married and decided to retire and have a family.

In September 1945, as already reported, I enrolled as an accountancy student at the International Correspondence School (Overseas) Ltd. For the next three years I pursued the course, taking the intermediate exam. From 1955 to 1991 this background expertise was to prove invaluable. With assistance from our accountants/auditors J Sampson & Son we quickly established a conventional book-keeping system after the Eric Scott debacle. As the years went by and the business grew, we moved through Kalamazoo ledgers, Rank Xerox systems, National Cash Registers and Sweda accounting systems to full computerisation by 1970.

As we were bringing the Willis business into the new commercial climate without the restrictions of war time and post war controls, many major world events were taking place between 1955 and the early sixties. Some of the most significant were associated with the closing down of the British Empire and the first wave of immigrants from the West Indies. Conflict with the Mau Mau in Kenya came to an end as this country moved to independence. In October/November 1956 we suffered the Suez crisis, with Harold Macmillan succeeding Anthony Eden as Prime Minister. In March 1957 the Common Market was founded by six European nations. Self service was fast taking hold over the whole country, led by the multiple grocery retailers. On 5 December 1958 Britain's first motorway was opened, by Harold Macmillan, the Preston bypass of just eight miles. 1959 saw the introduction of the Austin Mini, a car for the average family had arrived. In October 1961 the Berlin Wall was built. A year later, October 1962, we held our breath over the Cuba missile crisis. To our dismay on 22 November 1963 John Kennedy, US President, was assassinated. The Vietnam War was on the horizon and the Cold War was to continue until the fall of the Berlin Wall in 1989. Changes in the grocery world were equally dramatic and far reaching.

Left: The 1st staff party, Greengate Inn, High Green, 1957.

Above: Staff party, Newton Hall, Chapeltown, January 1958.
Back l-r S Corbishley, R Shaw, E Foster.
Centre l-r Rita Corbishley, Eileen Shaw, Elsie Foster.
Front l-r GRTW, Joan, FE Willis, Brenda Willis, Derek Willis.

Right: Mineral Water Factory, Rylands filler and carboniser (manufactured in Worsbrough Bridge in 1912 and sold to M.E., 1959.

Above left: Bacon processing department, Barnsley warehouse, March 1959.

Above right: 1st extension to New Street, 6000 sq ft, 1960.

Below: RT Willis & Son distribution fleet outside Foundry Street Mineral Water Factory, 1959.

Left: Racecommon Road, 1959.

Below: A new logo, 1960 following the move into VIVO later to merge with SPAR.

Controls were now in place, which over the years were constantly refined to measure shrinkage, margins, stock levels, sales and cash flow. I now turned to look at our credibility with suppliers. It soon became obvious that suppliers were nervous in dealing with a business managed by two trustees. In effect, we were still viewed as being a one man business, as if father was still alive. The terms of father's will gave full powers to the trustees to sell, convert or dispose of any assets in father's estate provided that any changes produced sufficient income to meet the needs of Mrs FE Willis. All such income, after operating expenses, was to be credited to the account of Mrs FE Willis for her to decide on its disposal. Through our solicitor, Mr AP

Thomas of Smith & Ibberson, Counsel's opinion was sought. The trustees were assured that using funds arising from the disposal of the Trust's assets to buy shares in a company, created to trade as RT Willis (Food Distributors) Ltd, did not infringe, in any way, the contents of father's will. The only infringements of the trustees' duty would arise if the investment in RT Willis (Food Distributors) Ltd did not provide a return to the satisfaction of the beneficiary, Mrs FE Willis.

RT Willis & Son (Food Distributors) Ltd was duly incorporated on 30 September 1963. On the same day, as a separate enterprise, Foodwise Ltd was incorporated to take care of our growing interest in operating and owning individual retail grocery stores. From 1956 to 1963 the whole of the Trustees' enterprise had been growing steadily and, following Counsel's advice and assurances, the soft drinks side of the business was transferred into RT Willis & Son (Soft Drinks) Limited, incorporated on 21 June 1961. Many changes were beginning to loom in the grocery world, most notably the introduction of self service by major multiples, as already mentioned, with Sainsbury's, in particular, leading the way as it moved into the Midlands from its south east base. We had a disparate and fragmented business, so when an offer came from Jehovah's Witnesses to acquire our warehouse in Lane End, Chapeltown, a quick sale was soon effected. The manager, Stanley Corbishley, transferred to New Street, ultimately becoming a Director and Company secretary to R T Willis & Son (Food Distributors) Limited. He became a most valued supporter of the writer to the date of his retirement on 9 September

1986. Enquiries were made resulting in all the machinery at the soft drinks plant in Foundry Street, Barnsley being disposed of at the same time. The closure of the soft drinks plant was inevitable as our funds for modernisation were strictly limited. Was capital to be invested in modernising the soft drinks plant, already over 50 years old, or in developing the wholesale and retail food business? The choice was obvious. The manager of the soft drinks factory moved to a similar position with a local competitor and proper compensation was paid to the very small but loyal staff, just four in number, who stayed to the end.

Right above: Staff Party, January 1959, Newton Hall, Chapeltown.

Right below: Staff trip to Blackpool, 1960.

Left above & below: Staff Party, 1960, Newton Hall, Chapeltown. Presentation to Ernest Foster on his retirement.

The soft drinks warehouse was now empty. For the time being it could be used as an extension to the warehouse in New Street, approximately 500 yards away. I built a small office on a mezzanine floor in these Foundry Street premises, to enable a permanent office to be built in 1963 at New Street, in place of the wooden structure installed in 1955 and subsequently expanded. We were now well on the way to a substantial expansion programme involving company owned retail stores and a new concept in food wholesaling, namely, cash and carry. Looking back over the past eight years, how had we performed financially?

As already reported sales and net profit before tax in the last full year before father's death were £242,942 and £5,439 respectively. In the trustees first full year to 11 February 1956 sales of £252,967 with net profit before tax of £2,803 was achieved. Four years later, with inflation running at less than 3% a year, sales had risen to £461,270 with net profit before tax at £1,106 for the year ending 13 February 1960.

RT Willis & Son Ltd was incorporated on 14 November 1956, with a paid up share capital of £2,000, provided in equal shares by myself and Derek. We assumed responsibility for developing a pre packaging business from the Trustees' premises at Gem Works, Chapeltown. In 1957 all brokerage business with RT Willis & Son at New Street, Barnsley, was terminated with the Barnsley business taking over responsibility for all the new suppliers and with the Limited Company taking over the Chapeltown business. In its first 43 weeks of trading, to 15 February 1958, the new company's sales were £93,718 with a net profit of just under £1. In the following full year to 15 February 1959, the sales were £145,183 with a net profit of £203. The success in building up the sales and profit in the new company was largely due to the diligence and honesty of the manager Stanley Corbishley, who I had recruited in 1954. Eight years later in the year ending 31 March 1967, sales had increased to £801,936 with net profit before tax of £4,701. On 1 April 1967 the stock in trade, and moveable assets of the company were moved from Chapeltown into the expanded premises at New Street, Barnsley. Gem Works was put up for sale and sold to Jehovah's Witnesses as previously reported.

The success of RT Willis & Son Ltd, as an independent profit centre, prompted a complete rethink of the total structure of the business. When RT Willis & Son (Food Distributors) Ltd was incorporated on 30 September 1963, it took over the wholesale grocery function of the business. As previously mentioned, Foodwise Ltd was incorporated at the same time and designated to invest in retail grocery outlets. RT Willis & Sons (Soft Drinks) Ltd was formed a little earlier on 21 June 1961, followed by RT Willis & Son (Shopfitters) Ltd and Foodwise (Cash & Carry) Ltd in 1962. The three key operating companies were RT Willis & Son (Food Distributors) Ltd, Foodwise Ltd and Foodwise (Cash & Carry) Ltd. By the year ending 4 April 1969 group sales had reached £3,099,976, with profit before tax of £40,538. Despite inflation of nearly 50% over the past 13 years, these results were quite an achievement, looking back to sales of just over £200,000 and net profit of just under £3,000 in 1956. These results were only possible through a trained and well motivated management team. In 1959 we had also joined forces with other similar companies in the UK in the quest to achieve improved buying power and a higher profile with potential customers. In 1960 Hyland House, Dodworth, Barnsley was sold for £5,000 and mother, at Derek's wish, moved to a pleasant bungalow, in her own name, in the village of Mosbrough, adjacent to Eckington. The plan was that Derek and his wife, Brenda, would keep an eye on mother and assist her as and when required.

Personnel recruited to take the company forward were Maurice Galloway, as General Sales Manager from 1958, Stanley Corbishley, as the Chapeltown Business was moved to

New Street, took over my retail customer base, which I had developed in the Dearne Valley area from 1949 to 1960. Norman Foster was recruited in 1964 to assume the position of chief buyer and merchandise controller. Perhaps the most important decision made in these early years was my brother's agreement that I be appointed Managing Director, with Derek assuming responsibility for the efficient operation of the central warehouse and the new cash and carry division. In 1964 the Managing Director's salary was £2,250 a year. In 1965, as the retail store division was developed, Eric Wadsworth, an ex Barnsley Grammar School pupil, previously employed by Yorkshire Traction, a local bus company, joined us to assume responsibility for the growth and profitability of the retail store division. As all these new staff members were being recruited and inducted into the ethos of the business, the warehouse and offices at New Street were being developed and partnerships created with other similar enterprises, all of which would have a profound impact in the years ahead. Due to our profit record we maintained very good relations with our bankers, the Midland Bank, who advanced sufficient funds to enable us to pursue a steady programme of office and warehouse development over the years. In 1959 I moved from Foundry Street into the first stage of a two storey office block facing onto Joseph Street, erected over a large loading bay for the main distribution warehouse. Negotiations with the local authority eventually resulted in either acquiring or leasing most of the site bounded by New Street, Joseph Street, Heelis Street and Wood Street. By 1971 we had a modern office block containing a large general office, printing department, computer room, conference room, executive offices and a large canteen. The warehouse exceeded 40,000 square feet and cost £40,600. It was a cantilever construction and housed modern pallet racking together with a bacon processing plant and frozen and temperate refrigeration. Apart from investment by the company, this development was supported by funds from the bank secured by a mortgage on the property.

Above left: Staff Party, Newton Hall, 1961, Mabel Shaw retires.
Above right: Hoyland Common opening 1965, l-r Miss VIVO, GRTW, John Simmons.

Above: RT Willis & Son football team 1961/62. Back l-r A Dewhirst (Soft Drinks), K Black (Chapeltown), ?, E Newton & R Pearson (New St), T Hardwick (ex New St), R Hemsworth (Soft Drinks); Front l-r B Thrumble (ex Soft Drinks), C Hollins, B Collins, R Hawley, M Butcher (all New St).

Left: Staff outing to Blackpool, 1965.

Right: Stairfoot Cash & Carry, 1969.

Below: Herringthorpe, 1968.

From 1959 the company started to advance with three major activities. Firstly we had the original core business, namely supplying small independent grocers in South Yorkshire, having available a full range of groceries and provisions. Two new activities, inspired by increasing competition in our market, were Cash and Carry wholesaling and company owned retail stores. For these initiatives to be successful it was essential that we improved our negotiating ability with suppliers. In 1959, following a contact made through an advertisement in the trade press, we became members of The International Wholesale Grocers and Traders Alliance based at 5 Suffolk Street, Pall Mall, London SW1. This Alliance was instrumental in introducing us to a large buying group, Grocery, Produce Importers and Distributors, always referred to as GPID, supporting a national marketing group, the Family Grocers' Alliance. It was a complex structure of many different organisations and companies connected with the grocery trade, but it did introduce us to a wide range of opportunities.

Within a few months, I was appointed by the wholesale members of the Family Grocers' Alliance to liaise with staff at the FGA office in Pall Mall on marketing policy. In 1961 FGA received a letter from a much larger but similar organisation, based in The Netherlands, by name of VIVO International, to enter into discussions with a view to a possible merger. Noel Quibell, the then Chairman of FGA and the managing director of Evershed (Food Distributors) Ltd, of Shoreham by Sea, Sussex and I were commissioned to travel to The Netherlands and Germany to report back to the members. Eversheds were a substantial wholesale distributor, considerably larger than the Willis enterprise. We were well received in Amsterdam and later at Frankfurt in Germany. VIVO International was a franchise operation which identified all its affiliated stores with the VIVO logo and image. Just 16 years after the end of the Second World War in terms of imagery, stock variety, self service and modern warehousing facilities, the German VIVO enterprise was well ahead of the average UK counterpart. We were offered membership of the group which covered all the Scandinavian countries and Western Germany. Initially Noel Quibell was reluctant to switch the FGA image to VIVO, but after outlining the advantages to Noel, I was asked to present the case for joining the VIVO organisation to a General Meeting of members, at the National Liberal Club in Whitehall Place, Northumberland Avenue, London W1. After much debate, the members unanimously agreed that we apply for membership and transfer all marketing imagery to VIVO. The role of the FGA central office remained unchanged apart from using the VIVO imagery instead of the FGA material. Although the role of the FGA central office was unchanged, the management had to be of sufficient calibre and expertise to bring the independent grocery sector in line with the best multiple store practice. Jack Ellis, from the Gateway Supermarket chain was recruited and appointed VIVO managing director. As managing director of Gateway he had established a large multiple operation in the Bristol area, later to become part of the Safeway chain. Jack Ellis was to have a profound effect upon the Willis business as he introduced us to The Union Corporation of South Africa, and its UK subsidiary, Greenhaven. Greenhaven were property developers who Jack Ellis persuaded to build and lease back to us our first company owned store in Birdwell, Barnsley and our first Cash and Carry warehouse in Mexborough, near Doncaster. The VIVO office was moved out of central London to Sheen Road, Richmond, Surrey where there was ample and much cheaper accommodation for staff and board meetings. At the same time the members decided that it would be beneficial to appoint an outside, experienced non executive chairman. Mr Norton, a retired insurance actuary, took up this post from Noel Quibell. At the same time I was elected to the board by the members.

The switch from the Family Grocer Alliance (FGA) to VIVO covered a period of 2 years from 1961 to 1963. At the time of the members' General Meeting in October 1963 the organisation comprised 25 wholesalers, 1900 retail members with a collective wholesale turnover of £19 million and a net profit of £110,000. There were too many wholesale companies competing for retail members with wholesalers' net profits too low at well under 1% of turnover. Over the ensuing years there was a steady decline in wholesale members, mainly through take-overs and mergers. The Willis business, fragmented as it was, arising from having to maintain trust status for the original core business, was at this time producing a net profit of only 0.7% on a turnover of just under £1 million.

If the Willis business was to survive, apart from joining the VIVO organisation, it was imperative that the business structure was simplified to reduce costs. Advice was sought from the Willis family solicitors who recommended that RT Willis Limited purchased for cash and at full balance sheet value the total assets of the RT Willis Trust. The cash received by the Trust was then reinvested in RT Willis & Son (Food Distributors) Limited through an ordinary share purchase which would ensure a dividend income to Mrs FE Willis. Full consent was given for this sale of Trust assets through two trading enterprises by Mrs FE Willis. Merging the two trading companies now demanded an up to date management structure and an effective business plan. In October 1963 I was appointed Executive Chairman of the board of RT Willis & Son (Food Distributors) Limited. New Accountants were appointed, namely Sampson Nicholson & Co, Chartered Accountants of Wakefield. With a Business Plan in place and support from the Midland Bank, CM Warren was recruited from VIVO Central Office as General Sales Manager in June 1964. As the company moved into 1966 all delivered business at the Eckington and Chapeltown depots was transferred to Barnsley. Eckington depot was converted to a Cash and Carry operation. Stanley Corbishley was appointed Company Secretary and the share capital of the company increased to £20,000 by the issue of 5,000 new ordinary shares at £1 each.

In August 1966 an agreed merger took place between WJ Hiscock & Son Ltd, a VIVO wholesaler based in Hessle, near Hull and RT Willis (Food Distributors) Ltd who purchased a controlling shareholding in the Hiscock business. I joined the board of WJ Hiscock whose management remained in place under Ivor Winetroube, the managing director. The merger was initiated to give the merged business greater buying power. All negotiations with the manufacturers, together with the overall marketing and pricing policy, were centred at the Barnsley head office under the control of Derek Morgan, the newly appointed Trading and Marketing manager, reporting to Cedric Warren, appointed to the board as Trading Director. To ensure good financial controls Derek Pitchford a Chartered Accountant was appointed Finance Director. The management structure, in early 1967, was now in place to develop three prime business objectives, namely development of company owned neighbourhood VIVO supermarkets, a VIVO franchised delivery supply service to affiliated retailers and a wholesale cash and carry business for independent grocery retailers and caterers. The prime strategy of the business for the next 20 years was now in place.

In 1967 a partnership agreement between VIVO and SPAR was agreed which would, over the long term, produce a much strengthened SPAR UK enterprise. One of the first results of this partnership was to produce a joint computer enterprise, namely Distribution Computer Services Ltd (DCSL) in which RT Willis (Food Distributors) Ltd took up a shareholding. At this time, as Chairman of VIVO, I took a seat on the board of this new enterprise. DCSL was established in 1968 as a computer bureau offering computer services on a national basis, including Northern Ireland and Eire. Shortly after its incorporation, I was appointed Chairman. At this time commercial computer development was in its early stages with most companies using a computer bureau to process simple applications such as pay-rolls and invoicing systems. This new computer company was based at Levenshulme, Manchester. On the shareholders behalf, it was set up by consultants, FB Trethewey and Partners of Quay Street, Manchester, who recruited and trained the original management and programmers.

Moving into 1969, a full programme of company owned retail store development was speeded up with the appointment of Derek Wem to the board of RT Willis (Food Distributors)

Ltd as Store Development Director. By 1972 over 20 company owned neighbourhood supermarkets, mostly of over 2,500 square feet, were in place all trading under the VIVO and later the SPAR fascia. At the same time, a cash and carry warehouse, established at Stairfoot, Barnsley a few years previously, was expanded to 40,000 square feet at a cost of £91,000, partially supported by a £20,000 loan from Old Broad Street Securities Ltd, a venture capital company based at Founders Court, London EC2. Quite unexpected and without warning but due to various health problems, my brother Derek relinquished his management of the central warehouse wholesale activities and the overall cash and carry management. Our son, Andrew, recently graduated from Bradford University in Business Studies, agreed to fill the management gap by taking over responsibility for the flagship cash and carry depot at Stairfoot.

Left: Andrew joins the company, July 1972.
Right: Andrew Willis, Trading Director, 1980.

I should mention that in the late 1960s Joan and I rented an apartment in Harrogate, which we used at weekends as often as possible. This apartment was designed to give Joan a break away from the smoke polluted atmosphere we suffered in Worsbrough Road. The benefit was very limited as on most weekends I had to catch up on paperwork and review the financial/trading results of the previous week. A permanent break with Worsbrough came when I gave myself a week to find a new house away from Barnsley's pollution and give Joan and the family a better base. We were fortunate to find a stone built bungalow in Emley, a pleasant village between Huddersfield and Wakefield. We moved in August 1971 paying £12,000 for a property which was two years old, but not fully completed. To complete another £6,000 had to be found to re-install the roof, improve the electrics, provide double glazing, roof insulation and other various improvements. 101 Worsbrough Road was sold for £5,000. We took out a mortgage with the Halifax, finally paid off in 1990.

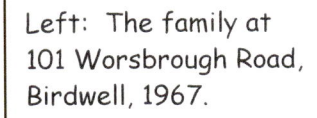

Left: The family at 101 Worsbrough Road, Birdwell, 1967.

Below: Greenways, Emley.

For the next few years much emphasis was placed upon building a skilful middle management team culminating in the company receiving an award in 1978 from the Distribution Industries Training Board. In 1976, at the suggestion of Andrew, his older brother Ian, a chartered accountant currently working in London, was invited to join the expanding family enterprise as Marketing Director and financial controller of the company's retail store division. Ian proved to be a most effective Financial Director. To support the continuing expansion of the business the Midland Bank provided overdraft facilities of £200,000 secured by a floating charge on the assets of the group. In 1979 Andrew was appointed as the director responsible for all training programmes and associated activity. Further board appointments in July 1980 were Ian, as Vice Chairman of the Group and Andrew as Deputy Group Managing Director. By 1980 the whole group was having to re-examine all marketing policies due to rapid changes in the retail food market, following the opening of out of town superstores, particularly by Asda, together with increasing competition from major cash and carry operators. All the group's major supermarkets were taken out of SPAR and rebranded under the 'Willis Discount' fascia. A significantly more competitive image, than that promoted by SPAR central office, was offered to affiliated SPAR retailers under the SPARTA scheme. SPARTA was a marketing plan specially designed to meet local competitive conditions under which affiliated retailers entered into a Spar Trading Agreement (SPARTA) with RT Willis (Food Distributors) Ltd. The take up was most successful.

1980 also saw a very close look at internal costs. The head office financial systems were transferred to a total in-house computer system, supported by DCSL. Consultants were engaged from Trethewey and Partners to measure and implement a more productive distribution system, culminating in successful negotiations with staff trade union representatives agreeing to standard working practices and reward systems. DH Pitchford resigned as Financial Director to take up a personal practice. Ian was appointed Finance Director in his stead. In early 1984 negotiations took place to acquire all the supermarkets operated by Sherwood Costcutter Ltd of Worksop. Six major supermarkets were acquired from Sherwood Costcutter, all for cash, partially financed by the sale of the Spar wholesale franchise to Alfred Jones of Warrington for £100,000. The group was now a major local food retailer, with 31 neighbourhood stores and supermarkets in Humberside, South Yorkshire, Derbyshire and into Lancashire, all trading as 'Willis Discount'. The group resigned from membership of SPAR (UK) Ltd but kept its affiliation to the cash and carry national group, affiliated to SPAR, under the trading name of Landmark.

1986 came in with the early retirement, for continuing health reasons, of my brother Derek and Stanley Corbishley, to be followed later in the year with the retirement of Ivor Winetroube. Mrs Joan Crofts was appointed Company Secretary. Membership of the Landmark cash and carry group was terminated. Membership of the British Retailers Association was confirmed. Marketing development included TV advertising and the development of Willis own label products. With the increasing consumer preference for fresh food products a major programme of refrigeration enhancement, at both warehouse and store level, was implemented. Also, to meet changing personnel needs, a staff pension scheme was implemented, supported by contributions from both staff and the company. The next few years were to be most testing and demanding in a period of high inflation and substantial economic changes.

Miss UK opens the East Hull store in 1970, queues form outside and the store is packed with keen shoppers.

Right: Into the Reception, Kensington Palace Hotel, London, 1970.

Left and below: Hoyland store, 1970.

Above: Glossop store, 1975.

Right: DP Willis and Florence Elsie Willis, 1979.

EXTRACT FROM THE BOARD MINUTES OF RT WILLIS FOOD DISTRIBUTORS (1963-1988)

Date	Details
01.10.63	GRTW elected Chairman of Company & Board of Directors. DPW other permanent Director.
	Certificate of Incorporation of the Company No.775637 dated 30 September 1963.
	£24,008/6/7 be paid to acquire business carried out by the Trustees of Robert Thomas Willis trading as RT Willis and Son.
01.07.64	6 Seniors Place, Lane End, Chapeltown mortgaged to Midland Bank Ltd to secure the account of RT Willis & Son Ltd.

11.01.65	Appointment of CM Warren as General Sales Manager to RT Willis and Son (Food Distributors) Ltd and associated and subsidiary companies from 16.11.1964 at £2,000 pa plus pension and company car. CM Warren appointed to Board as a Director.
	Authorised expenditure up to £25,000 in year 1965/66 on New St depot – new office block and warehouse extension. Office block 3,600 sq ft 2 storey over a loading and assembly area.
	GRTW elected to the Board of VIVO Ltd.
08.02.65	Agreed that the authorised capital of the Company be increased by £5,000 by issue of a further 5000 shares at £1 each.
	Managing Director's salary for financial year 65/66 be £3,000 pa.
	Warehouse/Cash & Carry Director's salary for financial year 65/66 be £2,500 PA (DPW).
23.03.65	Appointment of CM Warren and E Wadsworth as directors.
03.05.65	Negotiations to take place with Arndale Developments Ltd for renting a small supermarket to be erected in the Market Place development, Maltby during 1966.

26.07.65	Agreed that as soon as new premises available in Barnsley the Eckington depot be closed as a delivery depot. Chapeltown Branch operations to be incorporated into the Barnsley depot.
06.12.65	Contract from Wheelhouse & Co for £40,602 accepted for New Street Warehouse.
17.01.66	Share Capital of the Company increased to £20,000 by creation of 5000 new shares at £1 each.
14.03.66	Resolved to cease trading in the Soft Drinks Subsidiary from end of current financial year. RT Willis & Son (Soft Drinks) Ltd would then be put into liquidation.
	Instructions given to Spencers Estate Agents, Sheffield to negotiate sale or lease of Gem Works, Lane End, Chapeltown.
	All Directors waived dividend, as in previous years.
25.04.66	Mexborough Cash & Carry to open 9 May 1966.
08.06.66	Agreements reached with WJ Hiscock & Son Ltd to buy 2,001 ordinary shares in WJ Hiscock & Son Ltd at £5 per share. RT

	Willis & Son (Food Distributors) Ltd then have controlling interest with just over 50% of voting share capital.
	Mr I Winetroube of WJH & Son Ltd invited to join the Board of RTW & Son (FD) Ltd.
08.08.66	Management Training Residential Course in Scarborough for the week-end of 25-27 November.
28.02.67	Appointment of Mr DH Pitchford ACA as Group Accountant from 30 January 1967. Mr DP Willis appointed Cash & Carry Director. Mr E Wadsworth appointed Retail Store Director.
23.10.67	International Computers and Tabulators (ICT) with consultants Trethewey & Partners to review computer installation.
25.07.68	Support given for a proposed SPAR/VIVO computer operation to be incorporated as 'Distribution Computer Services Ltd'.
26.09.68	Retail store development at Penistone, Hoyland Common and Thorne be proceeded with.

05.12.68	Approval to complete supermarket development programme at Burncross, East Hull, Glossop and Normanton.
23.01.69	DH Pitchford ACA appointed as Financial Director.
28.02.69	DR Wem appointed as Development Director.
17.04.69	NCR machine 152/5S.431EN purchased from DCSL, as company installed its first computer system.
04.11.69	CM Warren and E Wadsworth resigned as directors.
24.02.70	Loan from United Dominions Trust in sum of £15,000 approved to finance shopfitting at Penistone, Woodthorpe and Southcoates Lane superstores.
15.05.72	Stairfoot C&C extension to a 40,000 sq ft unit at an overall rent of £18,000pa subject to lease of 21 years, with 7 year reviews.
24.07.72	Contract for development of Stairfoot C&C placed with Messrs CD Potter and Sons Ltd in estimated sum of £90,834.

22.02.73	Engrossment of a further charge between RT Willis & Son Food Distributors Ltd and Old Broad Street Securities Ltd as security for a loan by Old Broad Street Securities Ltd of £20,000.
10.09.73	Hoyland town centre developed as a VIVO superstore.
07.09.77	RI Willis appointed Marketing Director. AM Willis appointed Cash & Carry Director.
24.02.78	S Corbishley appointed a Director.
07.06.78	Purchased store at Baghill Lane, Pontefract together with stock, fixtures and fittings at their written down value.
19.07.78	DITB: Company qualified for the Distributive Training Award.
06.09.78	Midland Bank Ltd made an overdraft facility of £150,000 available.
09.05.79	AM Willis appointed Director of the Group's total wholesale activity.
30.11.79	Midland Bank Ltd overdraft facility increased to £200,000.

12.12.79	RI Willis appointed Vice Chairman with effect from 12 May 1980 and AM Willis as Deputy Group Managing Director with effect from 11 May 1981.
28.10.80	Company computer system replaced by a total in-house system from DCSL.
28.01.81	Board accepted the resignation of DH Pitchford.
10.05.84	Board approved the transfer of the company's interest in Spar, associated with the company's Spar Franchise area, to Alfred Jones (Warrington) Ltd for the sum of £100,000.
18.01.85	Letter from Midland Bank setting out terms for £600,000 overdraft for one month followed by £500,000 continuing – subject to acceptable financial results from the Company.
24.06.85	Approved purchase of store at Loundsley Green, Chesterfield for £42,500 plus legal costs.
10.06.86	Approved proposals by AMW to use TV advertising in the Yorkshire area.

03.09.86	S Corbishley resigned as Director and Company Secretary. Mrs J Crofts appointed as Company Secretary.
15.10.86	I Winetroube resigned as a Director.
14.10.87	Board approved introduction of Willis Own Label on fresh, chilled and frozen products.
14.10.87	Wilfred Wyatt & Co appointed Auditors.
27.01.88	DPW resigned as Director. Documents for registering Willis trademark were executed.
01.02.88	Agreed that RIW and AMW become Joint Managing Directors of RT Willis Group of Companies; GRTW as Chairman.
10.06.88	Agreed maximum capital budget to 31.12.88 be £254,000.
	25th anniversary celebrations on 30.09.88.
21.03.89	Business Plan: priority to improve liquidity and reduce costs. No further capital expenditure during financial year.

An appendix to the Board Minutes Summary

The Group was planned and conceived in 1955. Listed here are a few dates to supplement the Board Minutes.

1955	Turnover approximately £200,000 pa. Staff approximately 18.
1959	Turnover approximately £600,000 pa. Staff approximately 30. Joined Family Grocer Alliance – a buying group.
1962	Joined VIVO (Voluntary Chain). Turnover passed £1 million pa. Staff approximately 32. Started Cash and Carry operation in Racecommon Road, Barnsley.
1963	Opened 2nd Cash and Carry warehouse in Mexborough.
1963-1965	Operated a VIVO franchise system for independent grocers. Opened and developed four small Cash and Carry depots at Barnsley, Eckington, Mexborough and Sheffield.
1965	Opened first two company owned self service grocery stores at Birdwell and Rotherham.
1969	Opened Stairfoot Cash and Carry, Barnsley (15,000 sq ft). Opened the 13th company owned store at Glossop (VIVO Superstore).
1970-1984	Company stores now 30 in number. Developed the franchise system for independent grocers in VIVO, later SPAR.
1970	Opened the largest supermarket then trading in East Hull, Southcoates Lane store. Opened Cash and Carry in Hessle, Hull.

	Extended main Barnsley warehouse, plus new office block.
1971	Changed all VIVO stores to SPAR stores. Started concept of trading as 'Willis Discount'.
1972-1982	Grew company from a turnover of approximately £5 million to £20 million. Increased number of stores company owned to 20. Increased trading area to serve independent SPAR stores to cover all west and east Yorkshire.
1984-1988	Created and invested in new computer systems at head office and in retail stores and cash and carry depots. Changed company owned SPAR stores to Willis Discount.
1984-1985	Increased number of company owned stores to 31. Operating only as a franchiser for 'Willis Discount' after resigning from SPAR. Joined British Franchise Association. Total staff approximately 400.
1986	First TV advertising programme of 'Willis Discount'. Spent as a company well over £100,000 on media advertising.
1987	Commenced a substantial upgrade of all stores and depots. Promoted the policy of investment in people, premises and growth, supported by ten basic beliefs: 1. In being the 'best'. 2. In the importance of detail, in doing a job well. 3. In the importance of people as individuals. 4. In superior quality and service.

5. In informal and simple communication (team briefing).
6. In working hard to keep things simple.
7. In minimum of control reports but an overriding determination to make full use of those reports.
8. That management should be visible; management by 'walk-about'.
9. In the goals of the Company which in turn will stimulate excitement, enthusiasm and commitment.
10. That the customer is king.

Left: Evershed's office, Shoreham, Essex, 1975. Back l-r Peter Stubbs, Eddie Parr, John Bradfield, Bill Harris, GRTW, John Irish, ?, ?, John Beaumont, ?. Front l-r Dick Branston, ?, Len Jackson, ?, Cushin (Mars).

Above left & right: Baghill Lane, Pontefract, 1975.

Left: Michael Parkinson, Hoyland store, 1975.

Top right: Hoyland Common.
Bottom right: SPAR lorry, 1972.

Top: Head Office, Joseph Street, Barnsley, 1977.

Above left: GRTW 1980.
Above right: GRTW, New Street, 1977.
Left: GRTW FWD Conference, London 1979.

Top: Cash & Carry warehouse, Stairfoot, Barnsley, 1980.
Above: Willis Discount, Hoyland Town Centre, 1980.

Below left: RI Willis, 1980.
Below right: Stanley Corbishley.

Above: Stanley Corbishley retires, 1980, New Street canteen.

Right: Philip Steer, Warehouse Manager, New Street using the new product scanning technology, 1985.

Bottom right: Office block and loading bay, 1985.

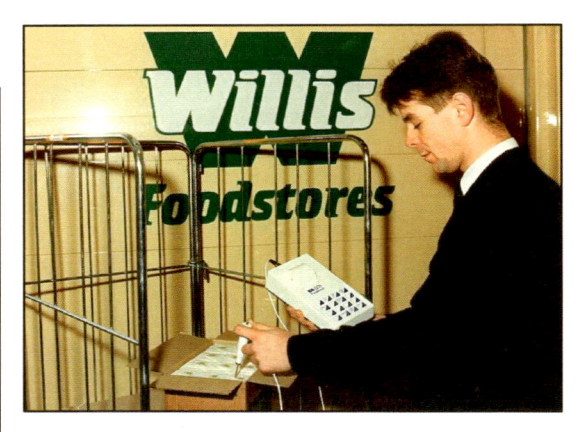

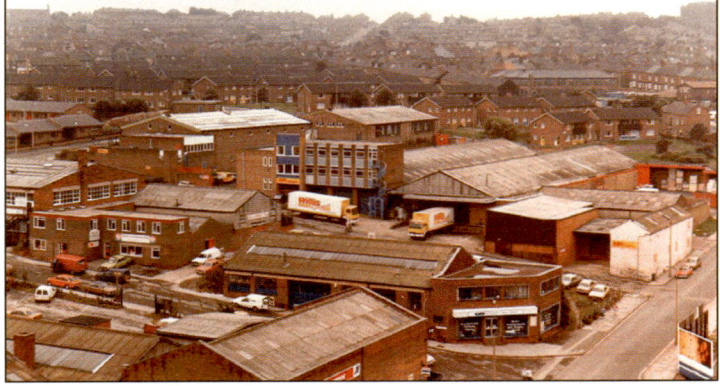

Top: Willis store, Crookes, Sheffield, 1985.
Centre: Willis Office and Depot, New St/Joseph St, 1985.
Bottom: Willis store, Wickersley, Rotherham, 1985.

CHAPTER 13

SUCCESS, THEN FACING DISASTER WITH A REWARDING CONCLUSION
A Testing Time for the Willis Wholesale/ Retail enterprise

The ten years from 1981 to July 1991 were to prove to be the most challenging in the Group's history when all was staked upon an expansion and modernising programme. The prime objective was to achieve such a critical mass that the Group could pursue a policy which would match more closely the daily needs of the consumer by providing convenience products, at competitive prices, in company stores located in urban areas. The group had to offer an attractive alternative to the giant out of town superstore. What was not foreseen was the dramatic upheaval which affected the Groups' trading area very adversely, due to the coal miners strike of 1984/85 and the subsequent pit closures. This national coal miners strike (apart from the Nottinghamshire coalfield) lasted 12 months from March 1984 and severely affected the spending power of the lower income groups in our trading area for many subsequent years.

In October 1987, following the retirement of Michael Nicholson, our auditor for many years, Wilfred Wyatt and Co, Chartered Accountants, were appointed the company auditors. The Group celebrated its 25th anniversary on 30 September 1988, at the same time embarking upon further warehouse and supermarket improvement programmes, with a capital budget of £254,000 for 1988. Board members in 1988/89 became increasingly aware that recycling, environmental and health and safety policies should become part of the Group's business plan. Active support was given at Board level to the Willis Sports and Social Club. Changing market conditions in the late 1980s and inflation pressures were making it imperative to reduce operating costs to enable the Group's modernisation programme to be adequately funded. A further factor we had to bear in mind, but difficult to understand, was the dishonesty by a very small minority of our staff who systematically stole from the business. The breakdown in honesty by some employees has to be contained by all traders to this day. The reality was that the businesses lost at least 1% of turnover in theft, either by staff or customers. In later years this loss would add up to approximately £300,000 a year. Theft would range from petty shop lifting to a bounced cheque of just over £10,000 from a retail customer, classified by the police as 'a long fraud'.

The decade from 1980 to 1990 could best be described as a period of substantial growth and general expansion for the Willis Group, followed by a financial crisis in July 1991, culminating in a highly successful reconstruction of the Willis business giving both Ian and Andrew new opportunities, backed up by adequate financial resources. It was a just reward for their individual contributions to the success of the Willis Group of companies. The reconstruction was so successful that all jobs were preserved across the Group. A further positive result of the sale and dismantling of the Willis Group in the early

1990s was the retirement of G R T Willis who was able to take up his full entitlement from the fully funded company pension scheme. With this introduction to the events of the 1980s it would be appropriate to summarise in a little more detail the development of the Willis Group in the 1980s, culminating in the director's decision to place the Group into members voluntary liquidation in 1991.

One has to ask what brought about the voluntary liquidation of the Willis Group? Clearly it was a step that was never planned or anticipated. The great success of the liquidation was viewed by the directors, at that time, as being a great disappointment after 36 years of high ambition and achievement. With the appointment of Grant Thornton, operating from their offices in Leeds, it should be noted that in reporting to the directors they stated on 29 July 1991 that the major factor leading to the company's liquidation was excessive capital expenditure, which the company was unable to fund, particularly with the unprecedented rise in interest rates from 1988 to 1991, culminating in a rate of over 15%.

During the immediate post war years, the wholesale grocery business was relatively stable, where much depended upon good personal relations with the customers, coupled with a reliable service. However, the RT Willis and Son business was a very minor player indeed, with a full time staff of less than 20. With the Second World War over, it seemed quite natural that son would succeed father and enjoy a comfortable life style. With the cessation of all food rationing in the early 1950s and the formation of the

Common Market in March 1957, real competition for market share was emerging. The refusal of RT Willis senior to look ahead and invest in the company created much tension between father and son, only resolved when RT Willis died of lung cancer in February 1955, aged 63 years. Two brothers, Robert Willis and Derek Willis had to work very hard indeed to recover some of the lost ground as the organisation struggled to produce sufficient profit to invest in future growth. It could be said that the seeds had already been sown in the immediate post war years for the ultimate sale of the business.

Despite the most strenuous efforts when inflation raged in 1990/91 and the ploughing back of all profits, after very modest dividends to shareholders, lack of capital to invest in modern warehousing and in the improvement of the retail store portfolio produced losses in 1991 which were unsustainable. The financial history of the business was well summarised by Grant Thornton, international accountants. In an extract from a letter to shareholders on 17 October 1991 by Grant Thornton they say, "You will note that the outcome of the receivership has been extremely successful and that there are sufficient funds to pay the claims of all creditors in full".

A letter of the same date as the above was sent to all suppliers and other creditors announcing the members voluntary liquidation of the Willis Group and setting out the history of the company. The letter also stated that the whole enterprise had been sold leaving sufficient funds to pay all creditors and professionals services, leaving a balance for the shareholders to reclaim their investment in the company in full. Again it is useful to quote extracts from this letter as circulated by Grant Thornton which summarises the history of the Willis Group from its foundation in February 1955 to its ultimate sale, completed on 11 October 1991.

From their Leeds Branch, Grant Thornton reported as follows on 17 October 1991:
> "The companies were incorporated in the early sixties and took over the operation of the Willis family's retailing and wholesale operation. Previously the Willis family had operated in South Yorkshire since the 1940s.
>
> The three main aspects of the companies operations were as follows:
> a) 3 wholesale cash and carry sites owned by RT Willis (Cash & Carry) Limited.
> b) 27 retail outlets in Yorkshire, Humberside, Lancashire and Derbyshire, this division was owned by RT Willis (Superstores) limited.
> c) A central distribution warehouse run by RT Willis (Food Distributors) Limited. The warehouse supplied the 3 Cash & Carry's, 27 stores and a few external retail outlets. This is also the ultimate holding company.
>
> The retail operations had previously been associated with the SPAR organisation. In the last few years

they purchased LIFESTYLE products through the SPAR LANDMARK organisation.

The trading performance of the companies is summarised as follows:

	Year ended 11.5.91 (Management) £ '000	Year ended 12.5.90 (Audited) £ '000	Year ended 12.5.89 (Audited) £ '000
Sales	23,093	23,345	23,099
Gross profit	3,790	3,886	3,632
Profit/(loss) before tax	(298)	101	67
Profit/(loss) after tax	(298)	96	65

It is apparent that even during the recent retailing slump the group continued to make profits until the year ended 11 May 1991 when a substantial loss was incurred. In addition, the group came under increasing financial pressure due to the need to implement systems and facilities required to distribute a variety of products in the most modern way. The cost of modernisation was borne by way of an increased overdraft. Consequently the group found itself under capitalised."

The directors and the Grant Thornton team quickly agreed that the way forward was to advertise and dispose of the whole Willis enterprise as a going concern at the earliest date. All the assets were sold very successfully within less than three months.

The overdraft facility was granted by the Midland Bank plc in the sum of £700,000 at an interest rate of 2% over bank base rate. Capital expenditure of £599,977 was paid in the year ending 11 May 1991 covering the ongoing store and distribution modernisation cost. As noted by Grant Thornton the expenditure coupled with the increasing rise in bank base rate, was the major cause of the company's financial crisis. During the period base rate had risen to 15% pushing the amount paid in interest to the bank, over the year to 11 May 1991, to £146,466. With a depressed nation-wide retail market and unemployment at over 2 million, the burden of funding the planned modernisation and marketing programme became impossible.

Despite much reduction in staffing levels and the disposal of unprofitable stores, the group both at its wholesale and retail level soon accumulated losses which became impossible to claw back, before the end of the financial year on 11 May 1991. Apart from the Midland Bank, the group had no long term debt. Over the previous 30 years the group had raised short term loans from Broad Street Securities plc and the linked Dominion Trust to fund retail store and distribution facilities. Prior to 1980 all this debt had been paid off. Apart from the debt to the Midland Bank plc, the group was able to produce an unencumbered balance sheet which led to a very quick sale by Grant Thornton of all retail outlets and all the distribution and Cash and Carry facilities. The retail outlets were in prime local locations with attractive leases or, in some cases, on freehold sites owned by the group. The main distribution warehouse in Barnsley, together with all the Cash and Carry outlets, found ready buyers. It had been a time of great anxiety, but thankfully the end result was very satisfactory. Main credit is due to Ian Willis and Andrew Willis who worked closely together at this time, with Geoffrey Gee, the joint liquidator, appointed by Grant Thornton.

WILLIS GROUP FINANCIAL SUMMARY 1954-1991

YEAR ENDING	ORGANISATION TRADING AS	SALES £	NET PROFIT BEFORE TAX £
31.12 1954	RT Willis & Son	232,000	5,440
11.02.1956	Executors of RT Willis & Son	253,000	2,803
15.02.1958	RT Willis & Son Ltd	93,700	100
14.02.1959	RT Willis & Son Ltd	145,200	800
13.02.1960	RT Willis & Son Ltd	245,460	790
10.02.1962	RT Willis & Son (Soft Drinks) Ltd (founded 2.8.1961)	11,700	160
16.02.1963	Trustees of RT Willis T/A RT Willis & Son	647,000	4,100
15.02.1964	RT Willis (Food Distributors) Ltd (1st year consolidated with Trustees of RT Willis & Son)	683,000	4,900
03.04.1965	RT Willis & Son (Soft	32,000	600

	Drinks) Ltd		
02.04.1966	RT Willis (Food Distributors) Ltd	583,000	9,700
02.04.1966	Foodwise (Cash & Carry) Ltd	561,000	2,800
02.04.1966	RT Willis & Son (Shopfitters) Ltd	4,500	150
02.04.1966	RT Willis & Son (Soft Drinks) Ltd	23,800 (52 weeks)	730
02.04.1966	RT Willis (Food Distributors) Ltd (Consolidated)		7,900
02.04.1966	Foodwise Ltd	76,000	700
23.04.1966	WJ Hiscock & Son Ltd		(200)
31.03.1967	RT Willis (Food Distributors) Ltd	495,000	8,600
31.03.1967	RT Willis & Son Ltd	802,000	4,700
31.03.1967	RT Willis (Food Distributors) Ltd (Consolidated)	2,577,000 (8 companies)	17,400
04.04.1969	RT Willis (Food Distributors) Ltd (Consolidated)	3,100,000	40,500
28.04.1973	RT Willis & Son (Food Distributors) Ltd (Group)	5,390,000	31,000
03.05.1975	RT Willis & Son (Food Distributors) Ltd (Group)	6,746,000	13,400
12.05.1979	RT Willis (Food Distributors) Ltd (Group)	12,674,000	54,500
09.05.1981	Willis Group	15,686,000	65,700

07.05.1983	Willis Group	16,657,000	30,200
12.05.1984	Willis Group	23,946,000	(11,900)
10.05.1986	Willis Group	30,886,000	203,500
07.05.1988	Willis Group	28,546,000	125,900
12.05.1989	Willis Group	23,099,000	66,700
12.05.1990	Willis Group	23,345,000	100,700
11.05.1991	Willis Group	23,088,000	(298,000)
13 weeks to 10.08.1991	Willis Group	4,695,000	(485,400)

From the early 1900s four generations of the Willis family had worked in the family's grocery enterprise, successfully sold in 1991, with all creditors paid in full and with all family shareholders receiving a fair price for their shares. It was a fitting conclusion, giving new opportunities in a changing world.

Right: Willis in the Alps, Venture Scouts & Guides, leaders Joan & Brian Crofts, 1985.
Below: On the buses in Bury, 1985.

Left above and below: Glossop store interior and exterior, 1986.

Willis Discount, Hoyland Common, 1985.

Funding the Barnsley Local Employer Network 1987 (left) and 1988 (right).

Above: Grant to engineering student, Barnsley College by Koyo Bearings, Dodworth, Barnsley 1987. L-r Koyo MD, David Eade, Principal Barnsley College, GRTW on right.

Above: Chairman's Prize, 1989.

Above: 'The Warriors', back l-r Irene Bray, AM Willis, Debbie Swift, Sandra Parker, Joan Foster, Beverley Russell, Joan Thornton; front l-r Mary Baker, Anne McHale, June Frost, Michelle Buckler, Joan Hill.

Right: Andrew and Joan Crofts, Long Service Award, Royal Hotel, Scarborough, 1989.

CHAPTER 14

NOT QUITE RETIREMENT
Challenges and Opportunities from 1991-2007

Far from being seen as a business failure, the sale of the Willis wholesale and retail enterprise was judged by the local business community to have been quite an achievement, in a rapidly changing food retailing market.

Following my resignation from the Willis Group of Companies, I quickly installed myself in an attractive office in Regent Street, Barnsley as I still had several commercial responsibilities, most notably the chairmanship of the computer company DCSL in Manchester. Although now well past the normal retirement age, I was encouraged to offer my experience and expertise for the benefit of small and medium sized enterprises. Additionally, the local authority, in particular the education department of Barnsley MBC, were anxious to keep my services as Chairman of the Barnsley Business Education Partnership, in which I had played a major role since its inception in 1989. During the 1980s the Thatcher government had created, across the country, a number of Training and Enterprise Councils with an individual annual income of approximately £20M. On the formation of the Barnsley and Doncaster Training and Enterprise Council in 1988, with its headquarters in Barnsley, I was invited to be a non executive director. Despite resigning from this position in 1991, as I no longer had a major company supporting me, the TEC, as it was always known, asked me to continue to give my services to the business community as a consultant. Fortunately, as I had an office in the centre of Barnsley, I was able to meet this request supported by secretarial assistance. Hence, Robert Willis Associates Ltd was established in 1991.

Above left: Tankersley Manor, 1992, l-r Joanne Beedon, Andrew, Yvonne, GRTW, Joan, Wayne Beedon.

Below left: Investors in People Award, 1997, Hovematch Ltd, Mexborough. Back l-r John Hills, John Green, GRTW>

My time was equally divided between an active consultancy role and the Barnsley Business Education Partnership of which I was chairman, ultimately becoming Chief Executive until I retired in 1995. As a consultant I was able to give some valuable assistance to several companies in the Barnsley/Doncaster area. One such company, was Hovematch Ltd of Mexborough, a supplier of building protection products, chiefly to the public sector. I was invited by the board to become a non-executive director, a post I held until retirement in 1998, when the business was merged with a French company. Advising companies was time well spent and certainly appreciated by several small enterprises, as demonstrated when I received a phone call in 2007 from Mr Dave Smith, a partner in Custom Kitchens of Thorne near Doncaster. He thanked me for all the advice I had given 12 years before which had pointed the company in the right direction and ultimately enabled him to sell his shares in the company and retire. In this period I was also heavily involved in such initiatives as The Local Enterprise Services (Lens), sponsored by the Barnsley Chamber of Commerce. For over 10 years I was a member of the Council of the Chamber and, together with support from the TEC, took part in many training and education programmes. Honours were never sought, so it was quite a pleasant surprise to be awarded an MBE in the Queen's Birthday Honours of June 1996, for these services. For many years, supported by the Chamber of Commerce, the Local Authority and the TEC, I had given help and advice to many small enterprises and to encouraging ambition and higher esteem in the young. Consultancy was challenging but very rewarding, especially to be contacted by former customers in later years thanking me for putting them on the right path to commercial success.

Perhaps this extract from a letter from John Edwards OBE, Chief Executive of Barnsley Metropolitan Borough Council presents a reasonably accurate description as to why I was honoured with an MBE.

"…………Your award is a well deserved recognition of the great personal contribution you have made to life in, and the regeneration of the town. I know you have enjoyed taking part but it must be very pleasing to have received such public recognition. You have, of course, still the highlight to come with the award ceremony and I hope you have as good a day as I did. Once again, well done and welcome to the membership of a rather select club…………."

Yes, it was a good day. Along with Joan and our two youngest sons Andrew and Howard, I was summoned to attend the investiture at Buckingham Palace at 10.30am on Tuesday 11 December 1996. We stayed at the Strand Palace Hotel overnight, which is about 15 minutes by taxi to the Palace. The message was that any late arrivals would be excluded! It was a cold, raw and overcast December morning as we got into our taxi at 9.45. We joined the other recipients, 135 in number, along with their guests who numbered about 400. We made our way in a long line across the Palace forecourt into the inner quadrangle and then into the Palace after security checks. We moved up the central staircase, lined by Life Guards, to our allotted locations. The guests were seated in the Ballroom where the investiture was to take place. The recipients waited in the Picture Gallery which did not boast any chairs, except a few settees for the more frail. Being a 'W' I was not called until 11.45am by which time I had enjoyed a good look at many of the Queen's pictures which included several Dutch masters.

We were instructed as to the procedures, which involved bowing and walking backwards! To explain, when you are

MBE Investiture, l-r Andrew, GRTW, Joan, Howard.

called you walk down a long corridor to step onto a large dais in the Ballroom. An usher checks your name and indicates when to move forward. Halfway across the dais you turn left to face the Queen, bow and walk forward. The Queen attaches the medal onto your jacket over a hook, previously placed there by a court official prior to entering the Ballroom. The Queen says a few words to every recipient, shakes your hand and then you walk backwards for about six paces, still facing the Queen, bow and then turn to walk out of the Ballroom. The Queen asked me who I had trained. I made a brief response, then handshake and it was all over, but I forgot to bow or walk backwards as I departed! The guests have the best day. They enjoy seeing all the recipients who are to receive a knighthood kneeling on a foot-stool as the sword is briefly placed on their shoulder by the Queen. My guests were seated on the second row from the front in the Ballroom, giving an excellent view of the various recipients who included service personnel of all ranks from senior officers to sergeants along with members of the police, fire service, the business community plus civil servants. I found the whole proceedings very moving, conducted in a very professional manner. Throughout a military band played quietly in the gallery of the Ballroom. No applause was allowed throughout the proceedings. When it was all over all present stood as the National Anthem was played and then the Queen departed with her escort of the Yeomen of the Guard. The day ended with photographs in the Palace courtyard.

From 1997 to 1999, I researched and wrote my RAF story as previously mentioned, which was published in a hardback edition in 1999 under the title of 'No Hero, Just A Survivor'. I was fortunate in being able to find an expert assistant in the village, Paulette Huntington, a former teacher and a local magistrate, who did all the type setting and interpretation of my indifferent handwriting. An additional bonus was that her husband Trevor, a local schoolteacher, continues to give me very welcome help in the garden. The book ran to three editions selling over 1200 copies in the UK and overseas. Without Paulette's assistance this family history publication would not have seen the light of day.

In 1996, as I wound down my consultancy, I closed down the Barnsley office to work from home. For many years, as a veteran Mosquito pilot, I had been a member of the Mosquito Aircrew Association. When, at short notice in 1998, Barry Blunt, the editor of their magazine The Mossie, resigned I volunteered to take over the editing and publishing responsibilities, again with the help of Paulette. From January 1999 I edited and published three copies a year, full of veterans' stories. The magazine's quality was much praised, being dispatched to many places around the world. On the closure of the Mosquito Aircrew Association in 2004, the final edition was published in June 2005. I had the privilege of organising the final reunions of the MAA and of the 'Old Boys' section of the 47 Squadron Association. Both events took place at the RAF Club, Piccadilly, London in 2006. I was now fully retired!

Left: Robert in a Mossie cockpit after 59 years.

Right: RAF Museum, Hendon, Robert with Mosquito veterans, 2004.

Left: Poix de Picarde, 24 February 2004, Michael Forster holding the RAFA Standard, Robert and Eric Atkins, Chairman of the Mosquito Aircrew Association.

Joan and I have four children, as detailed on the family tree, all married with families. I will always be very grateful for the unfailing support Joan and all the family gave to my commercial activities. Detailed curriculum vitae feature in a later chapter. All four children graduated very successfully. Catherine graduated from Newcastle with a first, married to Chris soon after university she gave him wonderful support as he was posted by Shell to many countries, with homes in Germany, The Netherlands and for nine years in Kenya before retirement. Their three children, Andrew, Richard and Annabel, are all prospering in their different fields. Catherine and Christopher live in Sevenoaks, Kent. Ian graduated from Manchester and went on to qualify as a chartered accountant, working in London where he met his future wife Jutta. Their two children, Susan and Martin, are both prospering and building their careers in London. Ian joined the Willis Group in 1973, ultimately becoming Finance

Director. He worked very successfully with Grant Thornton as the Willis Group was sold off in 1991. Ian went on to found his own company in partnership with a fellow IT consultant. The business has offices in Trentham near Stoke on Trent and trades under the name of Retail Accounting Solutions Limited. Ian and Jutta live in Macclesfield, Cheshire. Andrew joined the Willis Group in 1972 straight from Bradford University, with a business degree, to fill a very important gap as Cash and Carry Manager for the Stairfoot depot. Andrew progressed from this position to be the Group's Marketing Director. He was very supportive of the liquidation and sale of the Willis business in 1991. He went on to found his own company AM Willis Supermarkets Limited which he ultimately sold, very successfully, in January 2002 to United Norwest Co-operative Limited. Andrew has two children, by his second wife Gwynn, Sally and Simon, both in the early stages of their careers after graduating from University. Andrew firstly married Lynn, then Gwynn, but is now very happily married to Yvonne and finding new opportunities as a property investor. Andrew and Yvonne moved from Dodworth, Barnsley to live in Matlock, Derbyshire. Howard, the youngest of our children, graduated from Manchester University and then went on to law school where he qualified as a solicitor. Married to Fiona they have two children, Joshua and Maisie, with Joshua currently at Nottingham University and Maisie heading along the same path of higher education. Howard is currently a partner in Chadwick Lawrence, Solicitors of Dewsbury, Wakefield and Huddersfield.

Much blessed with a wonderful family, Joan and I have also had the great privilege of having many friends who have continued to support us in, our so called, retirement years. Going back to our early years at Middleton St George, George Baker a fellow instructor at the RAF base was a frequent visitor to our rooms in Yarm Road, Darlington. He yearned to go back to Canada, where he did pilot training, leaving behind a young lady Margaret to whom he promised to return. Leaving his family behind in Norfolk troubled him. We encouraged him to emigrate. He did so and was always grateful for our encouragement. We visited him and his wife Margaret and their family in Canada several times over the years. George died in January 1992 and Margaret in October 2001. We still keep in touch with family members. Other very valued family friends overseas are Mary and Bob Shearer, living in retirement near San Francisco. They have welcomed us warmly to their home in California on more than one occasion. We first met Mary Shearer on a Cosmos tour of the north east USA in September 1993. Other overseas journeys, apart from business visits, were to Catherine and Christopher in Holland and Germany and just once to Kenya in 1997.

Friends nearer home have included Jimmy Gibson, another RAF colleague, and his wife Audrey now both deceased, followed by Bill Powell a colleague on 47 Squadron who died in June 2007. We were also very sad to lose Tony Norris, the Intelligence Officer of 47 Squadron, who died in the early 1990s. For both Joan and I, with the war years of 1939-45 affecting our lives so much, these old RAF colleagues will always have a very special place in our hearts.

Left: The Second World War Experience Centre, 2002. L-r Robert, Peter Liddle, Jimmy Gibson.

Far right: Joan, Sevenoaks, 1990.
Right: Joan, Golden Wedding day, 24 November 1995.
Below: l-r Terry, Joan, Mary, Jennifer Gosse, Margaret.

Left: Joan, Mary Shearer, Doris Immethun, 23 February 1995.
Right: Jane Kastner & Joan, Jane's garden, 24 February 1995.

Joan & Charles Forster, Diamond Wedding, 24 May 2001. Back l-r Jason & Rolf Taunton-Rigby (Alison's sons), Andrew Brattle (Carolyn's son), Jason Ferguson (Sarah's husband), Richard Hoyland, Jonathan Taunton-Rigby (Alison's son). Middle l-r Carolyn Stone (Joan & Charles' daughter), Liv Taunton-Rigby (Alison's daughter), Lanis Taunton-Rigby (Jonathan's wife), Sarah Ferguson (Carolyn's daughter), Alison Taunton-Rigby (Joan & Charles' daughter). Front l-r Monica Hoyland (Joan's sister), Joan, Charles.

Above: Chris, Catherine, Howard, Joshua, Fiona, Maisie, Joan, Andrew & Sophie's wedding, Scotland, April 2003.

Above left: Andrew & Sophie, April 2003.

Above right: Yvonne, Andrew, Robert & Joan, Emley Show, August 2004.

Left: Joan, Ethel Thompson, Robert, 2004.

Right: Joan, Robert and Freddie House, December 2004.

Left: Richard Hoyland, 8 January 2000; Monica Hoyland, 2005.

Above: Monica Hoyland's 90th birthday, Bagden Hall. L-r Alison Taunton-Rigby, Joan, Monica, Richard, Carolyn and Bill Nickson.

Left: Simon & Sally, Coach House, Dodworth, summer 2005.

Above left: Joan
Above right: Joan, Greenways garden 2005.
Left: Joan & Robert, 47 Squadron Reunion, 2 September 2005.

Above: Diamond Wedding day, 24 November 2005.
Below: Diamond Wedding celebrations, Bertie's, Elland,
26 November 2005 – the assembled gathering.

Bertie's, Elland,
26 November 2005
Above: l-r Howard, Catherine,
Robert, Joan, Ian, Andrew.
Right: Robert and Joan.
Below: Dara and Susan.

Chris's 60th birthday
celebration at Rules,
23 December 2005.
Above: The assembled guests.
Left: Chris.
Below: Chris and Annabel.

Susan and Dara's wedding, September 2006.
Above & right: Susan and Dara.
Below: Ian and the Bridesmaids.

Above: Simon, Yvonne, Andrew and Sally.
Left: Catherine and Christopher.
Below: Fiona, Howard, Joshua and Maisie.

Above left: Freddie House, 2007.

Above right: Marjorie's 80th birthday, 8 January 2007.

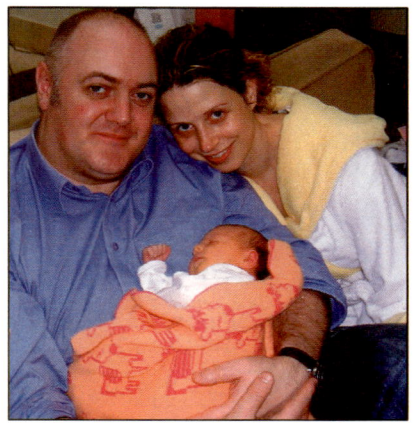

Above: Andrew and Yvonne, 2008.

Right: Dara, Susan and Orla, March 2008.

CHAPTER 15

THE WILLIS FAMILY 1701-2009

JOSEPH WILLIS
Spouse: Alice Johnson.
Married: 12 February 1701, Hathersage. Father of **WILLIAM** Willis, born 1701.

WILLIAM WILLIS 1701-12 June 1779.
Spouse: Abigail Hadfield, 1720-1993. Abigail was born on 5 May 1720 and died in Eyam on 10 September 1793, age 73. (*Daughter of Joseph Hadfield of Edale and Ann Woolley, married in 1713 at Sheffield, blessed at Edale.*)
Married: At Tideswell, 1749.
Children: 3
1. William, 1751-16 May 1817, age 66.
2. Rebecca, 1755-16 October 1821, age 66.
3. **DANIEL**, born 1757, died 28 September 1840, age 83.
General Information: William Willis lived at Grindleford Bridge, near Eyam in 1758 and was a farmer, probably a tenant on the Chatsworth Estate. He was possibly baptised at Stoney Stratford on 1 March 1721.

DANIEL WILLIS 1757-28 September 1840.
Spouse: Mary Townsend, 1767-21 April 1855, buried at Eyam.
Married: 12 April 1789, Sheffield.
Children: 10
1. Ellen, 31 August 1789-4 October 1811.
2. William, 4 February 1792-27 May 1824, married Anne(?) 1795-13 September 1845 and had 6 children: Ellen, Daniel (died in infancy), Mary Ann, Arthur (Lt Col?), Thomas, William.

3. Abigail, 12 August 1783-25 September 1829. Married James Dixon whose father James Dixon Snr founded the Cornish Works, Sheffield in 1804. Their son James Willis Dixon married and moved to New York in 1838 and stayed for 3 years. James Willis Dixon Jnr was born in New York in 1838, coming back to England with his parents.
4. Mary, 3 September 1795-?, married John Cocker and had 3 children; Mary, born July 1826; Hannah, born July 1828 (married John Batt in 1859 – 6+ children – William, Pollie, John, Horace, Annie, Fred and others names not known); Daniel married Mary Anne ? – one daughter Emily 1866-24 March 1935.
5. Joseph, 10 January 1798-2 June 1835, buried 5 June 1825.
6. Rebecca, 15 March 1800-21 June 1800, buried 24 June 1800.
7. Daniel, 16 May 1801-4 February 1836.
8. Ann, 11 September 1803, baptised 2 October 1803, married Henry Parker (had henry Parker possibly been married before to 1) ? Wolivin & 2) ? Moore).
9. Sarah, 5 October 1805-8 September 1845, baptised 6 October 1805.
10. **GEORGE**, 1 August 1808, baptised 14 August 1808.

GEORGE WILLIS 1 August 1808-1844.
Spouse: Elizabeth Hind of Cross Low Farm. *(Daughter of John Hind, born 8 January 1779, and Hannah Wright, baptised at Eyam 1786, married at Eyam on 6 March 1814).*
Married: 23 May 1836 at Eyam.
Children: 3
1. Daniel, 1838-15 September 1909, married Elizabeth Dane, 6 children (one son John Hind Willis married Mary Ann Heppenstall and moved to Meltham.)
2. **JOHN**, 21 December 1840-1898, died in Pontypool July/September?, married Emma Lowe 1849-1898, also died in Pontypool.

3. Mary, 26 December 1843-1920, married George Bennett.
General information: Elizabeth sailed for America in 1843 and was never heard of again. Did George go with her? Did he stay to look after the children?

JOHN WILLIS 1840-1898.
Spouse: Emma Lowe, born Newton Heath, Lancs 1849. *(Daughter of Isabella Hayes and Hamlet Lowe; her elder brother James (1836-1907) was a billiard table maker in Manchester).*
Married: 1867, in Eccles (according to 1881 census) registered in Chapel en le Frith Registered District.
Children: 6
1. **GEORGE HAMLET**, born Eyam 17 October, died 26 December 1950.
2. Henry (Harry), born 1870.
3. Edith, born 1873, died in infancy.
4. Bernard, born 1874 in Leeds.
5. John, born 1875 in Leeds.
6. Walter, died in infancy.

General information: John Willis was born in Eyam. 1871 Census – John Willis was a shoemaker living at 2 Court, 5 Buckley Street, Barnsley. Farming would not support growing families. Shoe factories in Eyam drew workers from the land. John Willis was believed to have walked from Eyam to Barnsley, a growing mining town. 1881 Census – living at 19 Ashfield Place, Leeds.

GEORGE HAMLET WILLIS 17 October 1867- 26 December 1950.
Spouse:
1. Mary Louisa Hyland, 1861-22 May 1894, age 33. (Daughter of Thomas Hyland born 1820, died 5 September 1901. Sister of James, d April 1853, Thomas, d March 1864, Jane, d September 1899, William, b 1865, Robert, d 1930 and Martha (Mattie) b 1862).

2. Charlotte Elizabeth Varley, born 1862 in Sheffield, married in 1895, died 1910.
3. Marianne Alice Hardy, 1890-18 July 1967, married in 1912.

Children: 3

Marriage 1: **ROBERT THOMAS**, born 4 January 1892, died 1955.
Marriage 3: Monica, born 18 April 1913, died 29 March 2008; Joan, born 20 September 1915, died January 2009.

ROBERT THOMAS WILLIS 4 January 1892-13 February 1955.
Spouse: Florence Elsie Martin, born 16 August 1894, died 2 July 1988.
Married: 24 July 1920.
Children: 5

1. **GEORGE ROBERT THOMAS**, born 20 June 1921.
2. Florence Maisie, born 22 May 1922, died 14 September 1949.
3. Derek Percival, born 13 December 1924, died 8 May 1989. Married Brenda Levick (b 14 May 1931) on 19 July 1954; 2 children – Mark and Paula (adopted).
4. Bertram Terence Martin, born 9 May 1927. Married 1. Nanette Goater, died 1975, 3 children – Michael, Alison, Jonathan. 2. Margaret Stella Helsby (nee Andrews) in 1978.
5. Mary Christine, born 17 January 1930, married Arthur Bellhouse. Marriage later dissolved.

GEORGE ROBERT THOMAS WILLIS 20 June 1921.
Spouse: Joan Nowell, born 23 September 1921.
Married: 24 November 1945 at St Mary's Church, Worsbrough Village, Barnsley.
Children: 4

1. Catherine Mary, born 30 August 1946, married Christopher House, born 23 December 1945 – 3 children: Andrew Christopher, born 1 April 1972; Richard James, born 9 April 1975; Annabel Sarah, born 11 June 1980.

2. Robert Ian, born 27 November 1947, married Jutta Hoole, born 22 December 1948 – 2 children: Susan Fiona, born 3 March 1976; Martin Patrick, born 6 December 1978.
3. Andrew Martin, born 25 March 1951, married 1. Lynn, born 11 September 1951 (dissolved); 2. Gwynne, born 5 October 1951 – 2 children: Sally, born 30 May 1982; Simon, born 3 June 1985, (dissolved); 3. Yvonne, born 16 August 1950, married 29 December 1994 at Bagden Hall, Scissett, Huddersfield.
4. Howard John, born 22 March 1957, married Fiona Elizabeth Longbottom, born 20 January 1962 – 2 children: Joshua Samuel, born 29 May 1988; Elizabeth Maisie, born 25 October 1990.

****

Transcript of a document held by the Ridgeway family in Eyam given to GRT Willis, by a local historian, when visiting Eyam in 2003.

THE WILLIS FAMILY

In the year 1758 William Willis, a farmer, lived with his wife at Grindleford Bridge, near Eyam, Derbyshire.

William had a son, Daniel, whose wife was named Mary. They had ten children, their names are in a register which was in the possession of Isaac Ridgeway of Eyam. Isaac married as his first wife, Anne Willis. After her death he married his late wife's sister, Edith Willis. The register came into her possession and now 1957 is probably in the hands of Joseph Ridgeway, her nephew, of Beechurst, Eyam.

The inscription in the book reads as follows:

THIS BOOK
which contains a register of Daniel and Mary Willis of Eyam from the year 1789 is given into the care and possession of Isaac Ridgeway of Eyam for his and his family's use, by his father in law, Daniel Willis, this 5th day of October 1903.

Taken from old register
Ellen, the daughter of Daniel and Mary Willis was born August 31st 1789
William, there (their) son was born February 4th 1792
Abigail there daughter was born August 12th 1793
Mary there daughter was born September 3rd 1795
January 10th 1798 Joseph was born
March 15th 1800 Rebecca was born
June 21st 1800 Rebecca died. Buried June 24th
May 16th 1801 Daniel was born
September 11th 1803 Ann was born. Baptised October.
October 5th 1805 Sarah was born. Baptised October 6th.
August 1st 1808 George was born. Baptised August 14th.
October 4th 1811 Ellen Died.
August 27th 1824 William Died.
June 2nd 1825 Joseph Died and was buried 5th.
February 4th 1836 Daniel died
September 25th 1839 Abigail died.
September 28th 1840 Daniel Willis died, father to the above named children in the 84th year of his age.
September 8th 1845 Sarah died.
April 21st 1855 Mary Willis, mother of the above named children died in her 87th year. Buried April 25th.

CHAPTER 16

THE NOWELL/PALFRAMAN FAMILY 1750-2008

THE NOWELL FAMILY

BENJAMIN NOWELL born 1750
Spouse: ?
Children: **GEORGE**, born 1773.
General information: Location of Benjamin Nowell's birth unknown, also details of his marriage unknown.

GEORGE NOWELL born 1773
Spouse: Martha Radcliffe.
Married: 1 January 1787 at Mirfield.
Children: 5
1. John, born 1793.
2. George, born 1796.
3. William, born 1798.
4. **JACOB**, born 1803.
5. Grace, born 1805.

JACOB NOWELL 1803-1849
Spouse: Mary Chadwick.
Married: 13 April 1823 at Dewsbury.
Children: 7
1. Mary Ann, born 1824.
2. Sarah, born 1825.
3. John, born 1829.
4. William, born 1831.
5. Joseph, born 1834.
6. Benjamin, born 1838.

7. **JACOB**, born 1839.
General information: Born in 1803 at Dewsbury and was christened on 22 March 1803 at Dewsbury, Jacob died in 1882 at Churwell. In the 1842 Census Jacob was listed as living in the parish of Batley, occupation Coal Loader.

JACOB NOWELL 1839-1882
Spouse: Harriet Hawkhead, 4 July 1836-1901.
Children: 6
1. Elizabeth Ann, born 9 February 1860, married Fred Woods and had a daughter Eliza, born 1881.
2. **JOHN CHADWICK**, born 5 December 1891.
3. Alice Hawkhead, born 24 July 1863.
4. Jacob, born 1868.
5. Miriam, born 1870.
6. Benjamin Orlando, born 4 July 1873.

General information: Born in 1839 at Dewsbury, christened on 25 July 1839 at Dewsbury, died 1882 in Leeds. In the national census he is listed as living in the parish of Batley in 1841, Churwell in 1851, 1861 and 1871 and in Morley in 1881. On John Chadwick's birth certificate Jacob's occupation is Fuller.

JOHN CHADWICK NOWELL 1861-1943
Spouse: Florence Annie Smith, born 16 December 1865.
Children: 3
1. **CLIFFORD**, born 11 March 1893.
2. Harold, born 1896, married to Doris and had a son Brian.
3. Marjorie, born 14 July 1904, married Clifford Cox, born 1895, on 31 January 1927 and had 3 daughters: Janet, born 28 October 1934; Judith, born 9 October 1940; Helen, born 26 July 1944.

General information: Born at Churwell, died in 1943. On his marriage certificate his occupation is Salesman. In the national Census he is listed as living in Churwell in 1871, Morley in 1881,

Armley in 1891 and Leeds in 1901 with the occupation of Woollen Rag Merchant.

CLIFFORD NOWELL 1893-1973
Spouse:
1. Lily Palframan, 1894-1939.
2. Elizabeth Ackroyd.
Children: 4
1st Marriage:
1. Joan, born 23 September 1921, married George Robert Thomas Willis on 24 November 1945 and had 4 children: Catherine Mary; Robert Ian; Andrew Martin; Howard John.
2. Dorothy Maiva, born 2 December 1924, married Theodore Bacon, born 21 February 1927, and had 2 children: Ruth, born 24 May 1960; Adam, born 3 March 1962.
3. Marjorie Alice, 8 January 1927-23 November 2008.

2nd Marriage:
1. Suzanne, born 18 July 1943, married Claude Costacurta (died 2008) and had 2 children: Serge, born 21 February 1965; Claire, born 30 April 1970. Serge in married to Lydie with one son, Titouan, born in 2007.

THE PALFRAMAN FAMILY

JOHN PALFRAMAN born 1833
Spouse: Susan Marshall, born 1833
Married: 1853.
Children: 8
1. William, born 1854
2. **ALBERT**, born 1855.
3. Samuel, born 1858.
4. Mary, born 1860.
5. Sarah, born 1862.

6. Caroline, born 1865.
7. Emma, born 1868.
8. Elizabeth, born 1870.

ALBERT PALFRAMAN 1855-1942

Spouse: Alice Bolton, 1855-14 October 1914.

Married: c1877.

Children: 10

1. Joseph Bolton, born 1878, married Gertrude and had 5 children: Joseph Burnett; Robert; Alice; Alan; Kenneth.
2. Susan, 1879-22 May 1919, married William Herbert Perkins with one daughter Mary Kerala (Morrie), born in India in 1917 who died on 9 September 2005. Morrie married Tony Callan on 18 October 1940 and had 5 children: Frances Mary; Moira; Joe; Teresa; Margaret.
3. Martha, born 1881, married David Braithwaite.
4. Albert Marshall, 1884-7 July 1916, KIA in WWl.
5. Alice, born 1886, married Bert Hughes after emigrating to Canada, and had 2 sons, Bert and Lennie.
6. Harold Atkinson, born 1890.
7. Annie, born 1892.
8. **LILY**, born 1893, married **CLIFFORD NOWELL** in 1919 and had 3 children: Joan; Dorothy Maiva; Marjorie Alice.

General information: Albert Palframan died on 28 February 1942.

CHAPTER 17

TODAY'S PLAYERS

GEORGE ROBERT THOMAS WILLIS MBE DFC

Date of Birth: 20 June 1921 at High Stile Cottage, Park Grove, Barnsley.
Married: Joan Nowell on 24 November 1945, four grown up children, Catherine, Ian, Andrew and Howard – all university graduates.

1932-1937	Attended Barnsley Holgate Grammar School (Scholarship). Left with School Certificate including a distinction in History and Geography.
1937-1940	Joined the family wholesale grocery and soft Drinks manufacturing business as a warehouse assistant, management trainee and from 1939, warehouse manager at the Eckington (Sheffield) warehouse.
1941-1946	Volunteered for pilot training in the Royal Air Force. Flew two tours of operations with 47 Squadron RAF, flying Beaufighters in North Africa, Mosquitos in India and Burma. Commissioned and awarded the Distinguished Flying Cross. The final year of service as a flying instructor on Mosquitos at Middleton-St-George near Darlington.
1947-1955	Returned to the family business, wholly owned

	by father, Robert Thomas Willis, but mainly managed by sister Maisie, brother Derek and GRTW. Maisie died 14 September 1949.
1955	Father died 13 February 1955 leaving family the business in trust.
1963	Founded R T Willis (Food Distributors) Ltd, 20 Employees, with the shares allocated between the RT Willis Trust, Derek Willis and GRTW. GRTW appointed Chairman and Chief Executive. Moved the new company into an international buying group, VIVO International.
1964	Appointed Chairman of the Rebecca Guest Robinson Charity, founded to support the community in Birdwell and Worsbrough Village, Barnsley.
	Appointed Chairman of the UK division of VIVO International.
1965-1970	Successfully developed RT Willis (Food Distributors) Ltd, together with its subsidiary companies.
	Appointed a director of the newly enlarged Spar (UK) Ltd following the merger of the UK division of VIVO International with Spar (UK) Ltd. Appointed non executive Chairman of Distribution Computer Services Limited, a computer bureau, founded by Spar members to offer nation-wide computer services to the wholesale and multiple grocery trade.
1971-1984	Moved from residence in Birdwell, Barnsley to Emley village near Huddersfield.
	Continued to develop RT Willis (Food

	Distributors) Ltd, eventually withdrawing from Spar to form an independent grocery multiple chain 'Willis Discount'.
1984-1985	Continued to develop and open supermarkets in Yorkshire, Lancashire, Derbyshire and Humberside.
1986	Appointed Chairman of the Barnsley Chamber of Commerce Education Committee.
1987	Sold the Wholesale Distribution business, supplying services to Independent Spar convenience stores, in order to concentrate on the Willis Discount supermarkets and the Cash & Carry business.
1987-1990	Actively involved, for the Barnsley Chamber of Commerce, in Business Education Links. Appointed Chairman of the government sponsored Local Employers Network (LENS). Appointed Chairman of the Barnsley COMPACT, a Department of Education initiative in partnership with the local authority's Education Department and the private sector. Appointed a director of the Barnsley and Doncaster Training and Enterprise Council, a central government funded organisation to develop effective training and the development of advisory services for Barnsley and Doncaster small and medium sized companies.
1991	Resigned, at the age of 70, as Chairman and Chief Executive of RT Willis (Food Distributors) Ltd, following which the directors sold 18 of the Company's supermarkets to Kwik

Save Limited. The family board members then agreed to place the main operating company into members' voluntary liquidation. The Cash & Carry business was also successfully sold. Two operating subsidiary companies were kept to enable Andrew Willis to continue as a multiple grocery operator with 13 supermarkets.

Appointed Chairman and later Chief Executive of the Barnsley Business and Education Partnership Limited.

Resigned as a director of the Barnsley and Doncaster Training and Enterprise Council, but continued as a member of the organisation's Education Board.

Created a consultancy and publishing business, Robert Willis Associates Limited. Appointed as an advisor and consultant to small and medium sized enterprises in the Barnsley and Doncaster area, under the overall direction of the Barnsley and Doncaster Enterprise Council.

1994	Retired as Chairman and Chief Executive of the Barnsley Business Education Partnership. Successfully closed down Distribution Computer Services Limited.
1996	Awarded the MBE in the Queen's Birthday Honours for services to training in Barnsley and Doncaster. Appointed a life member of the Institute of Grocery Distribution.
1998	Appointed a life member of Barnsley Chamber of Commerce.

	Appointed editor of the Mosquito Aircrew Association's magazine 'The Mossie'.
1999	Published 'No Hero, Just A Survivor', a personal Narrative of war time service running to three hardback editions.
	Appointed archivist to the Mosquito Aircrew Association in close liaison with The Second World War Experience Centre, a national museum based in Leeds.
2001	Commenced research into the family history and its associations with the textile, grocery, house building and manufacturing industries. Resigned as Chairman of the Rebecca Guest Robinson Charity.
2003	Appointed Secretary to the Mosquito Aircrew Association.
2004	Closed down Robert Willis Associates Ltd and retired from consultancy activity.
2005	Mosquito Aircrew Association closed down. Publication of 'The Mossie' ceased with the publication of the 37th edition.
2006	Continued as archivist and reunion organiser for the Mosquito Aircrew Association and 47 Squadron veterans to the end of 2006, when the activity ceased.
2007	With the onset of age related macular degeneration ceased to drive a car (from August 2006).
2008 onwards	Current priorities include watching the next three generations adapt to a challenging world, St Michael's Church and the local community,

Gardening and keeping in touch with family and friends of many years standing.

JOAN WILLIS (née Nowell)

Date of Birth: 23 September 1921, Chubb Hill, Whitby.

1926-1932	Educated at Dewsbury Moor Council School.
1932-1937	Attended the Wheelwright Grammar School for Girls with a scholarship.
1937	Achieved School Certificate. Achieved a high grade from the Guildhall School of Music. Sporting activity in hockey and tennis.
1938	Employed as a clerk in Borough Treasurer's Department, Dewsbury Town Hall.
1940	Volunteer Air Raid Warden (uniformed). Firewatching duties in Dewsbury Town Centre.
1944	Volunteered to become a hospital nurse. Chose to go to Edinburgh Royal Infirmary for training.
1945	Married George Robert Thomas Willis of Barnsley on 24 November 1945 at St Mary's Church, Worsbrough, Barnsley. Robert was a pilot in the RAF, recently returned from active service. Honeymoon for one week at the Wheatsheaf Pub, Carperby, Aysgarth, Wensleydale.
1946	Residence at Comeley Bank, Sunnyside, Whitwell, Worksop, Notts. Catherine Mary born 30 August 1946 in St Helen's Maternity Hospital, Barnsley.

1947	Robert Ian born 27 November 1947 at a Nursing Home in Worksop.
1948	Took up residence at 101 Worsbrough Road, Birdwell, Barnsley.
1951	Andrew Martin born 25 March at Pindar Oaks Nursing Home, Barnsley.
1955	Took over responsibility for the wages records and pay slips for the RT Willis Wholesale business.
1956	Howard John born 22 March at Pindar Oaks Nursing Home. Joan continued working out the wages of Willis staff whilst in the Nursing Home.
1957-1971	The family were attenders at St Mary's Church, Worsbrough Village, Barnsley with Catherine attending Sunday School and Robert for a time serving as Churchwarden. Business pressures and the desire to escape the industrial smoke from a nearby Coking Plant made attendance at Church quite spasmodic. During the whole period Joan continued to support Robert in the Willis enterprise through clerical work at home and attendance at important business or company social functions.
1967	Following the take up of a lease at a flat in Harrogate as many weekends as possible were spent there and where various business colleagues were entertained with Joan's support.
	'Greenways', 19 Rectory Lane, Emley, near Huddersfield was purchased from a Mr Thomas

	Hogg who had acquired this newly built dormer bungalow two years previously. All the family except Howard had now left home, but frequently returned either from university or for holidays. Joan continued to support Robert particularly in visits to the expanding retail store division.
1975-1980	Took up work as a part time volunteer teacher of Adult Literacy under Kirklees Education Department.
1980-2005	Attended a French conversation class firstly in Dewsbury and later in Holmfirth, organised by Kirklees Education Department.
1971 onwards	In partnership with Robert created the garden at Greenways. Joan was always a strong supporter for all members of the family as grandchildren came along, always with an open house and a smile of welcome.

CATHERINE MARY HOUSE (née Willis)

Date of Birth: 30 August 1946 at St Helen's Hospital, Barnsley, maternity unit located in the old workhouse, Gawber, Barnsley.

1951-1956	Educated at Birdwell Primary School
1956-1964	Attended Barnsley Girls High School with distinction, was an enthusiastic performer in school stage productions.
1964-1967	Newcastle University to read Botany.

	Graduated with 1ˢᵗ Class Honours.
1967-1968	Manchester University to research Plant Pathology with a view to obtaining a PhD. Resigned at the end of the first year.
1967	Married Christopher Frederick House on 19 October at St Mary's Church, Worsbrough, Barnsley. Left home in Birdwell and set up with Chris their first home at Shellhaven Cottages on the Thames, close to the refinery.
1968-1969	Employed by Porvair, a synthetic leather company, as an information officer for the lab and researchers at Dagenham Dock. Changed jobs to work for BP in London at their patents office when Porvair relocated to Norfolk.
1969	Moved in October to West Germany, setting up home with Chris, on the ground floor of Frau Nielson's house in Harburg, close to Hamburg and the Shell oil refinery. Not allowed to work in Germany. Dressmaking was an important skill, used with great effect over the years. When back in England, from Chris's many overseas assignments with Shell, Catherine was able, when time permitted, to pursue her main intellectual interest, namely archaeology, achieving an archaeology diploma from Birkbeck College.
1972	Andrew Christopher House born in Hamburg, 1 April.
1975	Richard James House born in Staincliffe Hospital, Dewsbury, 9 April.
1980	Annabel Sarah House born in Staincliffe

	Hospital, Dewsbury, 11 June.
1990	Acquired a TESOL qualification, i.e. qualified to teach English as a second language to foreign students, which was used in future years whenever the opportunity arose.
2005	Left Mombassa, Kenya in December to finally settle in Sevenoaks, Kent. Many memories of Mombassa, such as the winning of prizes in dressmaking competitions, or acting as hostess to family visits from England, with visits to national parks and game reserves and seeing life in an emerging African country.
2006 onwards	A new life in Sevenoaks, modernising the house in Ashley Road and much enjoying the company of grandchildren.

On 26 April 2003 Andrew married Sophie Elisabeth Boyer King (born 20 June 1972) in Edinburgh, now with three children, Frederick Thomas born 30 November 2004, Alexander Andrew born 20 October 2006 and James Louis born 14 May 2009. Andrew, a graduate of Bristol University, now a senior lawyer and director for Bank of America, the international investment bankers, based in New York. Andrew works in the legal department at the London headquarters. This family also lives in Sevenoaks, much to Catherine's delight.

Richard and Natalie Jill Adams (born 6 January 1975) were married near Beaminster, Dorset on 16 June 2007. Richard, a very successful music technologist, with his own music production company and music production studio. He is heavily involved with TV companies at home and overseas. They occupy a pleasant apartment in Bethnal Green, London.

Annabel works as a consultant in Social Development to public bodies, i.e. local authorities, etc. Annabel is based in and shares a flat in London. She is a keen runner having completed the London Marathon.

CHRISTOPHER FREDERICK HOUSE

Date of Birth: 23 December 1945 at Chelmsford, Essex, living there with his parents to age 3, when the family moved to Cranham, Essex. At age 11 the family moved to Gidea Park, Essex.

1950-1957	Oglethorpe County Primary School, Cranham.
1957-1964	Coopers Company School, Bow, London, travelling daily from home by train.
1964	Newcastle University to read Chemical Engineering, graduated in June 1967. He subsequently became a Chartered Engineer and Fellow of the Institute of Chemical Engineers. He first started employment in a trainee management post with Shell in September 1967, staying with Shell until retirement in December 2005.
1965	28 February – 1st date with Catherine.
1968	Married Catherine at St Mary's Church, Worsbrough, Barnsley on 19 October.
1968-1969	First home, Shellhaven Cottages, adjacent to

	Shell Haven refinery on the Thames.
1969	October, posted to Deutches Shell Refinery, Hamburg, moving with Catherine to Harburg, near Hamburg.
1969-2005	Hamburg and Deutches Shell was the first of many postings with Shell as Chris moved up the management ladder. Postings included a period at Shell Mex House, London; two periods at Shell International Head Office in The Hague; two further postings to Shell Haven Refinery; sundry assignments to Scandinavia, Switzerland, Taiwan, Saudi Arabia and Japan with a final posting as Chief Executive Officer of Kenya Petroleum Refineries Limited in Mombasa. For this last assignment to KPR Ltd Chris was seconded by Shell. CEO of KPR Ltd and responsible for restoring the company to a stable and profitable situation. This position required tact and exceptional personal skills, as Shell were a minor shareholder in KPR Ltd, with the Kenya government holding 50% of the shares.
1983	Purchased 3 Ashley Road, Sevenoaks, Kent whilst based at Shell Mex House in London. This house acted as a base to return to from overseas assignments. Above all it provided a home for the three children, who spent some of their educational years in boarding schools. Much to their credit all three children, Andrew, Richard and Annabel, graduated in their chosen subjects from university. Andrew

	graduated from Bristol University in Law and then went on to law school at Chester. Richard graduated from Manchester University with a first in Mechanical Engineering and then went to the Royal College of Art where he gained a Masters degree in Industrial Design Engineering. Annabel graduated from Edinburgh University with a degree in Sociology.
2005	December, retired from Shell to return briefly to Mombassa from time to time as a consultant and to renew old friendships. Current activity is to make 3 Ashley Road, Sevenoaks as comfortable as possible for Catherine and himself, enabling them to adjust hopefully to a slower pace of life, after Chris's achievements in several senior executive posts with Shell.

Congratulations to Catherine and Christopher in surviving so well the stresses and strains of many locations with much travel, and for creating homes in far away places.

ROBERT IAN WILLIS

Date of birth: 27 November 1947 at Worksop, Nottinghamshire; the family were living nearby at Whitwell before moving to Birdwell.

1953-1959	Educated at Birdwell Primary School.
1959-1966	Barnsley Holgate Grammar School.

1967-1970	University of Manchester, graduated with BA Honours in Modern History, Economics and Politics.
1970-1974	Qualified as a Chartered Accountant with Touche Ross, an international firm of Chartered Accountants based in the City of London. Involved spells of work on auditing, taxation and consultancy with major British companies and prospectus preparation for the listing of companies on the London Stock Exchange.
1973	Married Jutta Hoole (born 22 December 1947) on 20 January and lived intheir first home in Chiswick, West London.
1974-1991	Moved to South Yorkshire to live and to work in the family business until its sale in July 1991. Set up home in Barnburgh near Doncaster, a small mining village which saw much disruption during the miners' strike of 1984.
1974-1976	First role in the business was as Retail Accounting Manager ensuring that the small team of 4 people controlled the financial information for the company's wholly owned stores effectively.
1976	Susan Fiona Willis born on 3 March.
1976-1981	Next role was as Marketing Manager controlling the buying function and setting of prices and promotions for the company's wholesale and retail store business. This involved attending monthly regional promotion meetings with other wholesale business at the

	Valley Lodge Hotel (now a Holiday Inn) next to Manchester airport.
1978	Martin Patrick Willis born in Doncaster, 5 December.
1981-1985	Moved on to Administration Director. In charge of running an office of approximately 20 staff. Implemented change from a bureau based computer system to an in-house mini computer over a 2 year period. All office functions were streamlined and computerised. In this time the company's business increased $2\frac{1}{2}$ times and yet the number of office staff stayed the same.
1983-1990	Served as a director of Distribution Computer Services Ltd, a company which provided computer systems to UK wholesale distributors in the food industry. Assisted in implementing solutions to their customers' computing requirements.
1985-1988	At the family business moved to Operations Director, managing a team of 50 people operating a head office, warehouse, transport department and printing section. Obtained the Road Transport Industry Training Board Certificate of Professional Competence in Road Transport, a qualification which was necessary to run a fleet of lorries.
1988-1991	Became Joint Managing Director. At this point the company provided a wholesale distribution service to 100+ independent retailers, operated 4 cash and carry warehouses and ran 31

	company owned supermarkets. Managed the central operations of the company with an emphasis in the areas of finance, insurance, property management and computer systems.
1991	The family business was sold and went to work for the Costcutter Group, based in Dunnington, York.
1991-1993	Administration Director, Costcutter Supermarkets Group. Principal task was to set up modern computer systems for the company's operations and its customers. Introduced to the customer base of 500+ retailers computer technology in the form of hand held terminals for placing orders electronically with suppliers. Also 100+ retailers installed scanning systems Incorporating the full range of Epos and EFTPos functionality from systems providers recommended by RIW. Installed a UNIX/ Progress warehouse distribution system, an invoicing and accounting system using Platinum Accounts/Magic/Novell and a central price file to send product and price information to customers' scanning sites.
1993-1997	Moved to a company, Micro Retailer Systems Ltd. which specialised in supplying accounting software and Epos systems to independent retailers, as Finance Director based in Macclesfield, Cheshire. Managed the Administrative functions of the Company including finance, accounts, billing, taxation and VAT, personnel, contracts with customers and

	suppliers.
1997	Moved home to Macclesfield, Cheshire.
1998-2000	The Company changed its name to MRS Software Ltd. Undertook the task of providing the primary training service to the Company's department store and furniture store customers in its accounting and stock control software.
2000-2001	MRS Software was sold to the Alphameric Group in December 2000. Provided implementation and training services to the group's customers, which included some major national retailers.
2001-2002	Worked as an independent consultant to some of his previous employers' customers.
2002-2008	Set up new company Retail Accounting Solutions Ltd, to provide accounting software to retail businesses. By 2008 it had grown to a team of 7 people, moving to new offices based in Trentham near Stoke-on-Trent, and in May 2008 acquired another company which supplies Epos and e-commerce systems to retail businesses. In August 2008 the company rebranded and gave itself a new name, Touchretail.
2007	On 2 June Susan married Dara O'Briain in London and they live in Chiswick, West London. Their first child, Orla Clementine, was born on 25 March. Susan is a graduate of Leeds University Medical School and works as a hospital registrar at Guys Hospital, London.

2008	Martin is a graduate of the University of Gloucestershire, Cheltenham. He works as a graphic designer and took a year away from work to take a round the world tour. He is now living in Paris with his partner Aurélie Buon.
2009	Jutta retired from being a home carer and is now taking a well earned rest, but planning several activities.

ANDREW MARTIN WILLIS

Date of birth: 25 March 1951 at Pindar Oaks Maternity Home, Barnsley.

Married:
10 May 1975 Lynn Joyce Hodson (born 12 September 1951), divorced June 1982.
13 March 1984 Gwyn Davies, divorced March 1992.
29 December 1995 Yvonne Sylvia Wood (born 17 August 1950), finding much contentment.

Children:
Sally, born 2 June 1982, a graduate of Huddersfield University, working in Marketing.
Simon, born 30 May 1985, a graduate of University of Central Lancashire, working as a sports journalist.
Yvonne's son Stephen, born 1970, a graduate of Nottingham Trent University, working in Senior Management in manufacturing. Married to Catriona, a teacher, with two children, Sophie and Thomas.

Interests:
Football, playing until 25, winning Huddersfield Cup with Emley FC.
Squash, playing until 50. Skiing since 21. Cycling.
Season tickets holders at Barnsley FC.
Walking in Derbyshire Dales with Ramblers.
Holidays abroad and in the UK, breaks at holiday lodge in Bude, North Cornwall.
Gardening, shopping and DIY.

Education:
1957-1962   Birdwell Junior and Infant School.
1962-1969   Barnsley Holgate Grammar School.
1969-1972   Bradford University Management Centre, BSc(Hons) in Business Studies.

Business Career:
1972-1991   RT Willis (Food Distributors) Ltd.
Commenced by opening a 40,000 sq ft Wholesale Cash & Carry Depot in Barnsley which is still successfully trading.
Received from trade magazine 'Supermarketing', an award as the special runner up to Sainsburys as the Retailer of the Year 1983.
Joint Managing Director in 1988 with specific responsibilities for marketing, buying and operations. Developed Willis Discount.
Main contributor in members voluntary liquidation which obtained a surplus to shareholders and continuous employment for

	employees with Kwik Save, Blakemores and Costcutter.
1991-2001	<u>AM Willis Supermarkets Ltd.</u> New family business with AM Willis 60% shareholder. Commenced with 3 stores. Obtained Investors in People Certificate in June 1997. Expanded to 14 convenience stores, with annual sales of £10m and 180 employees. Sold company to United Coop with a surplus to shareholders.
2001-2004	<u>AMW Consultancy Ltd</u> Retained by Coop to integrate Willis Supermarkets and acquire 10 new Coop stores in Yorkshire.
1991 to date	<u>WJ Hiscock & Son Ltd</u> New family business, AM Willis and YS Willis 85% shareholders, remaining 15% with children. Property investment company specialising in freehold convenience stores and betting shops with multiple retailers as tenants.

HOWARD JOHN WILLIS

Date of birth: 22 March 1957 at Pindar Oaks Maternity Home, Barnsley.

1962-1967	Educated at Birdwell Primary School.
1967-1975	Barnsley Holgate Grammar School, a 1st XI

	footballer.
1975-1978	Manchester University, graduating in Economics.
1978-1979	Chancery Lane, London – Law College.
1979-1980	Leeds Metropolitan University to prepare for and pass Law Society final examinations.
1980-1982	Maurice Smith, Solicitor, Castleford – 2 years training contract.
1982	Pursued law career with Fitzpatrick Jones for 2 years in Wakefield. Moved to Chadwick Son and Nicholson of Dewsbury which became Chadwick Lawrence working in Ossett, Wakefield and Huddersfield, becoming a partner specialising in Litigation, licensing and personal injury claims.
1985	4 December, appointed non executive director of RT Willis (Food Distributors) Ltd.
1986	6 April married Fiona Elizabeth Longbottom, born 20 January 1962. 2 December appointed a Director of Rialco Securities Ltd.
1988	Joshua Samuel born 29 May, currently in 2009 at Nottingham University.
1990	Elizabeth Maisie born 25 October.

BERTRAM TERENCE MARTIN WILLIS

Date of birth: 9 May 1927
Place of birth: Corrawallen, White Cross, Worsbrough Dale, Barnsley.

Profession: Research Physicist, University Professor.
Marriages:
1. 1950 to Nanette Goater (1928-1975). Two sons and one daughter: Michael Joseph (1952-), Alison Mary (1954-1981), Jonathan Timothy (1956-).
2. 1978 to Margaret Stella Helsby née Andrews (1921-). Three stepsons and one step-daughter: Richard John Stephen (1949-), James Thomas Randle (1953-), Mary Rachel (1955-), William Hugh Endacott (1958-).

Education:

1932-1938	Wilthorpe Primary School, Barnsley.
1938	Winner of Carnelley Scholarship (£150) of borough of Barnsley.
1938-1945	Attended Barnsley Holgate Grammar School.
1945	Awarded State Bursary and Exhibition Standard of Cambridge University.
1945-1948	Attended Cambridge University (Emmanuel College).
1947	Class 1 in Part I of Natural Science Tripos.
1947	Awarded Senior Scholarship of Emmanuel College.
1948	Class II-2 in part II of Natural Science Tripos.
1948-1951	London University: post-graduate student at Royal Holloway College studying for PhD in optics.
Degrees:	BA (Cantab), MA (Cantab), MA (Oxon), PhD (London), DSc (London).

Appointments in the UK:
1951-1954   Member of research staff of General Electric

	Company, London.
	Research on new magnetic materials.
1954-1984	Group Leader at Harwell Research Establishment, Berks.
	Research on radiation damage, neutron Scattering and nuclear materials.
1966-1974	Honorary Professorial Fellow of University College, Cardiff.
1970-1975	Honorary Professor of the University of Birmingham at Aston.
1984-2002	Senior Research Fellow, Inorganic Chemistry Laboratory, University of Oxford.

Overseas Appointments (each for one academic term):

1977	Visiting Professor of Chemistry at the University of Aarhus, Denmark.
1980	Visiting Professor of Physics at Banares Hindu University, India.
1983	Visiting Professor of Crystallography at the University of Lausanne, Switzerland.
1985	Visiting Professor of Physics at the University of Kyushu, Japan.

Career:

1961-1963	Designed and constructed the first instrument ('automatic four-circle diffractometer') for studying the molecular structures of actinides, proteins, enzymes. The work was undertaken in collaboration with Dr Ulrich Arndt of Cambridge University and Ferranti Ltd of Dalkeith, Edinburgh.
1966	Founder and first chairman of the biennial

	'Harwell Summer Schools' on Neutron Scattering. The Schools are attended world-wide by 50 young post-graduate students. The fortieth anniversary of the Schools was celebrated in 2006.
1975	Suffered from manic depression after death of first wife. Six week period in Fairmile Psychiatric Hospital, Wallingford.
1980-1990	British co-editor of the journal Acta Crystallographica published by the International Union of Crystallography.
1981	Manic depression after death of daughter, Alison in climbing accident. Restored to health thanks to the loving attention of wife, Margaret.
1984-1987	Chairman of the Neutron Diffraction Commission of the International Union of Crystallography.
1986	Elected Fellow of the UK Institute of Physics.
1990	Elected Honorary Member of the British Crystallographic Association '..for important contributions to neutron scattering, thermal motion and the properties of uranium compounds.' (Membership restricted to ten Members: three are Nobel Prize Winners.)
1997-2005	Invited by the Royal Swedish Academy of Sciences to submit proposals for the award of the Nobel Prize in Chemistry.
2002	Resigned as chairman of Harwell Summer Schools.
2002	Emeritus Professor of Chemistry in the University of Oxford.
2004	Inauguration by the UK Institute of Physics of

the annual 'Willis Prize' and the annual 'Willis Lecture'. The prize is awarded to any scientist under 35 years of age. It has been awarded so far to a Scottish chemist (2004), to a French physicist (2005) and to an Italian biologist (2006).

Books:
1966	Single Crystal Diffractometry with U. W. Arndt (Cambridge University Press).
1969	Thermal Neutron Diffraction with A. W. Pryor (Oxford University Press).
1971	Chemical applications of Neutron Scattering (Oxford University Press).
1975	Thermal Vibrations in Crystallography (Cambridge University Press).
2005	Experimental Neutron Scattering with C. J. Carlile (Oxford University Press).

Other Publications:
About 130 scientific papers and review articles published in journals of physics, chemistry and crystallography.
(Oxford, 4 August 2006)

MARY CHRISTINE BELLHOUSE (née Willis)

Date of Birth: 17 January 1930.
Married: 1960 to Arthur Edward Bellhouse, marriage ended in 1966.

1983 shared a house with colleague Jennifer Gosse (+ dogs!)
1990 retired from teaching.

Education

1935-1941	Wilthorpe Primary School.
1941-1948	Barnsley Girls' High School.
1948-1951	University College, London BA in English.
1956-1957	University of Oxford, Diploma in Education.
1976-1979	St Anne's College, Oxford BA degree in Chinese.

Work

1952-1956	Taught English at St Hilary's School, Sevenoaks.
1957-1960	Taught English at Christchurch Girls' Grammar School.
1960-1966	Head of English Department St Hilary's School, Sevenoaks.
1968-1976	Head of English Department Westwood School, Reading.
1980-1990	Taught English at Downe House, Cold Ash.

(English teaching divided between State and Private Schools).

Lectured in Reading University's Extra-mural department:
    1980 – English Literature
    1992-93 – Chinese History

W.E.A. Lecturing   1982-83 – Chinese History.

Newbury College Adult Studies Department, 1995 – Chinese History.

Current activities

Walk, garden, dog walk, read etc!

Also researched and wrote a biography of Thomas Manning 1772-1840, Sinologist, who travelled to Lhasa among other exploits. This was published in 2006 as a hard back, 225 pages, titled 'My Friend M'.

DOROTHY MAIVA BACON (née Nowell)

Date of Birth: 2 December 1924, daughter of Lily and Clifford Nowell. Born at 445 Leeds Road, Dewsbury, West Yorkshire.
Married: Theodore Bacon at the Friends Meeting House, Oxford on 2 April 1955.

Attended Dewsbury Moor Council School, followed by a scholarship to the Wheelwright Grammar School for Girls 1936-1943.

1943-1947	Manchester University, graduated in Geography and Geology.
1947-1951	Teacher at Eldon Road Infants School, Edmonton, London, average class size 45 infants in a school of 13 classes.
1951-1952	Advanced Nursery Training course, Darlington, Co Durham.
1952-1956	Cutteslowe Infants School, Oxford. Taught in 1-6 year old nursery class.
1960	Daughter Ruth born, 24 May.
1962	Son Adam born, 3 March.
1961-1963	The family moved to Leicester as Theodore took up a new accountancy position.

1963-1987	Family moved to Bishopsworth, Bristol where Theodore headed up the finance department at Arrowsmiths Book Printers and Dorothy did part time nursery teaching from 1969-1985.
1987	With Theodore, moved to York as their retirement destination.
1988	Took up residence in a bungalow at the Hartrigg Oaks Community Centre, New Earswick, York founded by the Joseph Rowntree Foundation. Supporting the family and the community it is an ideal base.

As practising Christians in the Quaker tradition Dorothy and Theodore support many activities in the community.

THEODORE SIDNEY BACON

Date of birth: 21 February 1927.
Married: Married 2 April 1955 Dorothy Maiva Nowell at the Friends Meeting House, Oxford.

1927-1931	Birmingham.
1931-1937	Newcastle on Tyne.
1937-1943	Friends School, Great Ayton, Near Middlesborough (home was in Newcastle).
1943-1945	Accounting training as an articled clerk with a practice in Newcastle.
1945-1946	Served with the Forestry Commission in Kent. Served with Dartington Hall forestry department in Devon.

1946-1948	Completing education.
1948-1951	Articled Clerk in the City of London.
1951-1953	Two years in Austria engaged in social work with refugees.
1953-1961	Resumed accountancy training in Oxford. Qualified as a Chartered Accountant in 1956. Employed by Oxford University Press.
1961-1963	Chartered Accountant with Ashwell & Nesbitt Engineers, Leicester.
1963-1987	Finance Director, Arrowsmiths book printers, Bristol. Set up home at Bishopsworth, Bristol.
1987	Retired with Dorothy to York.
1998	Took up residence at Hartrigg Oak Retirement Community, New Earswick, York founded by the Joseph Rowntree Foundation.

MARJORIE ALICE NOWELL

Date of Birth: 8 January 1927.
Youngest daughter of Clifford and Lily Nowell. Born at 14 Moorend Lane, Dewsbury, West Yorkshire.

Attended Dewsbury Moor Council School, followed by a scholarship to the Wheelwright Grammar School for Girls.

Left the Wheelwright Grammar School at age 17 in 1944 to work in a wartime nursery. Stayed a short time, leaving to take up nursery nurses training (15-18 months) at Rugby. At age 19 became a Nanny at Limpsfield, Surrey where she was rather unhappy, resulting in her father, Clifford, bringing her home to Moorend Lane, Dewsbury.

1946	Having been certificated at Rugby, employed at a day nursery at Hillingdon, Uxbridge.
1947	Enrolled at Hillingdon General Hospital.
1950	Qualified as a State Registered Nurse. Went to St Giles Hospital, Camberwell for Part 1 Midwifery.
1951	To Lewisham General Hospital for Part 2 Midwifery where qualified as a State Registered Midwife.
1953-1954	Attend Ridgland Bible College, Bexley, Kent paid for by legacy from Uncle Harold.
1954	One year's night duty as an SRN at Bermondsey Medical Mission.
1955	Resigned from Bermondsey Medical Mission, having received a call from God to join the Overseas Missionary Fellowship. Applied in March 1955 and reported to Newington Green for preparation. In October disembarked at Singapore from SS Corfu. In Singapore contracted Diabetes, diagnosed in Singapore General Hospital. Stayed in Singapore to be stabilised.
1956	To Bangkok, Thailand in April under the care of Dr Christopher Maddox. Studied the Thai language in Bangkok. Moved to Uthai to work with leprosy patients. In August to Manorom Hospital, 150 miles north of Bangkok. Duties were nursing and midwifery to 1963.

1963	Moved to Saiburi, south near the Malayan border, on the coast. Became a teacher of 'Nurse Aides', mostly Thai, some Malay. Stayed 14 years with leave back to UK every 3 years or so. During these years the missionaries all received equal pay, depending upon funds received by the Mission. Whilst at Saiburi had to prepare lectures in Thai as there were no Thai text books at that time. Students were trained over 3 years. They worked in the OMF hospital and studied in their spare time.
1978	Returned to the UK to work in the office of the OMF at Sevenoaks, Kent.
1985	Retired after 30 years with the OMF. Lived with Naomi Kelly, retired widow of the Revd Leslie Kelly (C of E), as a companion from 1978 to 1991.
1991	Moved to a flat at Cornford House, Pembury, Tunbridge Wells.
2005	She was very happy at Cornford House, giving help where needed to the residents. In the early hours of the night 21/22 November Marjorie suffered a severe heart attack. She died very peacefully on Sunday 23 November 2008.

The certificates and photograph reproduced below are contained in the family archives supporting this family history.

China Inland Mission

Marjorie A. Nowell

received into the Fellowship of the Mission on 12th September 1955

George A Scott, Home Director
Norman ...., Secretary

Above: On the reverse of this certificate Marjorie has written an extract from Psalm 139 v 9/10.
Below: 14 December 1961, Marjorie promoted to Senior Missionary status for her work at Manorom Hospital.

Overseas Missionary Fellowship
of the
China Inland Mission
Senior Certificate

This is to certify that

Miss M. Nowell

was recognized as a Senior Missionary at a Meeting of the Headquarters Staff held in Singapore on December 14, 1961.

Arnold Lea, Director
............., Director
Herbert F. Rowe, Secretary

"Being confident of this very thing, that he which hath begun a good work in you will perform it until the day of Jesus Christ" Phil. 1:6

Above: Certification ceremony Saiburi Hospital 1972, Marjorie far left back row.
Below: A lifetime achievement.

Certificate of Appreciation

Presented to

Marjorie A. Nowell

who has completed 31 *years of faithful active service with*

The Overseas Missionary Fellowship

(formerly China Inland Mission)

The family members wish to express their gratitude

10 May 1991
Date of issue

James Hudson Taylor III
General Director

EPILOGUE

Putting together this family history has not been an easy task, made increasingly difficult with failing eyesight. Without the ability of Paulette to read and interpret my scribble the task would have been impossible to complete. Deteriorating eyesight has made it virtually impossible to read what I have just written, but Joan, as always, has helped with interpretation, spelling and dictionaries. To both these ladies and all the contributors to this family history my sincere thanks indeed for your support.

When reading this family history, with its many personal stories, I am aware that individuals who share the same experiences often take a different view or interpretation of the events described. Our memories are selective and our knowledge of individual circumstances often limited. I hope that future generations will be able to use this compendium of family stories and statistics as a basis for future research on where we came from and what contribution our forebears made to society.

Since compiling the above I have had an operation on my right eye, by Mr ET James, an eye surgeon, who has inserted two lenses, one in front and one behind the iris. The operation was in August 2008 and should halt further sight deterioration for some time. As I write in May 2009, the operation has proved a great success and now enables me to read typescript, albeit at a fairly slow pace.

I close with a favourite photograph as we sit in the front garden at Greenways, a location which continues to give us much pleasure, peace and joy.

APPENDIX

Joseph Willis (m 1701) to Daniel Willis 1757-1840

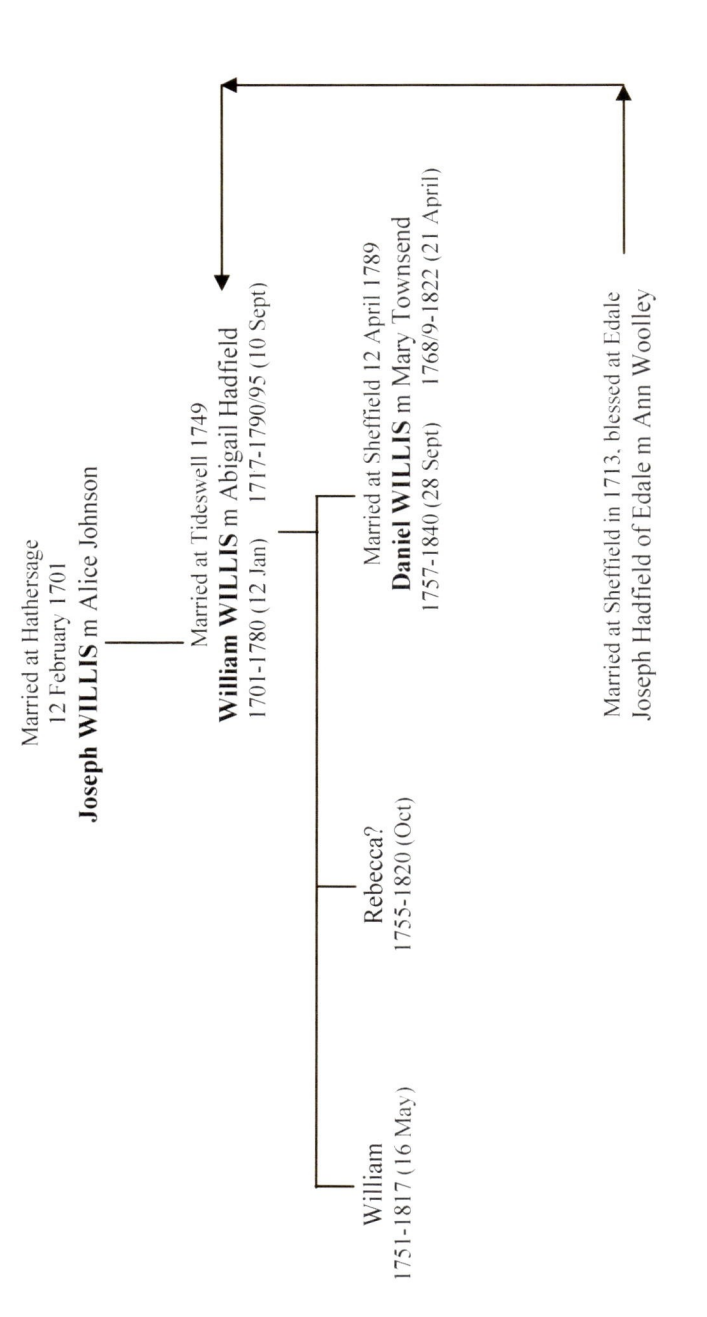

Married at Hathersage
12 February 1701
Joseph WILLIS m Alice Johnson

Married at Tideswell 1749
William WILLIS m Abigail Hadfield
1701-1780 (12 Jan)   1717-1790/95 (10 Sept)

Married at Sheffield 12 April 1789
Daniel WILLIS m Mary Townsend
1757-1840 (28 Sept)   1768/9-1822 (21 April)

Married at Sheffield in 1713, blessed at Edale
Joseph Hadfield of Edale m Ann Woolley

Rebecca?
1755-1820 (Oct)

William
1751-1817 (16 May)

Daniel Willis 1757-1840 to George Willis 1808-1844

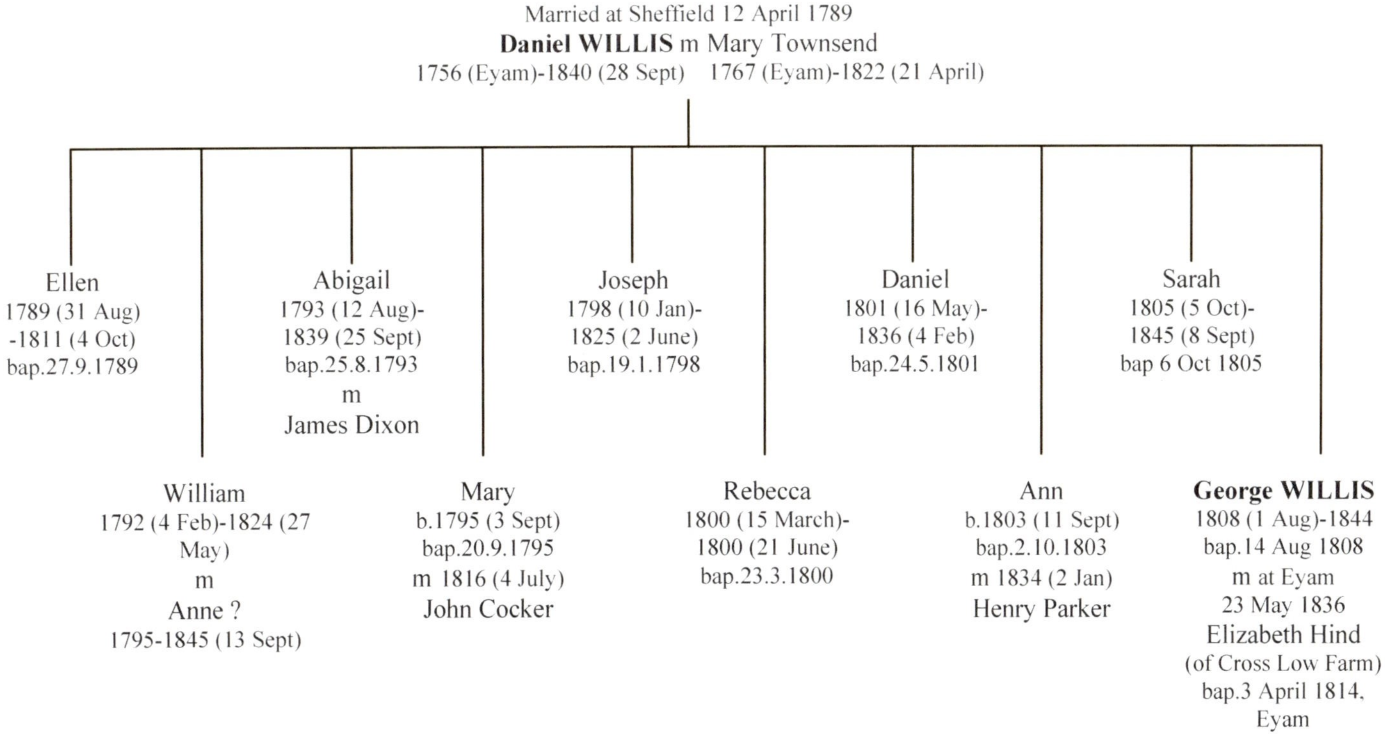

Married at Sheffield 12 April 1789
Daniel WILLIS m Mary Townsend
1756 (Eyam)-1840 (28 Sept)   1767 (Eyam)-1822 (21 April)

Ellen
1789 (31 Aug)
-1811 (4 Oct)
bap.27.9.1789

Abigail
1793 (12 Aug)-
1839 (25 Sept)
bap.25.8.1793
m
James Dixon

William
1792 (4 Feb)-1824 (27 May)
m
Anne ?
1795-1845 (13 Sept)

Mary
b.1795 (3 Sept)
bap.20.9.1795
m 1816 (4 July)
John Cocker

Joseph
1798 (10 Jan)-
1825 (2 June)
bap.19.1.1798

Rebecca
1800 (15 March)-
1800 (21 June)
bap.23.3.1800

Daniel
1801 (16 May)-
1836 (4 Feb)
bap.24.5.1801

Ann
b.1803 (11 Sept)
bap.2.10.1803
m 1834 (2 Jan)
Henry Parker

Sarah
1805 (5 Oct)-
1845 (8 Sept)
bap 6 Oct 1805

George WILLIS
1808 (1 Aug)-1844
bap.14 Aug 1808
m at Eyam
23 May 1836
Elizabeth Hind
(of Cross Low Farm)
bap.3 April 1814.
Eyam

George Willis siblings

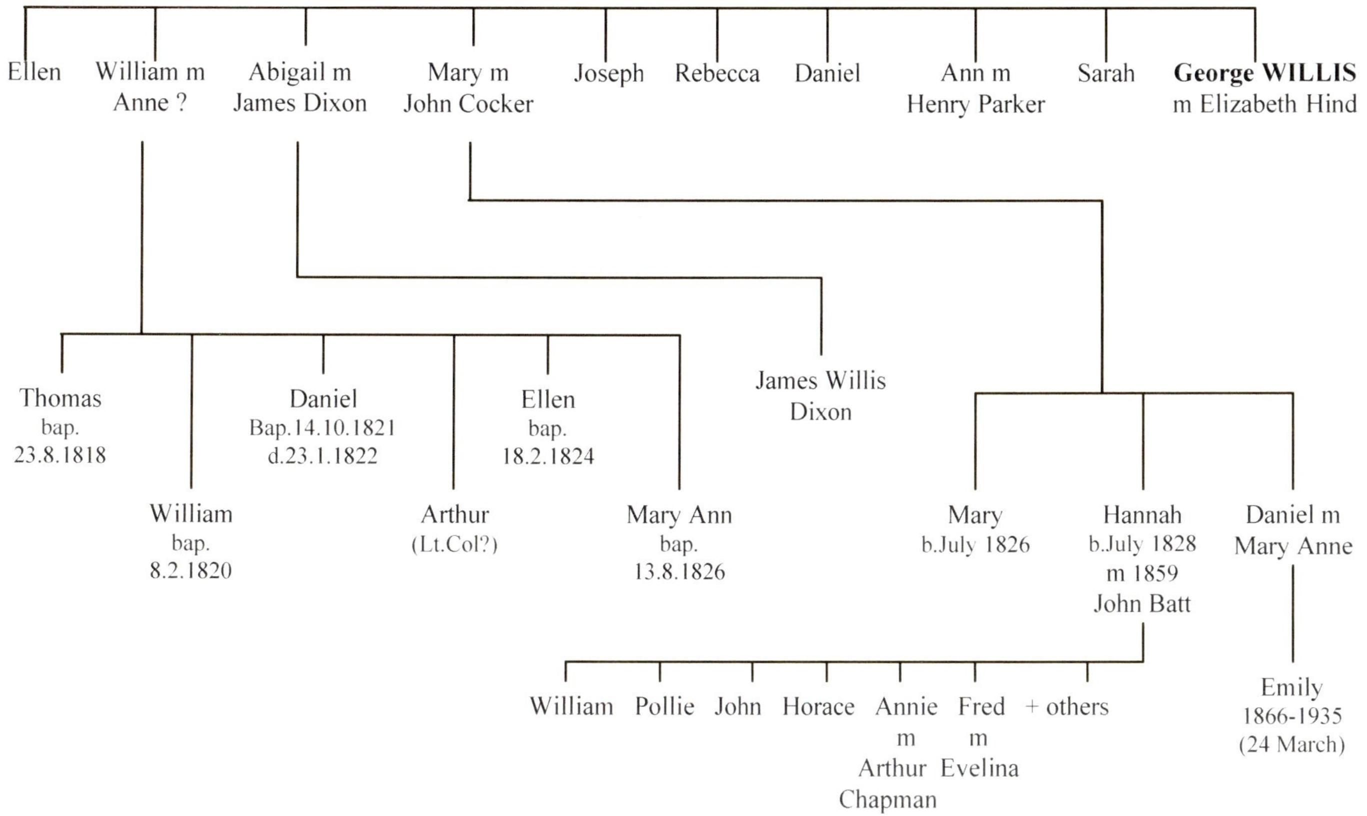
Ellen
William m Anne ?
Abigail m James Dixon
Mary m John Cocker
Joseph
Rebecca
Daniel
Ann m Henry Parker
Sarah
George WILLIS m Elizabeth Hind
Thomas bap. 23.8.1818
William bap. 8.2.1820
Daniel Bap.14.10.1821 d.23.1.1822
Arthur (Lt.Col?)
Ellen bap. 18.2.1824
Mary Ann bap. 13.8.1826
James Willis Dixon
Mary b.July 1826
Hannah b.July 1828 m 1859 John Batt
Daniel m Mary Anne
William
Pollie
John
Horace
Annie m Arthur Chapman
Fred m Evelina
+ others
Emily 1866-1935 (24 March)

**George Willis 1808-1844 to
George Hamlet Willis 1840-1898**

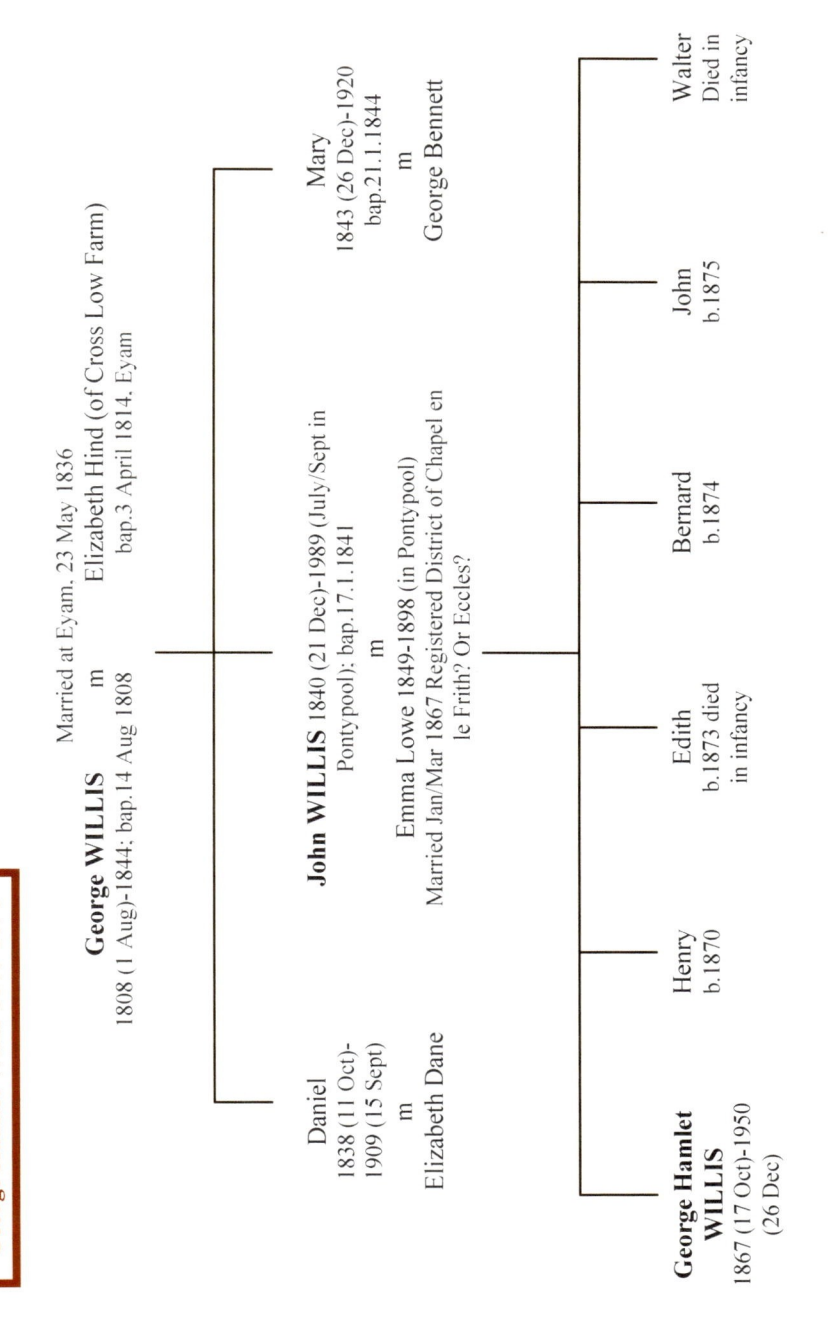

Married at Eyam. 23 May 1836

George WILLIS   m   Elizabeth Hind (of Cross Low Farm)
1808 (1 Aug)-1844; bap.14 Aug 1808   bap.3 April 1814. Eyam

Daniel
1838 (11 Oct)-
1909 (15 Sept)
m
Elizabeth Dane

John WILLIS 1840 (21 Dec)-1989 (July/Sept in Pontypool): bap.17.1.1841
m
Emma Lowe 1849-1898 (in Pontypool)
Married Jan/Mar 1867 Registered District of Chapel en le Frith? Or Eccles?

Mary
1843 (26 Dec)-1920
bap.21.1.1844
m
George Bennett

Henry
b.1870

Edith
b.1873 died
in infancy

George Hamlet WILLIS
1867 (17 Oct)-1950
(26 Dec)

Bernard
b.1874

John
b.1875

Walter
Died in
infancy

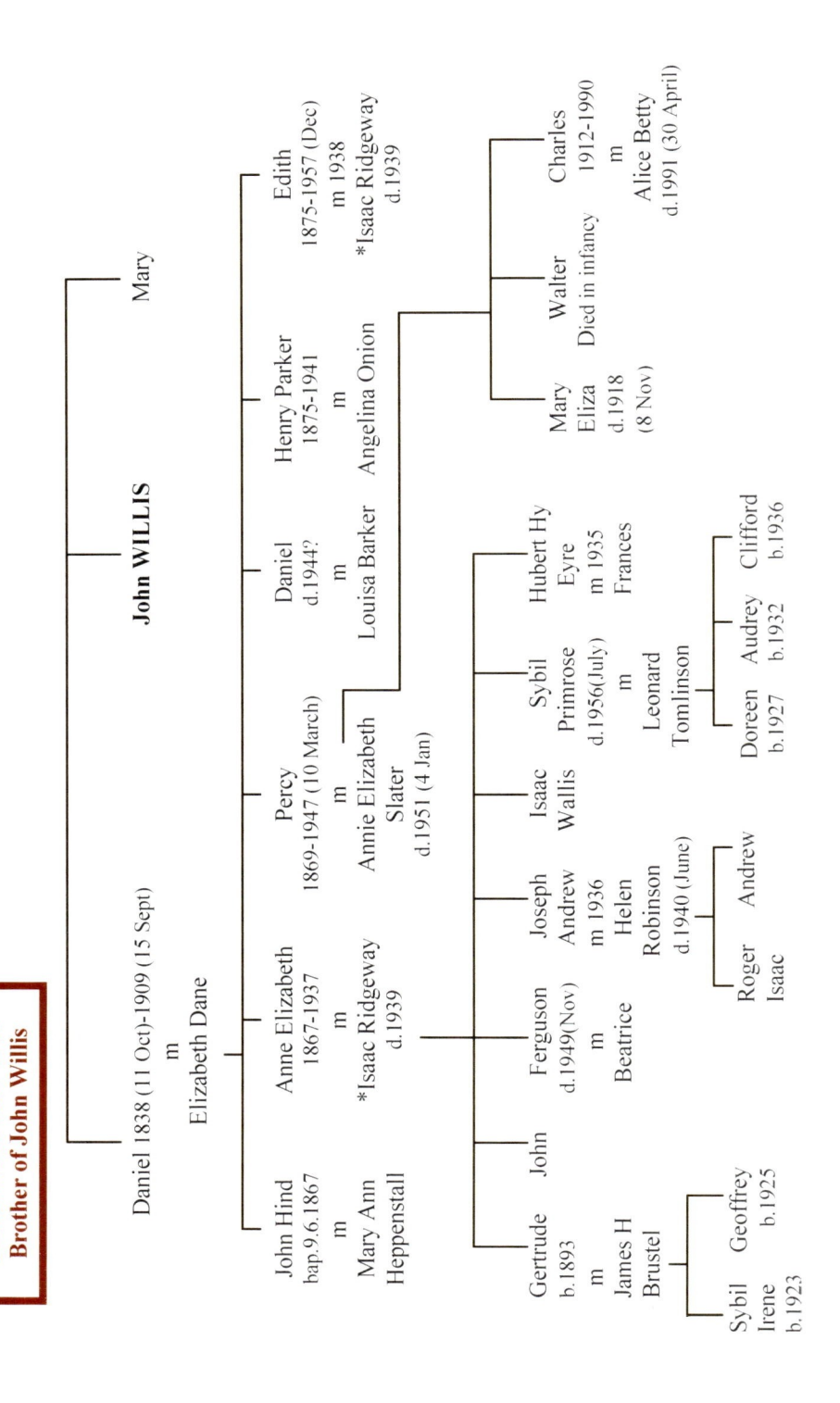

**Daniel Willis 1834-1909
Brother of John Willis**

Daniel 1838 (11 Oct)-1909 (15 Sept)
m
Elizabeth Dane

John WILLIS

Mary

- Anne Elizabeth
  1867-1937
  m
  *Isaac Ridgeway
  d.1939

- Percy
  1869-1947 (10 March)
  m
  Annie Elizabeth Slater
  d.1951 (4 Jan)

- Daniel
  d.1944?
  m
  Louisa Barker

- Edith
  1875-1957 (Dec)
  m 1938
  *Isaac Ridgeway
  d.1939

- Henry Parker
  1875-1941
  m
  Angelina Onion

John Hind
bap.9.6.1867
m
Mary Ann Heppenstall

John

Gertrude b.1893
m
James H Brustel

- Sybil Irene b.1923
- Geoffrey b.1925

Ferguson
d.1949(Nov)
m
Beatrice

Joseph Andrew
m 1936
Helen Robinson
d.1940 (June)

- Roger
- Andrew Isaac

Isaac Wallis

Sybil Primrose
d.1956(July)
m
Leonard Tomlinson

- Doreen b.1927
- Audrey b.1932
- Clifford b.1936

Hubert Hy Eyre
m 1935
Frances

Mary Eliza
d.1918 (8 Nov)

Walter
Died in infancy

Charles
1912-1990
m
Alice Betty
d.1991 (30 April)

George Hamlet Willis 1867-1950 to
George Robert Thomas Willis b.1921

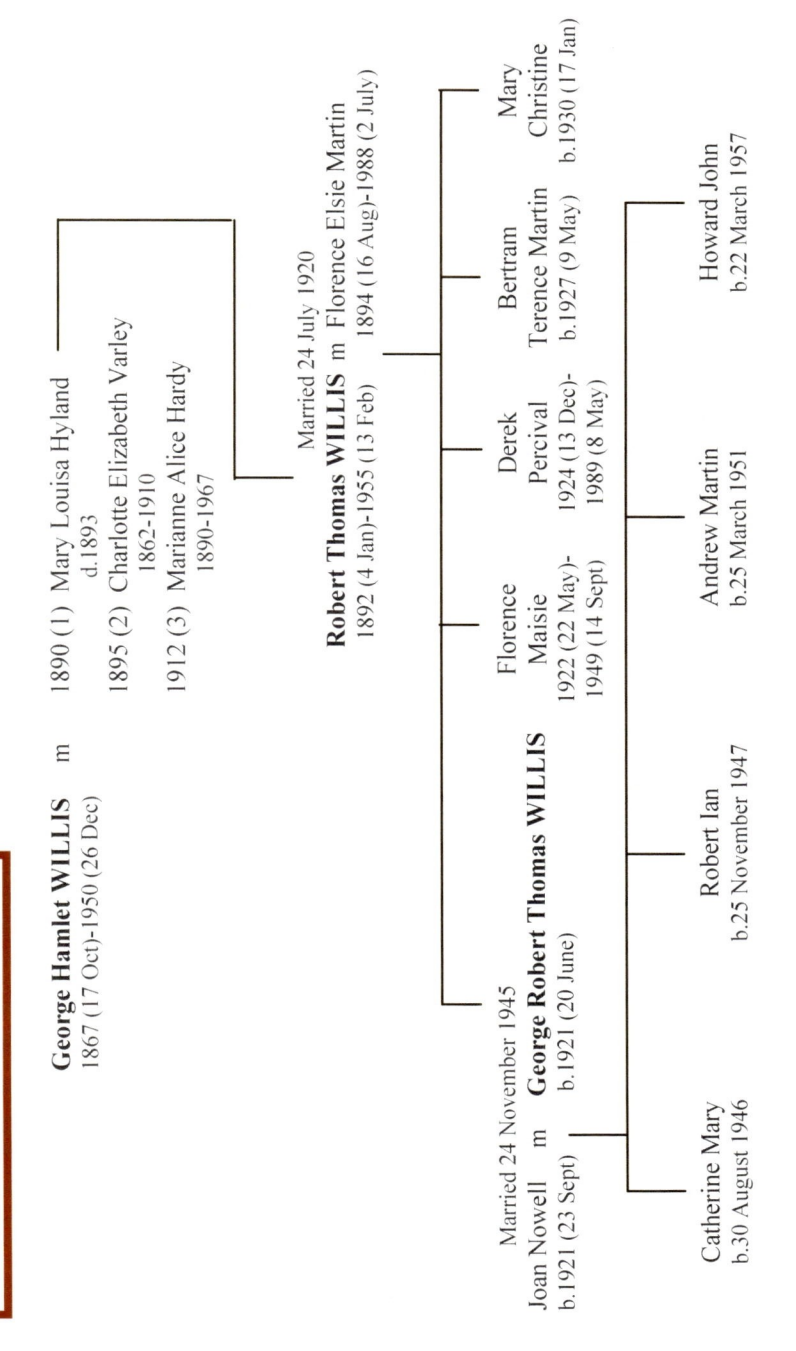

George Hamlet WILLIS   m   1890 (1) Mary Louisa Hyland
1867 (17 Oct)-1950 (26 Dec)   d.1893
                                         1895 (2) Charlotte Elizabeth Varley
                                                 1862-1910
                                         1912 (3) Marianne Alice Hardy
                                                 1890-1967

Married 24 July 1920
Robert Thomas WILLIS m Florence Elsie Martin
1892 (4 Jan)-1955 (13 Feb)   1894 (16 Aug)-1988 (2 July)

| Florence Maisie 1922 (22 May)-1949 (14 Sept) | Derek Percival 1924 (13 Dec)-1989 (8 May) | Bertram Terence Martin b.1927 (9 May) | Mary Christine b.1930 (17 Jan) |

Married 24 November 1945
Joan Nowell   m   **George Robert Thomas WILLIS**
b.1921 (23 Sept)   b.1921 (20 June)

| Catherine Mary b.30 August 1946 | Robert Ian b.25 November 1947 | Andrew Martin b.25 March 1951 | Howard John b.22 March 1957 |

George Hamlet Willis 1867-1950 to
Monica 1913-2008 and Joan 1915-2009

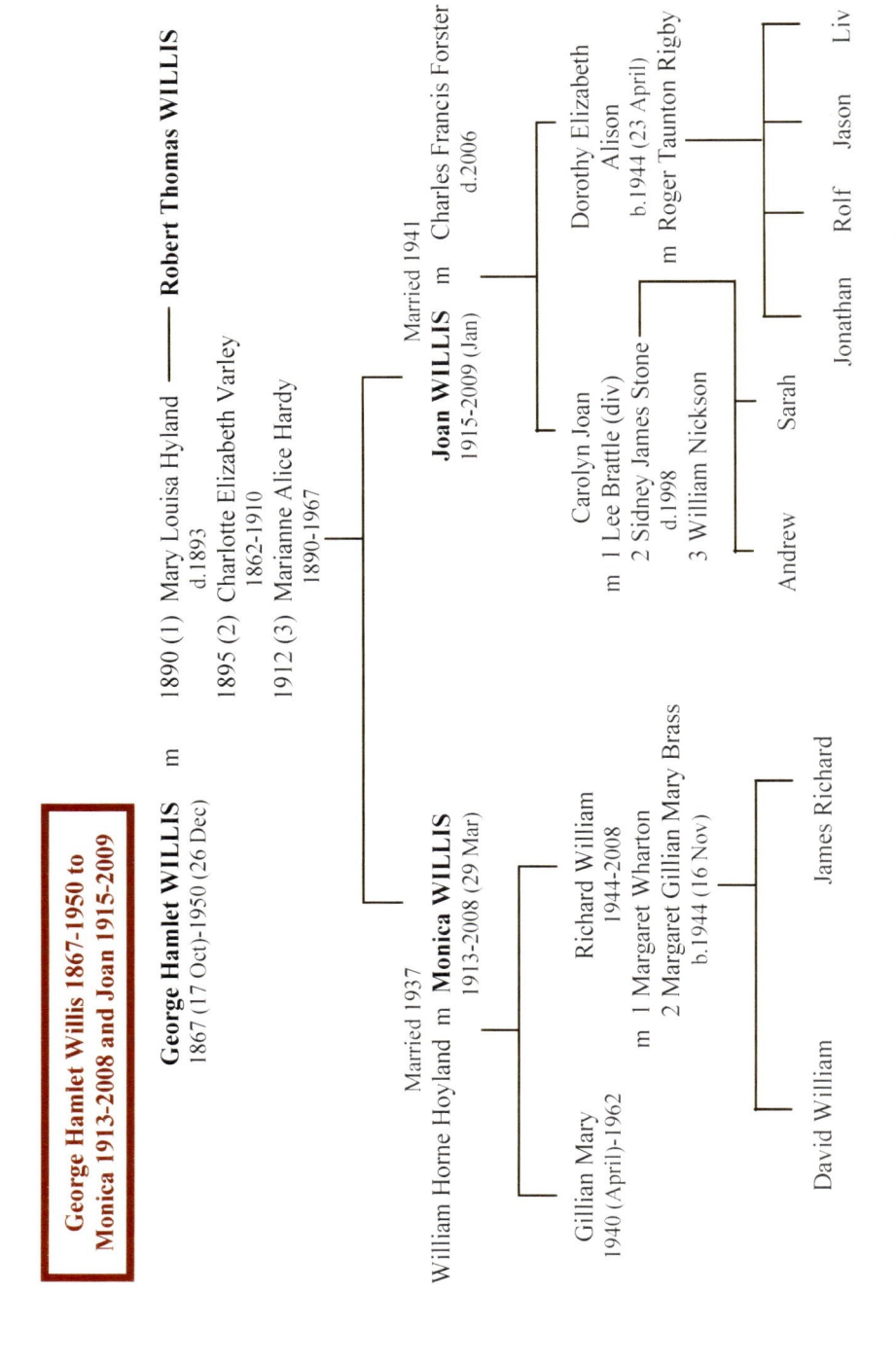

George Hamlet WILLIS m 1890 (1) Mary Louisa Hyland ——— **Robert Thomas WILLIS**
1867 (17 Oct)-1950 (26 Dec)   d.1893
                                1895 (2) Charlotte Elizabeth Varley
                                         1862-1910
                                1912 (3) Marianne Alice Hardy
                                         1890-1967

Married 1941
Joan WILLIS m Charles Francis Forster
1915-2009 (Jan)   d.2006

Carolyn Joan   Dorothy Elizabeth
m 1 Lee Brattle (div)   Alison
  2 Sidney James Stone   b.1944 (23 April)
    d.1998   m Roger Taunton Rigby
  3 William Nickson

Andrew   Sarah   Jonathan   Rolf   Jason   Liv

Married 1937
William Horne Hoyland m **Monica WILLIS**
                          1913-2008 (29 Mar)

Gillian Mary   Richard William
1940 (April)-1962   1944-2008
                          m 1 Margaret Wharton
                            2 Margaret Gillian Mary Brass
                              b.1944 (16 Nov)

David William   James Richard

George Robert Thomas Willis b.1921

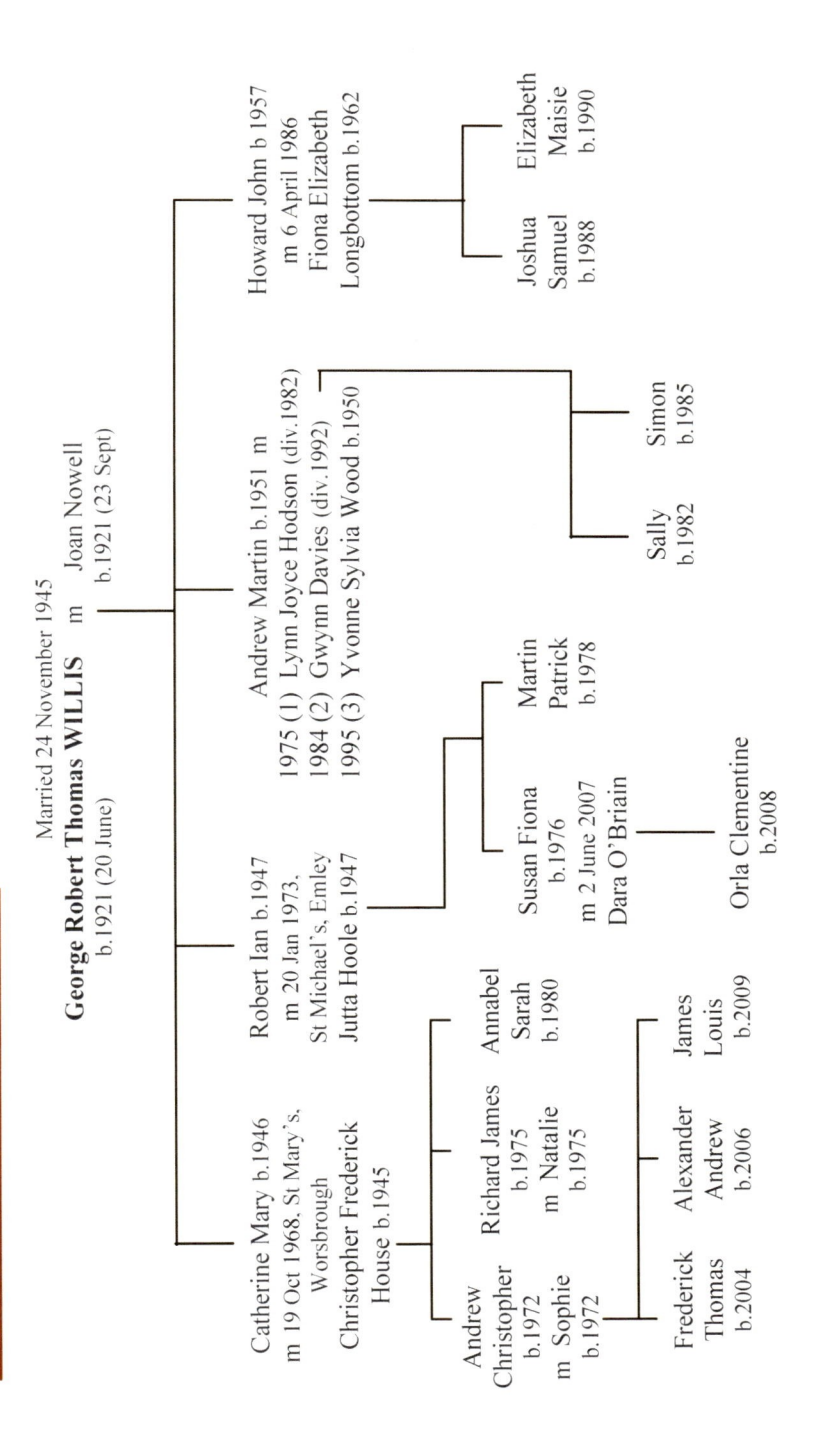

Married 24 November 1945
George Robert Thomas WILLIS m Joan Nowell
b.1921 (20 June) b.1921 (23 Sept)

Catherine Mary b.1946
m 19 Oct 1968, St Mary's, Worsbrough
Christopher Frederick House b.1945

- Andrew Christopher b.1972 m Sophie b.1972
  - Frederick Thomas b.2004
  - Alexander Andrew b.2006
  - James Louis b.2009
- Richard James b.1975 m Natalie b.1975
- Annabel Sarah b.1980

Robert Ian b.1947
m 20 Jan 1973, St Michael's, Emley
Jutta Hoole b.1947

- Susan Fiona b.1976
  m 2 June 2007
  Dara O'Briain
  - Orla Clementine b.2008
- Martin Patrick b.1978

Andrew Martin b.1951 m
1975 (1) Lynn Joyce Hodson (div.1982)
1984 (2) Gwynn Davies (div.1992)
1995 (3) Yvonne Sylvia Wood b.1950

- Sally b.1982
- Simon b.1985

Howard John b.1957
m 6 April 1986
Fiona Elizabeth Longbottom b.1962

- Joshua Samuel b.1988
- Elizabeth Maisie b.1990

**George Martin c.1830 to
William Alfred Martin 1856-1947**

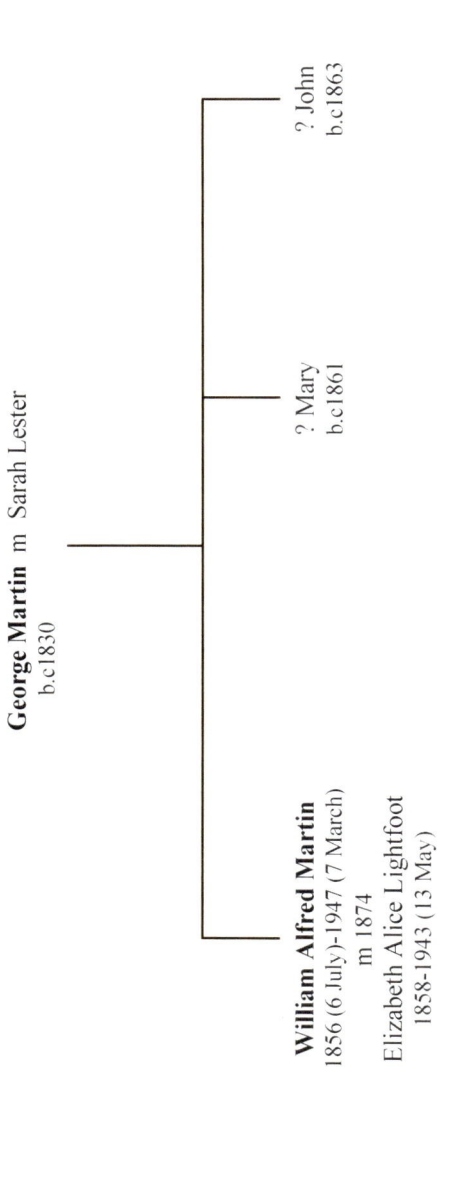

George Martin m Sarah Lester
b.c1830

- **William Alfred Martin**
  1856 (6 July)–1947 (7 March)
  m 1874
  Elizabeth Alice Lightfoot
  1858–1943 (13 May)
- ? Mary
  b.c1861
- ? John
  b.c1863

William Alfred Martin 1856-1947

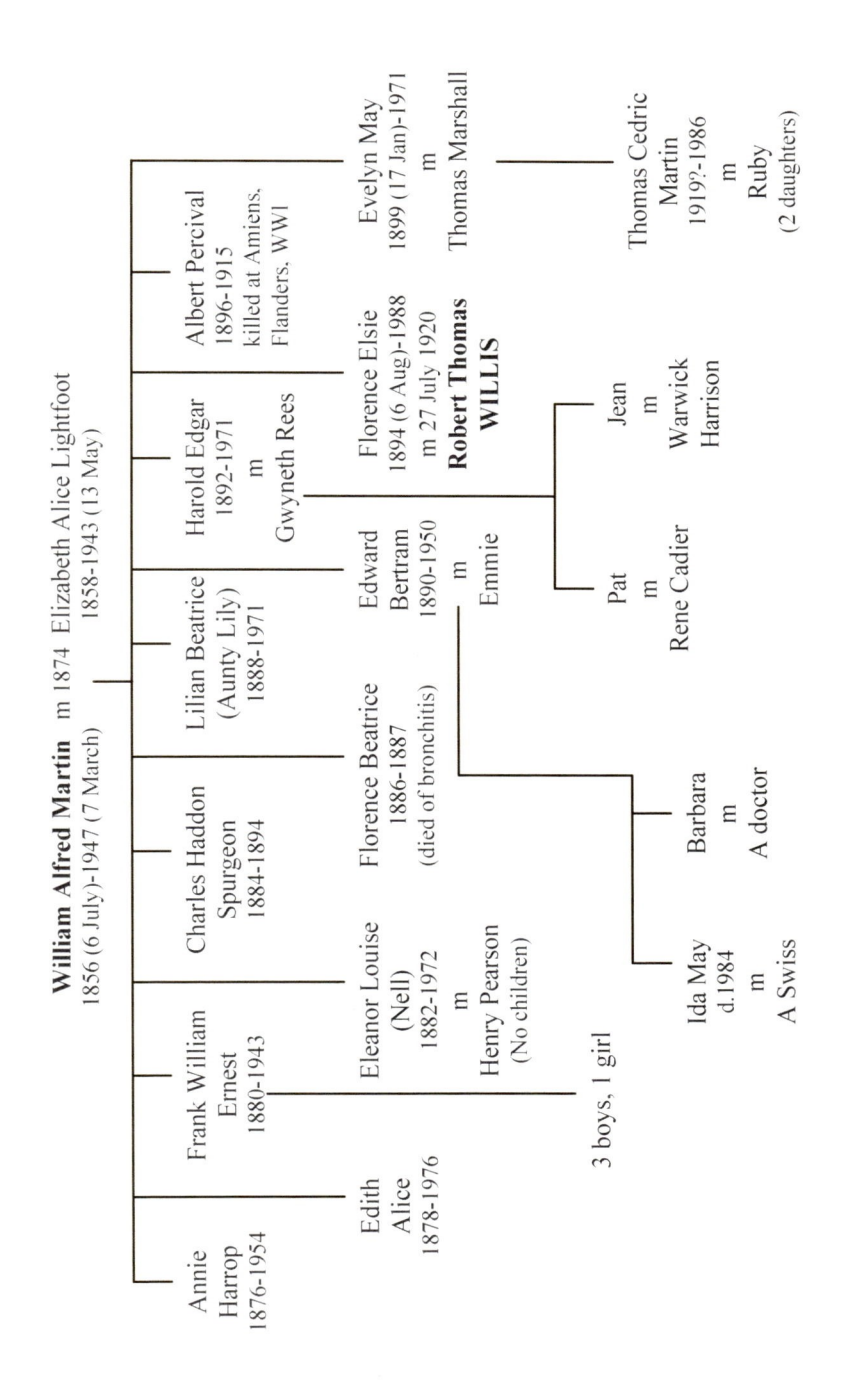

William Alfred Martin m 1874 Elizabeth Alice Lightfoot
1856 (6 July)-1947 (7 March) 1858-1943 (13 May)

- Annie Harrop 1876-1954
- Edith Alice 1878-1976
- Frank William Ernest 1880-1943
- Eleanor Louise (Nell) 1882-1972 m Henry Pearson (No children)
- Charles Haddon Spurgeon 1884-1894
- Florence Beatrice 1886-1887 (died of bronchitis)
- Lilian Beatrice (Aunty Lily) 1888-1971
- Edward Bertram 1890-1950 m Emmie
- Harold Edgar 1892-1971 m Gwyneth Rees
- Florence Elsie 1894 (6 Aug)-1988 m 27 July 1920 **Robert Thomas WILLIS**
- Albert Percival 1896-1915 killed at Amiens, Flanders. WWI
- Evelyn May 1899 (17 Jan)-1971 m Thomas Marshall

3 boys, 1 girl

- Ida May d.1984 m A Swiss
- Barbara m A doctor

- Pat m Rene Cadier
- Jean m Warwick Harrison

- Thomas Cedric Martin 19l9?-1986 m Ruby (2 daughters)

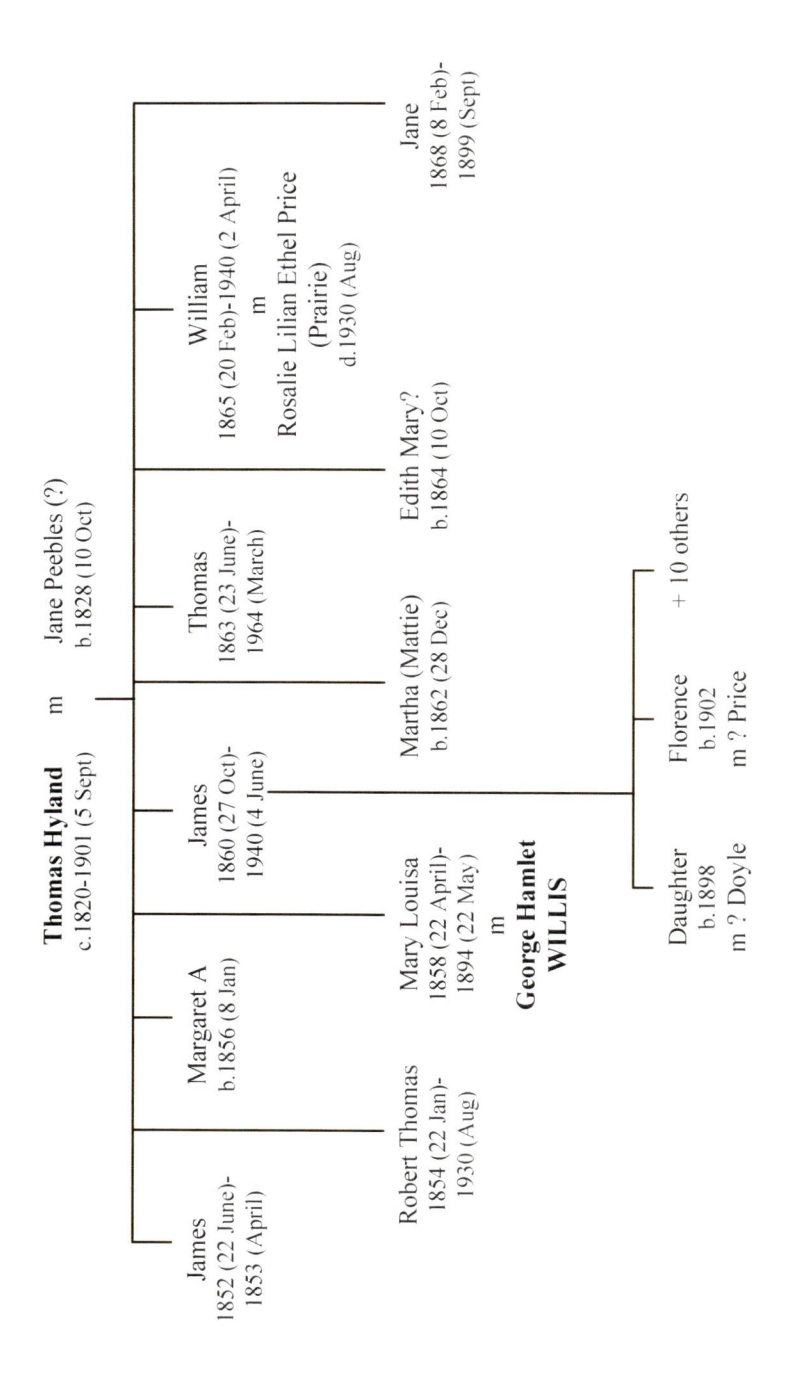

Thomas Hyland c.1820-1901

Thomas Hyland c.1820-1901 (5 Sept) m Jane Peebles (?) b.1828 (10 Oct)

- James 1852 (22 June)-1853 (April)
- Robert Thomas 1854 (22 Jan)-1930 (Aug)
- Margaret A b.1856 (8 Jan)
- Mary Louisa 1858 (22 April)-1894 (22 May) m **George Hamlet WILLIS**
- James 1860 (27 Oct)-1940 (4 June)
- Martha (Mattie) b.1862 (28 Dec)
- Thomas 1863 (23 June)-1964 (March)
- Edith Mary? b.1864 (10 Oct)
- William 1865 (20 Feb)-1940 (2 April) m Rosalie Lilian Ethel Price (Prairie) d.1930 (Aug)
- Jane 1868 (8 Feb)-1899 (Sept)

Children of Mary Louisa and George Hamlet Willis:
- Daughter b.1898 m ? Doyle
- Florence b.1902 m ? Price
- + 10 others

William Hyland 1865-1940

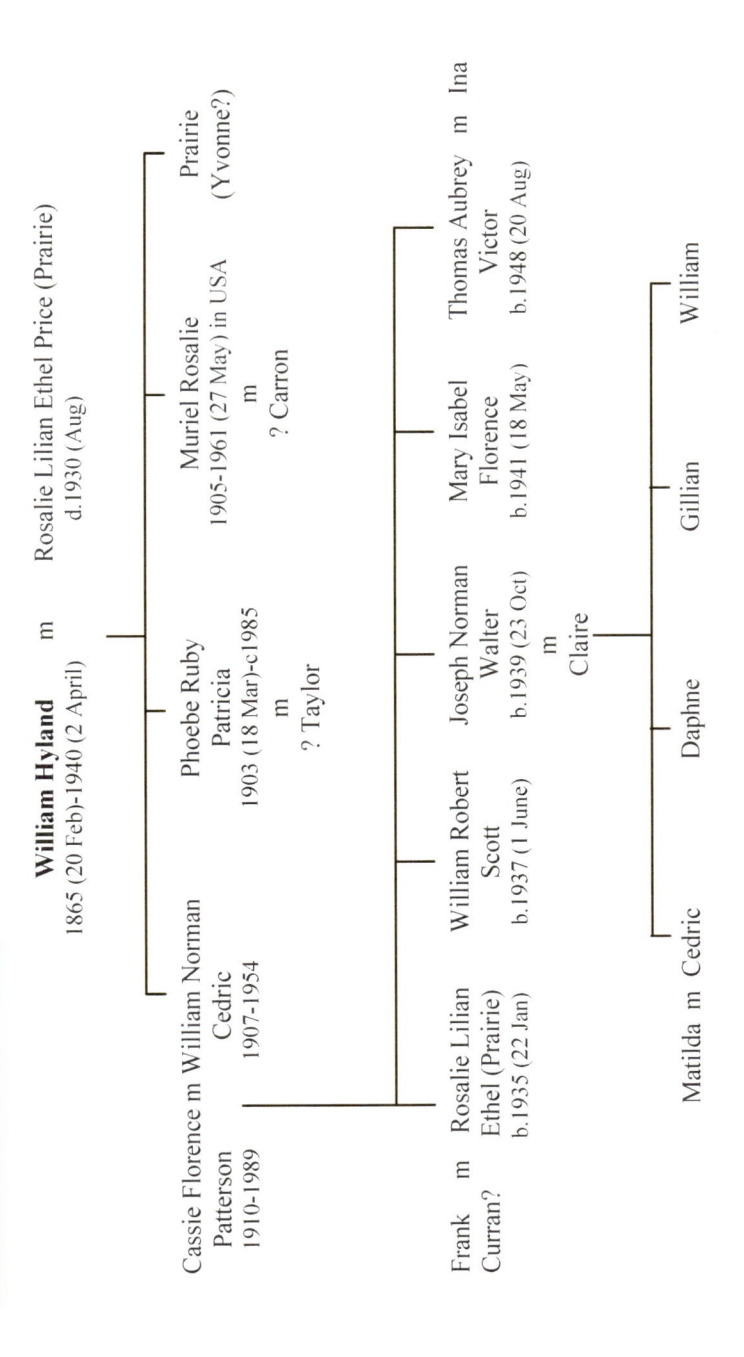

William Hyland m Rosalie Lilian Ethel Price (Prairie)
1865 (20 Feb)-1940 (2 April)   d.1930 (Aug)

Children:
- Cassie Florence Patterson 1910-1989 m William Norman Cedric 1907-1954
- Phoebe Ruby Patricia 1903 (18 Mar)-c1985 m ? Taylor
- Muriel Rosalie 1905-1961 (27 May) in USA m ? Carron
- Prairie (Yvonne?)

Children of Cassie Florence and William Norman Cedric:
- Rosalie Lilian Ethel (Prairie) b.1935 (22 Jan) m Frank Curran?
- William Robert Scott b.1937 (1 June)
- Joseph Norman Walter b.1939 (23 Oct) m Claire
- Mary Isabel Florence b.1941 (18 May)
- Thomas Aubrey Victor b.1948 (20 Aug) m Ina

Children of Joseph Norman Walter and Claire:
- Matilda m Cedric
- Daphne
- Gillian
- William

The Lowe Family

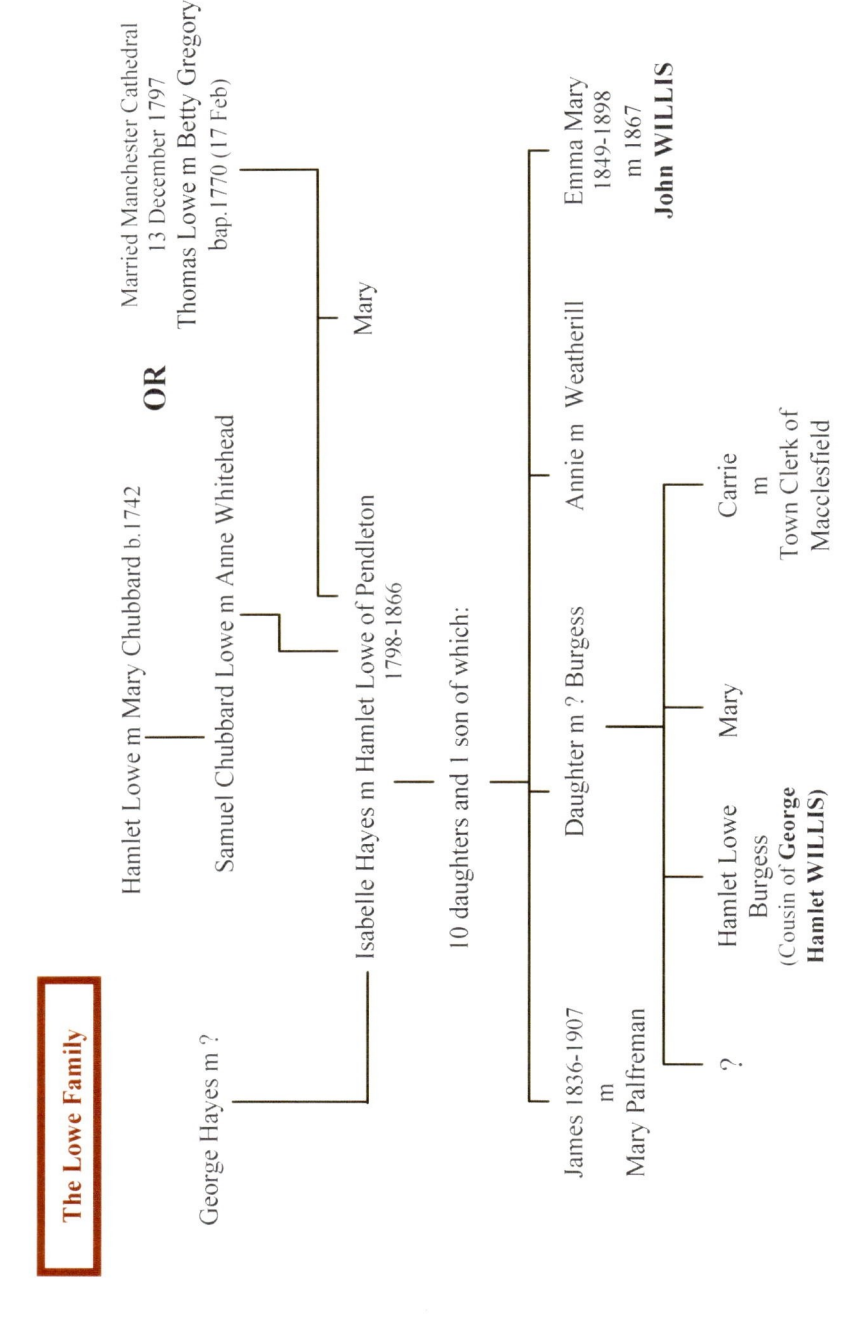

Hamlet Lowe m Mary Chubbard b.1742

Samuel Chubbard Lowe m Anne Whitehead

OR

Married Manchester Cathedral
13 December 1797
Thomas Lowe m Betty Gregory
bap.1770 (17 Feb)

Mary

George Hayes m ?

Isabelle Hayes m Hamlet Lowe of Pendleton
1798-1866

10 daughters and 1 son of which:

James 1836-1907
m
Mary Palfreman

Daughter m ? Burgess

Annie m Weatherill

Emma Mary
1849-1898
m 1867
John WILLIS

?

Hamlet Lowe Burgess
(Cousin of **George Hamlet WILLIS**)

Mary

Carrie
m
Town Clerk of Macclesfield

The Hind Family

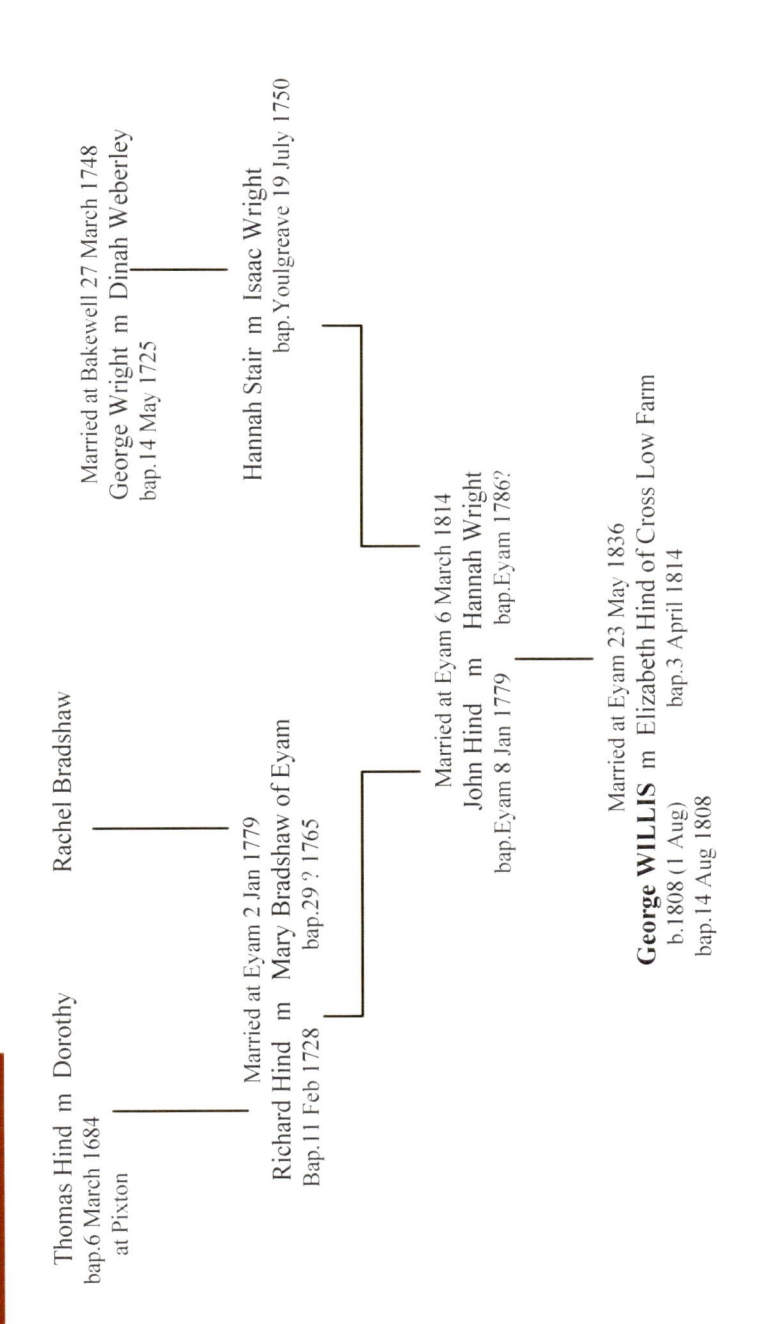

Thomas Hind m Dorothy
bap. 6 March 1684
at Pixton

Rachel Bradshaw

Richard Hind m Mary Bradshaw of Eyam
Bap. 11 Feb 1728   bap. 29 ? 1765
Married at Eyam 2 Jan 1779

Married at Bakewell 27 March 1748
George Wright m Dinah Weberley
bap. 14 May 1725

Hannah Stair m Isaac Wright
bap. Youlgreave 19 July 1750

John Hind m Hannah Wright
bap. Eyam 8 Jan 1779   bap. Eyam 1786?
Married at Eyam 6 March 1814

George **WILLIS** m Elizabeth Hind of Cross Low Farm
b. 1808 (1 Aug)   bap. 3 April 1814
bap. 14 Aug 1808
Married at Eyam 23 May 1836

Benjamin Nowell b.1750 to Jacob Nowell 1839-1882

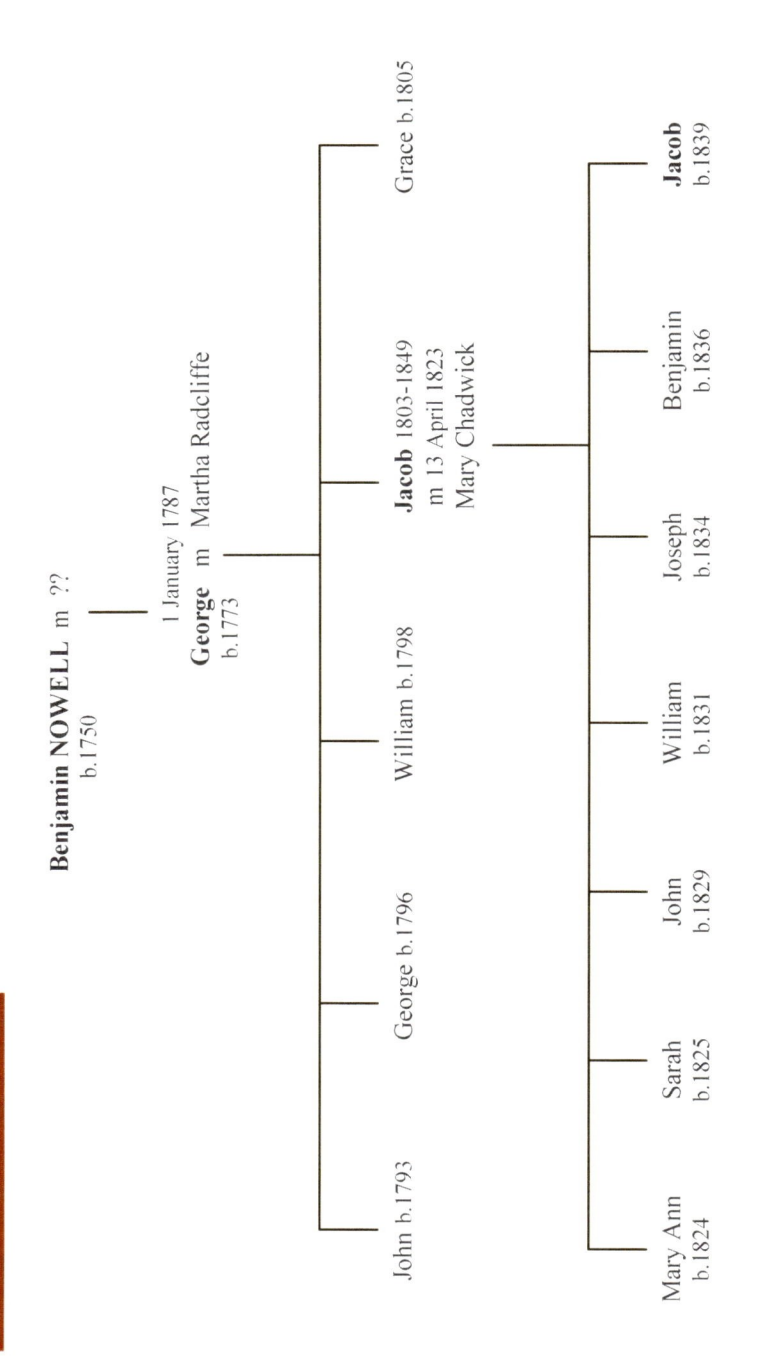

Benjamin NOWELL m ??
b.1750

1 January 1787
George m Martha Radcliffe
b.1773

- John b.1793
- George b.1796
- William b.1798
- Jacob 1803-1849 m 13 April 1823 Mary Chadwick
- Grace b.1805

Children of Jacob and Mary Chadwick:
- Mary Ann b.1824
- Sarah b.1825
- John b.1829
- William b.1831
- Joseph b.1834
- Benjamin b.1836
- **Jacob** b.1839

Jacob Nowell 1839-1882 to Clifford Nowell 1893-1973

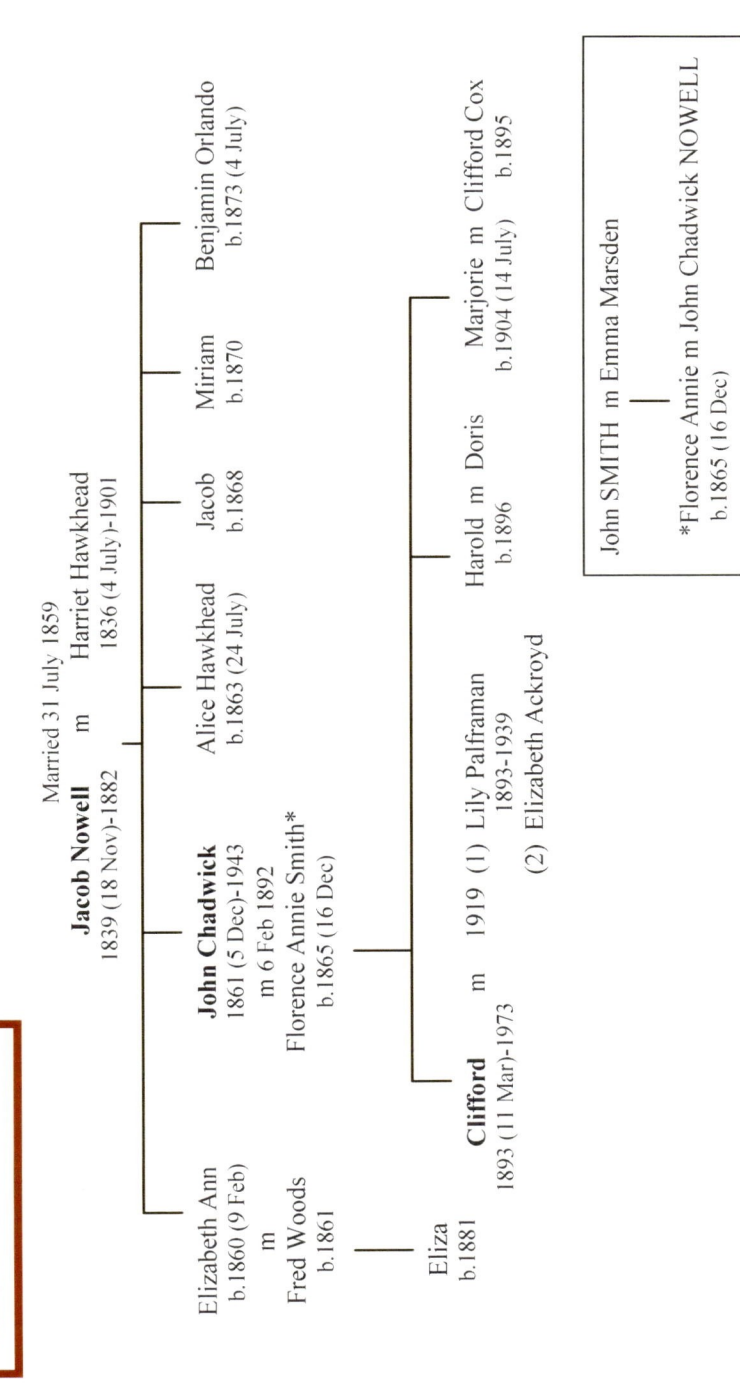

Married 31 July 1859

Jacob Nowell m **Harriet Hawkhead**
1839 (18 Nov)-1882   1836 (4 July)-1901

- Elizabeth Ann b.1860 (9 Feb) m Fred Woods b.1861
  - Eliza b.1881
- **John Chadwick** 1861 (5 Dec)-1943 m 6 Feb 1892 Florence Annie Smith* b.1865 (16 Dec)
  - **Clifford** 1893 (11 Mar)-1973 m 1919 (1) Lily Palframan 1893-1939 (2) Elizabeth Ackroyd
    - Harold m Doris b.1896
    - Marjorie m Clifford Cox b.1904 (14 July) b.1895
- Alice Hawkhead b.1863 (24 July)
- Jacob b.1868
- Miriam b.1870
- Benjamin Orlando b.1873 (4 July)

John SMITH m Emma Marsden

*Florence Annie m John Chadwick NOWELL b.1865 (16 Dec)

Clifford Nowell 1893-1973

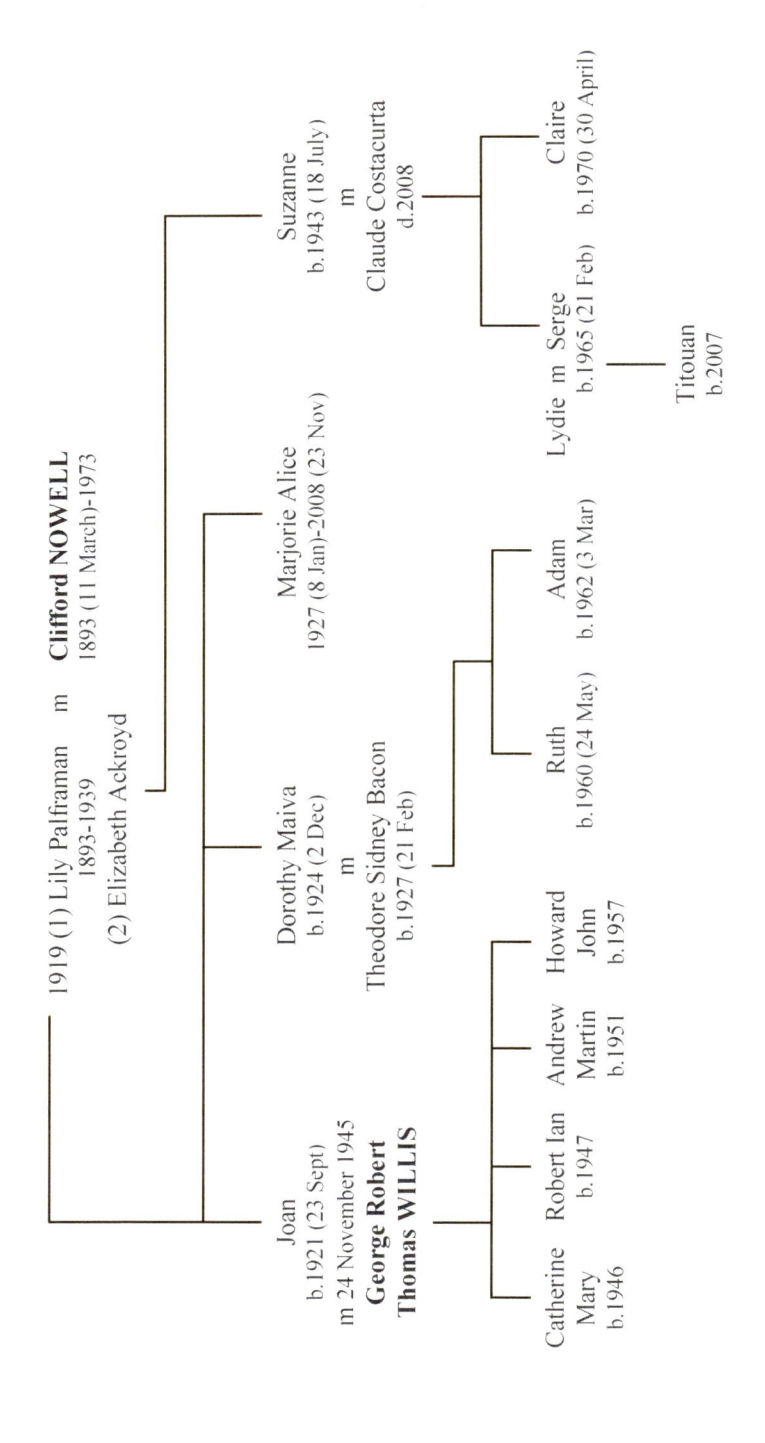

Clifford NOWELL 1893 (11 March)-1973

1919 (1) Lily Palframan m 1893-1939
(2) Elizabeth Ackroyd

- Joan b.1921 (23 Sept) m 24 November 1945 **George Robert Thomas WILLIS**
- Dorothy Maiva b.1924 (2 Dec) m Theodore Sidney Bacon b.1927 (21 Feb)
- Marjorie Alice 1927 (8 Jan)-2008 (23 Nov)
- Suzanne b.1943 (18 July) m Claude Costacurta d.2008

Children of Joan and George:
- Catherine Mary b.1946
- Robert Ian b.1947
- Andrew Martin b.1951
- Howard John b.1957

Children of Marjorie Alice:
- Ruth b.1960 (24 May)
- Adam b.1962 (3 Mar)

Children of Suzanne and Claude:
- Lydie m Serge b.1965 (21 Feb)
- Claire b.1970 (30 April)

Titouan b.2007

Harold Nowell b.1896 and Marjorie Nowell b.1904

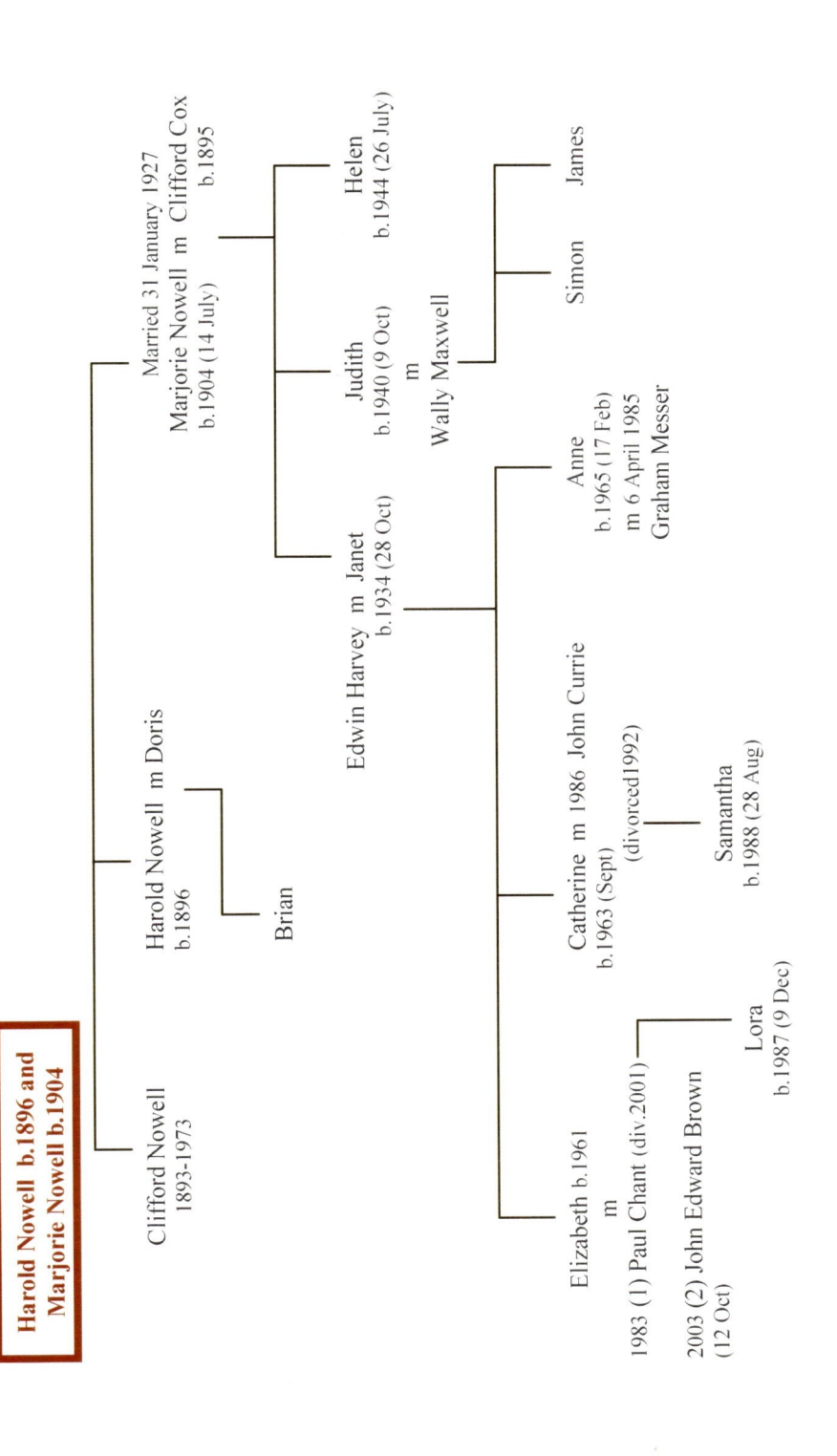

Clifford Nowell
1893-1973

Harold Nowell m Doris
b.1896

Brian

Married 31 January 1927
Marjorie Nowell m Clifford Cox
b.1904 (14 July)   b.1895

Judith
b.1940 (9 Oct)
m
Wally Maxwell

Helen
b.1944 (26 July)

Simon   James

Edwin Harvey m Janet
b.1934 (28 Oct)

Catherine m 1986 John Currie
b.1963 (Sept)
(divorced 1992)

Samantha
b.1988 (28 Aug)

Anne
b.1965 (17 Feb)
m 6 April 1985
Graham Messer

Elizabeth b.1961
m
1983 (1) Paul Chant (div.2001)
2003 (2) John Edward Brown
(12 Oct)

Lora
b.1987 (9 Dec)

John Palframan b.1833 to Albert Palframan 1855-1942

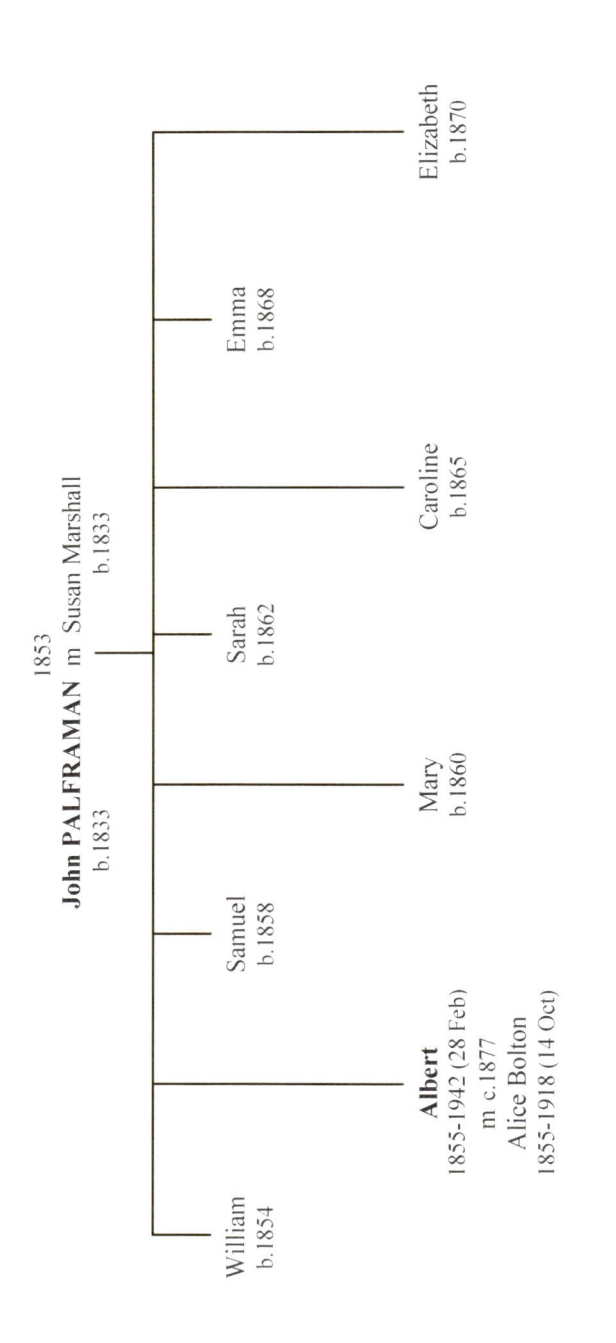

John PALFRAMAN m Susan Marshall
b.1833 — 1853 — b.1833

- William b.1854
- **Albert** 1855-1942 (28 Feb)
  m c.1877
  Alice Bolton
  1855-1918 (14 Oct)
- Samuel b.1858
- Mary b.1860
- Sarah b.1862
- Caroline b.1865
- Emma b.1868
- Elizabeth b.1870

**Albert Palframan 1855-1942
to Lily Palframan 1893-1939**

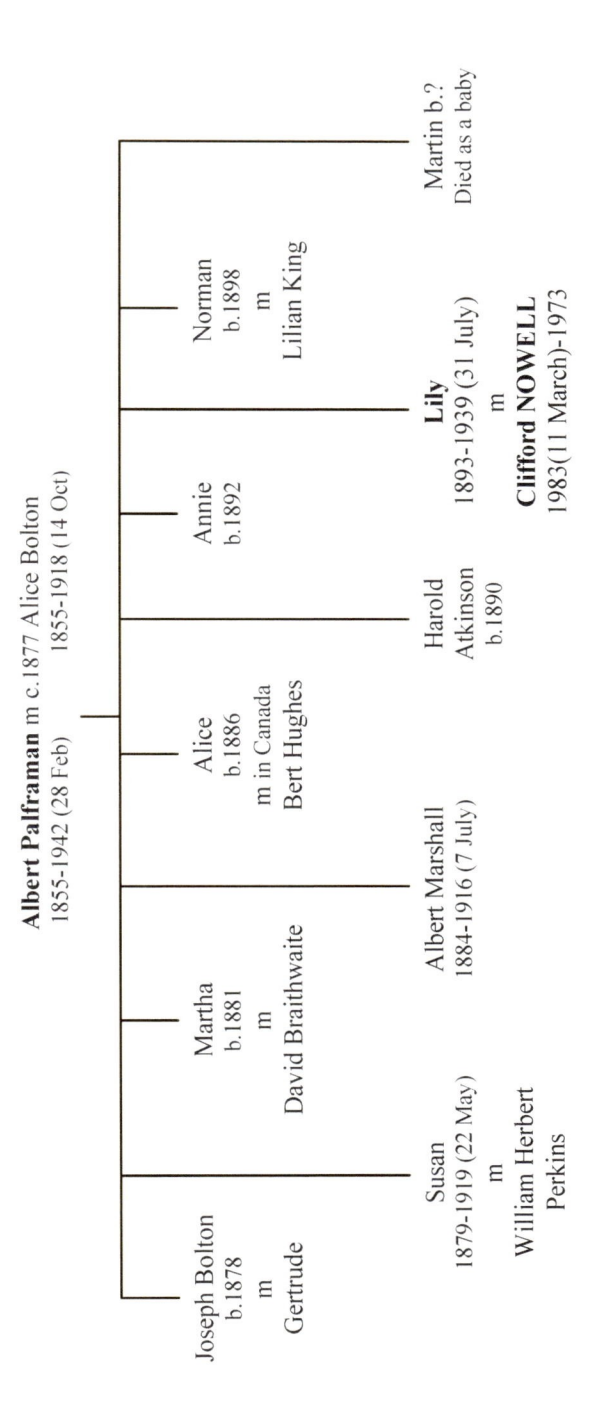

Albert Palframan m c.1877 Alice Bolton
1855-1942 (28 Feb)   1855-1918 (14 Oct)

- Joseph Bolton
  b.1878
  m
  Gertrude

- Susan
  1879-1919 (22 May)
  m
  William Herbert Perkins

- Martha
  b.1881
  m
  David Braithwaite

- Albert Marshall
  1884-1916 (7 July)

- Alice
  b.1886
  m in Canada
  Bert Hughes

- Harold Atkinson
  b.1890

- Annie
  b.1892

- **Lily**
  1893-1939 (31 July)
  m
  Clifford NOWELL
  1983(11 March)-1973

- Norman
  b.1898
  m
  Lilian King

- Martin b.?
  Died as a baby

Lily Palframan 1893-1939

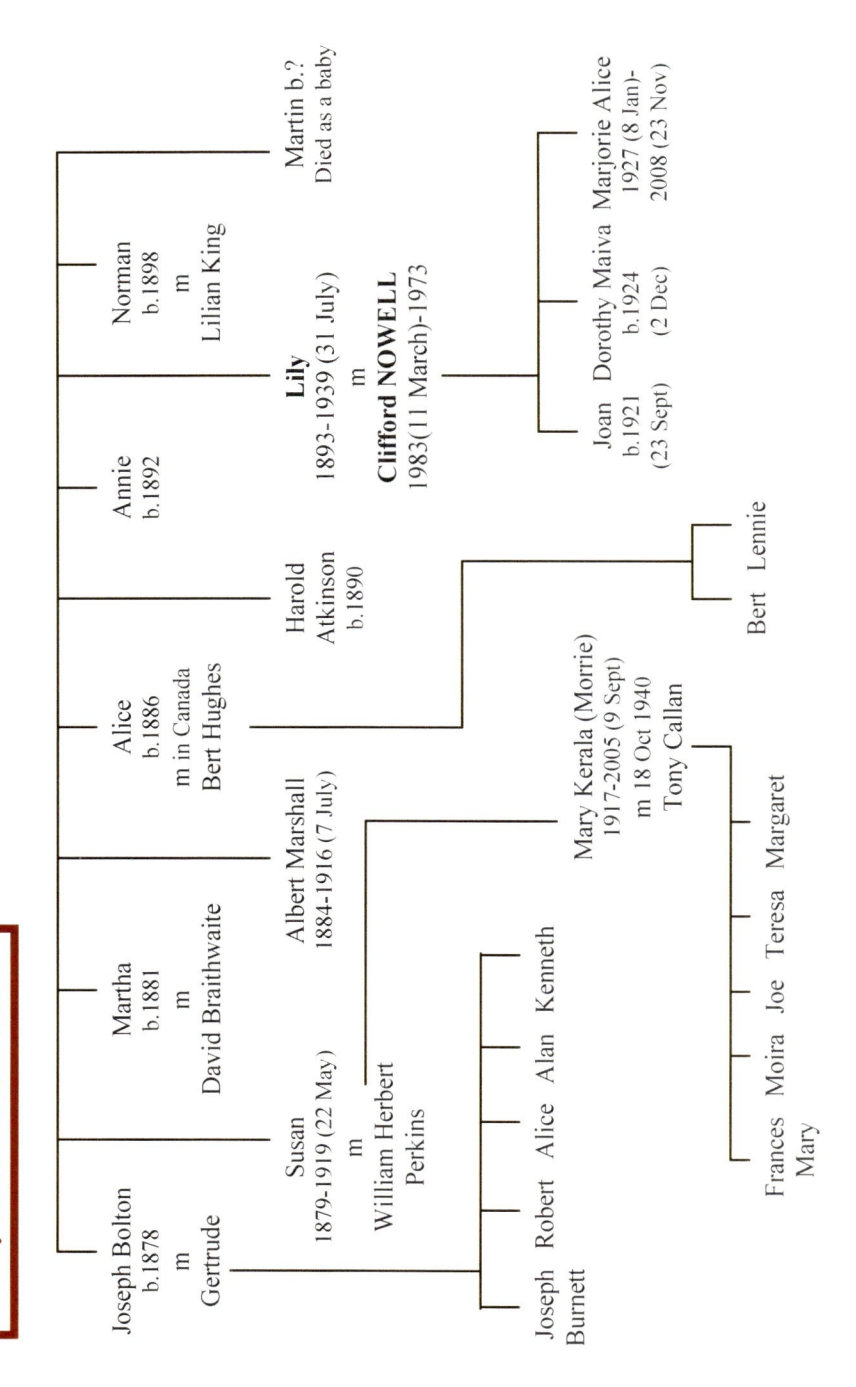

Joseph Bolton b.1878 m Gertrude

- **Susan** 1879-1919 (22 May) m **William Herbert Perkins**
  - Joseph
  - Robert
  - Alice
  - Alan
  - Kenneth
  - Burnett
- **Martha** b.1881 m **David Braithwaite**
- **Albert Marshall** 1884-1916 (7 July)
  - **Mary Kerala (Morrie)** 1917-2005 (9 Sept) m 18 Oct 1940 **Tony Callan**
    - Frances
    - Moira
    - Joe
    - Teresa
    - Margaret
    - Mary
- **Alice** b.1886 m in Canada **Bert Hughes**
  - **Harold Atkinson** b.1890
    - Bert
    - Lennie
- **Annie** b.1892
- **Lily** 1893-1939 (31 July) m **Clifford NOWELL** 1983 (11 March)-1973
  - Joan b.1921 (23 Sept)
  - Dorothy Maiva b.1924 (2 Dec)
  - Marjorie Alice 1927 (8 Jan)-2008 (23 Nov)
- **Norman** b.1898 m **Lilian King**
- Martin b.? Died as a baby